Medieval Fantasy as Performance

The Society for Creative Anachronism and the Current Middle Ages

Michael A. Cramer

THE SCARECROW PRESS, INC.
Lanham • Toronto • Plymouth, UK
2010

Published by Scarecrow Press, Inc.
A wholly owned subsidiary of The Rowman & Littlefield Publishing Group, Inc.
4501 Forbes Boulevard, Suite 200, Lanham, Maryland 20706
http://www.scarecrowpress.com

Estover Road, Plymouth PL6 7PY, United Kingdom

British Library Cataloguing in Publication Information Available

Library of Congress Cataloging-in-Publication Data
Cramer, Michael A., 1964–
  Medieval fantasy as performance : the Society for Creative Anachronism and the current
Middle Ages / Michael A. Cramer.
    p. cm.
  Includes bibliographical references and index.
  ISBN 978-0-8108-6995-0 (pbk. : alk. paper) — ISBN 978-0-8108-6996-7 (ebook)
  1. Middle Ages. 2. Europe—Social life and customs. 3. Europe—Social conditions—
To 1492. 4. Civilization, Medieval. 5. Historical reenactments. 6. Fantasy drama. 7.
Society for Creative Anachronism. I. Title.
  D117.C74 2010
  940.106—dc22   2009032089

⊖™ The paper used in this publication meets the minimum requirements of American
National Standard for Information Sciences—Permanence of Paper for Printed Library
Materials, ANSI/NISO Z39.48-1992.

Printed in the United States of America

For Gracia

CONTENTS

ACKNOWLEDGMENTS

I would like to give thanks to several people who helped me survive this book.

To the SCA members I interviewed and corresponded with. I especially need to thank Thorsen for having the good grace to win crown for Svava as I was in the middle of this project, giving me a wealth of material to draw upon. Thanks also to my SCA household, Ost Thorpe, and to the members of Serpentius, House Wilmot, and the rest of Tribe Rôt Mahne. And, of course, I need to thank the populaces and the crowns of the Kingdoms of the West and the East

To Ken Meyer/Master Hirsch von Henford, who maintains the West Kingdom History Project (http://history.westkingdom.org), where I did a huge amount of research.

To James Saslow, Dan Gerould, and particularly, Pam Sheingorn, for dozens of readings and invaluable advice.

A special thanks to Jim Cherry, Kurt Taroff, and Ed Lingan, my comrades in arms.

Inspiration came from Ray Charles Cramer, Willis Harman, Brad Stuart, Dean Harman, Rick Davis, Ward Harman, Elliot Beard, Gerry Boyle, and William Hazelton, and also from Fred Hollander, David D. Friedman, Heather Rose Jones, Dana Kramer-Rolls, Katherine Helm-Clark, and Steven Muhlberger.

Thanks to my parents, James Cramer and Ruth Cramer, and to my stepparents, Billie Harman and Jerry Nichols, for their love and support.

To Jenifer Tifft and Renée Camus, my very patient editors.

To the numerous conference panels and audiences who have sat through portions of this book as I worked it out.

To the editors of *The Year's Work in Medievalism,* who published a portion of Chapter in Volume XXII, Summer, 2007 under the title "Psychedellic Medievalism: Berkeley, the 60s, and the SCA".

Thanks to you, my readers for bearing with me through this book. Some of this work is based on oral history, tradition, and the sometimes faulty memories of myself and others, which often contradict one another. Any errors or omissions are all my own.

And finally thanks to Hanna Edwards, who was there when I first sat down to write and, amazingly enough, was still there when I finished, and who put up with me through it all.

INTRODUCTION

In the cover story of the issue of *Time* magazine for December 2, 2002, author Lev Grossman wrote about the resurgence of fantasy in popular culture. Grossman cites the film version of J.R.R. Tolkien's *The Lord of the Rings* trilogy, the *Harry Potter* movies, the computer game *EverQuest,* the card game *Magic: The Gathering,* and other films, books, games, and television shows as evidence of a trend in American popular culture: the replacement of science fiction with fantasy, particularly medieval fantasy, as our main form of escapism. By fantasy I mean not only escapism or unrealistic situations, but a genre of literature and film rooted in medievalism and in which magic, not science, is the governing paradigm. Writes Grossman:

> Popular culture is the most sensitive barometer we have for gauging shifts in the national mood, and it's registering a big one right now. Our fascination with science fiction reflected a deep collective faith that technology would lead us to a cybertopia. With *The Two Towers*, the new installment of *the Lord of the Rings* trilogy, about to storm the box office, we are seeing what might be called the enchanting of America. A darker, more pessimistic attitude toward technology and the future has taken hold, and the evidence is our new preoccupation with fantasy, a nostalgic, sentimental, magical vision of a medieval age.[1]

Grossman cites as his prime example of this fascination with the medieval an organization known as the Society for Creative Anachronism (SCA), a "medieval re-creation" society, in which people perform premodern roles in what is truly a postmodern fantasy about the Middle Ages. They dress in historic costume, take medieval names, practice medieval arts and crafts, and often fight in medieval-style armor with rebated weapons like Arthurian heroes. They have laid their own geography over the contemporary world, dividing it into "kingdoms," each ruled by rotating mock kings who, rather than having been born to the job, must win a "Crown Tournament" held two or three times each year. They have knights and other peerage orders: "the Order of the Laurel" for arts and sciences and "the Order of the Pelican" for service. In other words, they play at being medieval nobility. Grossman suggests that the impetus behind their game is a longing for a simpler time with clear moral values. SCA members he quotes mention an antitechnology nostalgia and a sense that honor, courtesy, and chivalry are missing from contemporary society as reasons for their participation.

If Grossman is right, and contemporary culture truly has developed a fascination with the medieval and with medieval fantasy, then looking at the SCA as a case study will allow us to examine some ways how and reasons why that fantasy is being played out, as well as allowing us to analyze the dissatisfaction with contemporary culture that leads people into these realms of fantasy. This book will examine the Society for Creative Anachronism in detail to discover how SCA members adapt and employ ideas about the Middle Ages in performance, ritual reenactment, living history, and re-creation. In doing so I hope to shed some light on the wave of medievalism Grossman mentions as causing a significant change in American culture. By looking at various ideas about medievalism, as well as contrasting medieval reenactment and living history with medieval re-creation as performance genres, I intend to analyze the performance of identity through ritual, sport, drama, and personal interaction. Placing this performance in the context of contemporary American society, I will show how the SCA, rather than reenacting the Middle Ages, uses performance to construct a postmodern counterculture that is framed as medieval and is centered around a reconstruction of the medieval king game.

I may not be the best person to write this book because I might be too involved. I have been in the SCA for more than thirty years. For a long time now it has been both my hobby and my subject of study. Victor Turner, discussing the influence that the work of Wilhelm Dilthey had on his own studies, says that "experience, in its formal aspect, is richer than can be accounted for by general formal categories."[2] Although traditional anthropologies favored observation, considering experience to be untrustworthy, Turner, after Dilthey, believed that only through experience and those very aspects of experience that the traditional anthropologists disdained—emotional involvement, value judgment, etc.—could true understanding be gained. I have been around the SCA in one way or another most of my life. I hold some of its titles and ranks myself. I have even won two royal tournaments, as a result of which I have been both "prince" of a principality and "King of the West." Obviously I am not an objective observer, and my methods and conclusions should be questioned throughout; however, my involvement gives me a knowledge and experience with the subject that provide valuable insights into the methods and means of SCA performance.

Grossman is right about the new wave of medievalism and fantasy that was popular in the first decade of the new millennium. November 2003 saw the opening of a new Michael Crichton film, based on his book *Timeline,* in which, in a tried and true formula, scientists travel back in time to the Middle Ages. Ridley Scott, fresh from his success with the Roman epic *Gladiator,* released *The Kingdom of Heaven,* a movie about the Crusades. 2004 saw a new *Harry Potter* film and yet another *King Arthur* movie. And in December 2003, the third installment of *The Lord of the Rings, The Return of the King*, opened with a box office total of $125.1 million in its first five days (these figures are for the US gross. The worldwide box was estimated to be $246 million for the same five day period).[3] It went on to be one of the top grossing films of all time and tied the record for number of academy awards won. But perhaps even more emblematic than all of these examples was the 2002 film *A Knight's Tale,* which fused medieval epic with rock and roll in a way recognizable to many members of the SCA (Lee Forgue/Mistress Eilis O'Boirne, a longtime SCA member and past member of the SCA Board of Directors, whom I interviewed for this project, joked that the party scene from *A Knight's Tale* looked just like the first SCA Twelfth Night celebration she attended). The SCA is an extreme and therefore clear example of this trend in contemporary society.

According to its official documents, the SCA, which was incorporated in 1968, is "a nonprofit educational organization dedicated to the study of the Middle Ages and Renaissance. Most of its activities take place in the context of a social structure adapted from the forms of the European Middle Ages, which allows participants to take a firsthand look at various aspects of the life, culture, and technology of the times under study."[4] However, SCA members often say they are "re-creating the Middle Ages as they should have been." (This phrase is part of a litany most people hear when they first encounter the SCA and is used to describe it to newcomers. It appears on several fliers and handouts, but I have not found the original source.) To members of the SCA this usually means the Middle Ages without plague, religious intolerance, or real war. They often refer to their game as "The Current Middle Ages," placing themselves not in history but as part of a contemporary utopian counterculture.[5] This utopian view leads most SCA members to a very selective and often incomplete view of medieval society, so that what they end up with is a fantasy about the Middle Ages rather than an accurate representation.

In referring to the SCA as a counterculture I mean both that the SCA was part of the counterculture movement of the 1960s and that it is a counterculture by definition: "the culture and lifestyle of those people who reject the dominant values and behavior of society."[6] The values being rejected in this case are self-interest, greed, and modernism, which are replaced by a romantic notion of chivalry. The SCA is more closely related to the hippie movement than it is to the Free Speech Movement (which began on the Berkeley campus in 1964) because as a body the SCA does not engage in the politics of the larger world. Like those elements of the counterculture that wanted to create their own better worlds and didn't care much what the rest of the world did, the SCA was not and is not overtly political. It should be noted, however, that identifying anything as part of the counterculture has some inherent risks since, as John C. McWilliams notes, "The counterculture is nearly impossible to define."[7]

Like the hippie movement, the SCA created an alternative utopian world where contemporary strictures and mores were relaxed. In her dissertation comparing the SCA to buckskinning, Wendy Erisman notes that behaviors that would not be accepted in much of America—homosexuality, casual sexual encounters, polyamory, open marriages, and pluralistic marriages—are not only tolerated in the SCA but are much more public there than in the general society.[8] Although society as a whole is more open to alternative relationships and nonconformist practices than it once was, the SCA is decidedly more so. However, this acceptance of alternative lifestyles is not universal within the SCA and creates some tensions, which I address. As the SCA has aged it has in some ways gotten more conservative, so that there is an increasing tension between people who see the SCA as a free and open society sexually and those who wish the SCA to be more conservative and "family friendly." There is also a great deal of heteronormativity in some segments of the SCA.

The SCA provides a social structure that mirrors that of a late medieval or renaissance court, in which people occupy various positions on a social hierarchy that begins with a king and queen at the top with various dukes, duchesses, knights, peers, and nonarmigerous nobles beneath them. Members play the roles of the king and his court, and although many of them study and re-create earlier parts of the Middle Ages or even nonmedieval or non-European cultures, donning the garb or armor of a twelfth-century Norman, a tenth-century Viking, or a Mongol warrior, the social structure of the SCA more closely parallels the late medieval courts of the dukes of Burgundy or the renaissance courts of the Medicis and the Tudors, courts in which power was centralized in an efficient bureaucracy and the nobility was kept close at hand to the prince. Titles and rank are either awarded (rather like merit badges) or earned in the case of the royal peerages that are given out to those who have reigned as either king/queen or prince/princess of one of the SCA kingdoms or principalities. The awards structure in the SCA is therefore wholly modern but coded medieval.

Very little about the SCA was actually planned; it just sort of happened. The method of choosing the kings in the SCA's kingdoms, for instance, is based on a romantic ideal that comes primarily from Sir Walter Scott's *Ivanhoe*. At the party that became the first SCA event a tournament was held, the winner of which was to crown his lady "fairest," establishing her as a type of queen of love and beauty. This was supposed to be a one-time party, but participants, primarily the combatants, wanted to do it again, so another tournament was held and then another. Soon the winners of the tourney were invested with the title of "king," and a whole court, and culture, developed organically around these rotating monarchs. Such a practice, in which a person is chosen "king" based on a competition or a game, or in some other way was proclaimed "king for a day," existed both among the nobility of the Middle Ages (in certain chivalric tourneys) and the peasantry (the king game).[9] This is the part of the Middle Ages that the SCA, more or less accidentally, stumbled onto and re-creates enthusiastically.

Theatrical Approaches to and in the SCA

The SCA has already been examined through the fields of anthropology, social studies, and leisure studies. It has been the subject of news magazine shows and documentaries. It is the setting for at least one mystery novel (*Murder at the War* by Mary Monica Pulver) and one fantasy novel (thinly disguised in *The Folk of the Air* by Peter S. Beagle) and is the inspiration for a popular series of science fiction novels (the *Greymere* series by Peter Stasheff). It inspired an important cult film of the early eighties (George Romero's *Knightriders*). It has been profiled in both *Smithsonian* and *Penthouse*. But it has not been explored from the point of view of performance studies and theatricality. The SCA is highly theatrical. Participation involves the adoption of names, the wearing of costumes, and the performance of attitudes that are not common in contemporary society. Some types of SCA performances I've witnessed include:

Introduction of fighters	Storytelling
Challenges	Poetic recitation
Invocation ceremonies	Campfire singing
Salutes	Dancing of all types
The fights themselves	Plays
Acknowledgment of defeat	Instrumental performance
Celebration of victory	Masques
Armorial display	Stickball
Armor and costume	Hurley
Mass battles	Wrestling
Court	Archery
Awards ceremonies	Fencing
Elevation ceremonies	Football
Coronation	Soccer
Oaths of fealty	Rounders
Ambassadorial presentations	Lawn bowling
Giving of royal gifts	Weddings
Bardic presentations	Memorial services
Choirs	

Not only is nearly everything about the SCA theatrical, but it is so much so that the participants are often not even aware that they are performing.

People in the SCA are encouraged to adopt a "persona," that is, to invent a character who could have lived in the Middle Ages, to portray at SCA gatherings (although many members steadfastly refuse to do this). Furthermore, the central activities of the SCA mirror theatrical activities common to the Middle Ages—tournaments, processions, coronations, courts, plus mimetic activities such as masking and the performance of plays. They constitute, for all intents and purposes, an ongoing, roving work of performance art, which has been running nonstop since 1966.

The SCA is one of the most active groups in the world in performing both medieval plays and contemporary plays written in medieval style. Masques, period farces, miracle plays, and court dramas are all common theatrical forms in the SCA. Commedia dell'arte is extremely popular. Because of its faux medieval social structure, the SCA is an excellent laboratory for the type of performance reconstruction experiments discussed by Robert Sarlos. It mirrors the hierarchical structure of the Renaissance much better than did the faculty of UC Davis when Sarlos did his reconstruction of the "Triumph of Peace."[10]

SCA performance becomes the dominant interaction in the lives of many of its participants, and many people's most lasting relationships exist within the group. The emotions engendered in the SCA's "make-believe" performance are very real, and the question that has to be asked is: If the emotions are real, how unreal can the actions be? As Marvin Carlson says, "it is extremely difficult, and ultimately perhaps not useful, to try as Wilshire does to draw a clear distinction between the 'real' world of 'responsible' human action, and the 'imaginary' world of play or performance."[11]

Postmodernism and the SCA

It is notoriously difficult to pin down exactly what postmodernism is. The term is usually defined in its relationship to modernism, but critics as varied as Francois Lyotard, Linda Hutcheon, and Frederic Jameson differ as to what its characteristics are.

In *The Cultural Turn* and *Postmodernism, or, the Cultural Logic of Late Capitalism,* Jameson's approach to postmodernism is highly critical. He objects to postmodernism's embrace of nostalgia, important in looking at the SCA, and opposes nostalgia to historicism, preferring the latter. He sees the fragmentation of ideas that comes with postmodernism as particularly harmful. Because it has no firm grounding in an idea of what is good or bad, Jameson sees postmodernism as contributing to the creation of an amoral society. He maintains that postmodernism's nostalgia is based, at least partially, in a frustration with the fragmentation of contemporary society. In other words, Jameson takes a modernist view of postmodernism. As an avowed Marxist, it is impossible for Jameson to embrace postmodernism, since it undermines his own master narrative as well as that which he opposes.

By contrast, Irene Eynat-Confino in *Space and the Postmodern Stage* takes a much more positive view, noting, "Unlike other trends in art, postmodernism has not invalidated the past but incorporated it with a zest."[12] She quotes Ihab Hassan's article "POSTmodernISM: a Practical Bibliography," in which Hassan lists some of what he considers to be postmodernism's features, among which are "Irony [that] becomes radical, self consuming play, entropy of meaning."[13] In *Postmodernist Culture* Steven Connor notes that performance is possibly the most postmodern of all art forms. He cites Michel Benamou's statement that performance is "the unifying mode of the postmodern."[14]

Like Jameson, Connor links performance and postmodernism to the 1960s, the era that also produced the SCA, noting:

> Postmodern theatre is often dated from the upsurge of performance in the 1960s, with its happenings, spectacles, dance-theatre, etc. One strain of radical theatre theory at that time and afterwards sought to free up performance from its degrading subservience to the pre-existing script.[15]

Among the radical theorists of sixties postmodern performance, none is more prominent than Richard Schechner, who in *The End of Humanism* eschews narrative in performance:

Finding ways to organize bits of information so that these bits exist both as experience—what performing art is always dealing with—and as what underlies, is the foundation of, experience. A very difficult job of doubling. Postmodern performance abandons narrative as its foundation. Narrative = experience-as-action.[16]

What the SCA has done is to take Schechner's theories one step further by doing away not only with the script but also with the audience. In place of the traditional audience is the membership itself. Each member of the SCA, as in life, is both performer for and audience to everyone else in the group. In place of a written script the SCA has created its own customs, history, traditions, and ritual that serve to bind the whole together into a community that is neither medieval nor contemporary nor fantastic but has elements of all three.

Theories of postmodernism are very useful in examining the SCA because the SCA, from events to each individual participant, is made up of layers upon layers of coding, some contemporary and some medieval, in constant interplay. The culture of the SCA is a negotiation between the historical and the contemporary, filtered through both academic and pop culture notions of the Middle Ages. It is a pastiche. In *The Cultural Turn* Jameson places the beginnings of postmodernism during the emergence of performance in the 1960s, which would make it concurrent with the beginning of the SCA.[17] Jameson insists that pastiche is one of the most significant features of postmodernism, noting:

Pastiche is, like parody, the imitation of a peculiar or unique style, the wearing of a stylistic mask, speech in a dead language: but it is a neutral practice of such mimicry, without parody's ulterior motive, without the satirical impulse.[18]

The difference is significant. Often, playful representations of earlier periods, including the Middle Ages, are performed in a mocking fashion, to show how silly the rustic medieval peasants or the pompous medieval nobles were when compared to normal, contemporary Americans. This is the approach at renaissance faires, a type of festival in which performers create a renaissance environment, usually centered around a market fair, for a paying audience. Unlike most living history enterprises, renaissance faires are often for profit businesses that place a higher value upon entertainment than upon historical reenactment.

The SCA, by contrast, is playing not to an audience of outsiders but to its own members, and thus it takes an approach that is much more complex.[19] On the one hand it is very nostalgic. Most people in the SCA talk about the Middle Ages not as a strange and backward "dark age" (one popular contemporary image of the Middle Ages) but as an era of romance and chivalry that presents a desirable alternative to contemporary society (a different but equally popular version). At the same time many people within the group complain that these ideals are seldom attained. Like the Middle Ages, the SCA is full of stories of people who are less chivalrous, honorable, and courteous than the romantic knights they are supposed to be emulating. In gossip, in song and story, and in

SCA plays, kings are sometimes mocked as being despotic, knights are often perceived as a group of uncontrollable frat boys, and women are often portrayed as golddiggers or groupies ("hat hunters," referring to the crowns worn by SCA royalty, is the common term).

These subjects are also constantly debated on internet newsgroups throughout the SCA. On the discussion list for SCA knights the two most common topics are conduct and authenticity, and the two subjects are often linked. Interestingly, many of the more serious reenactors are among those who say that knights in the SCA are held to an unrealistically high standard of conduct. The type of chivalry many in the SCA wish to recreate is a Victorian fantasy about chivalry, and those who want to re-create a more historical ideal of chivalry argue that such romantic notions should be jettisoned, even if it means accepting a society that is not so kind and gentle.

Between these two extremes are people who take the ideals of the SCA seriously but treat them in a tongue-in-cheek fashion. SCA members often joke about the plague, religious wars, and the despotism of medieval nobility while at the same time celebrating the romantic notions of the Victorians. It is revealing that most SCA members can quote huge sections of *Monty Python and the Holy Grail.* That film's juxtaposition of the medieval and the contemporary and the way it profanes ideas that the central characters seem to take seriously is very like much of the SCA. Not to mention the film's silliness. The SCA is, let's face it, a very silly activity: dressing up in tights, pretending to be knights, and bowing to somebody wearing a crown, a mock king without an actual kingdom, who might drive a beer truck for a living on weekdays but who, in this context, is a king; what could be more silly—or more postmodern—than that?

Medievalism and the SCA

Norman Cantor's *Inventing the Middle Ages*, which discusses how the twentieth century's view of the medieval world is based more or less on twentieth-century experience, provides a good starting point for looking at SCA medievalism. Cantor looks at the work of the twentieth century's most prominent medievalists and attempts to show how their own life experiences colored their interpretations of the medieval.

Because of his status both in medieval studies and in performance studies, Umberto Eco is particularly important. His concept of "Ostentation" (which as Marvin Carlson points out is closely related to Erving Goffman's concept of the frame[20]) is useful in looking at the various signs employed by the SCA and how they are coded by the way the group employs them in performance. Also important are theories about the medieval king game, in which peasants set up a mock king, often with a mock court. Scholars who discuss such theories include David Wiles *(The Early Plays of Robin Hood)*, E.K. Chambers *(The Medieval Stage)*, Richard Axton *(European Drama of the Early Middle Ages)*, Lawrence Clopper *(Drama, Play, and Game)*, and Sandra Billington *(Mock Kings in Medieval So-*

ciety and Renaissance Drama). On the whole, these present two different views of the king game. One view is based on the human impulse toward play (Wiles, Clopper), whereas the other sees the king game as stemming from the Celtic tradition of human sacrifice (Chambers, Axton). Although I favor the former I think the latter needs to be examined (though the whole dichotomy can be summed up in an exchange I had with Stephen Knight at the International Conference on Robin Hood Studies in 2001: when I pointed out that Chambers would say that dunking of Robin Hood by Friar Tuck in *Robin Hood and the Friar* was a reenactment of a ritual human sacrifice by drowning, Knight said to me, "If your name was E.K. Chambers you would say that too, but the simple fact of the matter is that dunking somebody in a river is just plain fun.").

Everyone who writes academic studies of the SCA looks at two important sources, Johan Huizinga's *Homo Ludens* and Mikhail Bakhtin's *Rabelais and his World.* In these two works medieval studies and performance studies intersect, and they are highly influential in both disciplines. While writing *The Autumn of the Middle Ages*, Huizinga proposed the idea that everything in the Middle Ages, at least from the point of view of the aristocracy, was a type of game, and from this he developed his theory, expanded upon in *Homo Ludens,* seeking to examine, as he puts it "the play element of culture."[21] Bakhtin's project was to take the qualities he saw as belonging to carnival and examine ways in which they were employed in literature. His theories have influenced everything from medieval studies to the study of popular culture, leading to the common use of the word "carnivalesque," an adjective used to describe activities that have some of the characteristics Bakhtin found in medieval carnival. These include an inversion of the social order, a relaxing of societal rules and strictures, abundance, overindulgence, and a sense of play. It is important that the carnivalesque be separated from carnival, since the latter has a specific religious meaning as a time of excess coming right before Lent, whereas the former is more general. Chris Humphrey in *The Politics of Carnival,* suggests using the term "festive misrule" in place of carnival, especially since in English tradition carnivalesque activities took place throughout the year. According to Humphrey, "transgression" is the one quality that is universal to festive misrule and carnival. As Humphrey puts it, "to transgress is to break the boundaries or to mix up elements of culture that are supposed to be kept separate."[22]

These two theoretical formations, medievalism and performance theory, work to place the SCA in a contemporary context while at the same time demonstrating how the game the SCA plays has precedents in the very time period its members are trying to re-create. It was primarily a reference to one source, Sir Walter Scott's *Ivanhoe*, that first led the SCA to have a queen of love and beauty, from which grew its own version of the mock king. The most interesting thing about this is that early SCA members did not consciously set out to re-create the king game, but the medieval tropes that they decided to employ in their game led them quite naturally to what Fred Hollander/Duke Frederick of Holland described as "a fairly good re-creation of a period recreation."[23]

[1] Lev Grossman, "Feeding on Fantasy," *Time*, 2 December 2002, 90.

[2] Victor Turner, *From Ritual to Theatre* (New York: New York Performing Arts Journal Publications, 1982), 13.

[3] *The New York Times*, 22 December 2003.

[4] The Society for Creative Anachronism, *The Society for Creative Anachronism, Inc., Organizational Handbook* (Milpitas, CA: The Society for Creative Anachronism, Inc., 2003), 1.

[5] The phrase "Current Middle Ages" comes from the title of a popular SCA song, "Welcome to the Current Middle Ages" by Darek Foster/Mastrer Baldwin of Erebor, which extols the "joys of gentle dalliance within a dream that has not passed away." This is the source of the SCA concept of "the Dream," meaning the shared dream of all SCA members—a concept which is highly controversial.

[6] *Random House Webster's College Dictionary,* rev. ed. (2001) s.v. "Counterculture."

[7] John C. McWilliams, *The 1960s Cultural Revolution.* (Westport, CT: Greenwood Press, 2000), 67.

[8] Wendy Erisman, "Forward into the Past: The Poetics and Politics of Community in Two Historical Recreation Groups" (Ph.D. diss., University of Texas, 1998), 131.

[9] See E.K. Chambers, *The Medieval Stage*, 2nd ed., vol. 1 (Toronto: Dover, 1996), 260. Originally published by Oxford University Press, London, 1903. Also see Richard Barber and Juliet Barker, *Tournaments* (Woodbridge, UK: The Boydell Press, 1989), 31.

[10] See Robert K. Sarlos, "Performance Reconstruction," in *Interpreting the Theatrical Past: Essays in the Historiography of Performance*, ed. Thomas Postlewait and Bruce A. McConachie (Iowa City: University of Iowa Press, 1989), 198-229.

[11] Marvin Carlson, *Performance* (New York: Routledge, 1996), 52.

[12] Irene Eynat-Confino, "A Stage Upon a Stage: Postmodern Stage Design and Opera," in *Space and the Post Modern Stage*, ed. Eynat-Confino and Eva Sormova (Prague: The Prague Theatre Institute, 2000), 93.

[13] Ihab Hassan, "Postmodernism: A Practical Bibliography," in *From Modernism to Postmodernism*, ed. Lawrence Cahoone (London: Blackwell, 1997). Quoted ibid.

[14] Michel Benamou, "Presence as Play," in *Performance in Postmodern Culture*, ed. Michel Benamou and Charles Carmello (Milwaukee: Center for Twentieth Century Studies, 1977), 1-26. Quoted in Steven Connor, *Postmodernist Culture: An Introduction to the Theories of the Contemporary* (Cambridge MA: Basil Blackwell, 1989; reprint, 1992), 134.

[15] Fredric Jameson, "Postmodernism and Consumer Society," in *The Cultural Turn*, ed. Fredric Jameson (New York: Verso, 1998), 84.

[16] Richard Schechner, *The End of Humanism* (New York: Performing Arts Journal Publications, 1982), 97.

[17] Fredric Jameson, "'End of Art' or 'End of History'," in *The Cultural Turn*, ed. Fredric Jameson (New York: Verso, 1998), 84.

[18] Jameson, "Postmodernism and Consumer Society," 4.

[19] It is worth noting however that the first renaissance faire was founded in California a few years before the SCA, and many people were involved in both: see William Keyes, *The West Kingdom History Project* (Golden Stag, 2001, accessed 4 February 2004); available from http://history.westkingdom.org.

[20] Carlson, *Performance,* 52.

[21] Johan Huizinga, *Homo Ludens* (Boston: The Beacon Press, 1950), Foreword.

[22] Chris Humphrey, *The Politics of Carnival: Festive Misrule in Medieval England*, ed. S. H. Rigby, Manchester Medieval Studies (Manchester, UK: Manchester University Press, 2001), 42.
[23] Fred Hollander, "SCA Culture," panel discussion at the Society for Creative Anachronism Thirty Year Celebration June 1996.

1

A BRIEF HISTORY OF THE SCA

A lot of things came out of the San Francisco Bay Area in the 1960s: the hippies, the Black Panthers, the Grateful Dead, the Free Speech Movement, each of them in some way challenging the norms of contemporary society. To this should be added a group of college students and science fiction fans who threw a medieval theme party that became their own utopian fantasy. The confluence of the counterculture and fantasy literature in Berkeley was the genesis of the SCA.

Carey Lenehan in a thesis on the SCA identified what he called a "taste group" centered around science fiction fandom that included role playing gamers and computer hobbyists, as well as the SCA, as subsets.[1] All four of these groups were concentrated in the Bay Area in the late sixties and through the seventies, the SCA's formative years.[2] Furthermore, the SCA could not have existed without the circle of writers in Berkeley that eventually became known as Greyhaven. Greyhaven (a clear reference to Tolkien and the Grey Havens from which the elves set sail when they leave Middle Earth at the end of *The Return of the King*) is the name of a house in the Berkeley hills owned by SCA founder Diana Paxson/Mistress Diana Listmaker, the now popular fantasy author who threw the party that became known as the SCA's first tournament. It is also the name of a literary circle that grew up around Paxson and Marion Zimmer Bradley/Mistress Elfrida of Greenwalls concurrent with the SCA. Bradley, her brother Paul Edwin Zimmer, Poul Anderson, Paxson, and many other well known science fiction and fantasy authors were among the SCA's founders, and it was through science fiction circles that the SCA first spread beyond the Bay Area.

Phase One: Berkeley in the Sixties

Although the official reckoning of the SCA puts its beginning on May 1, 1966[3], it actually traces back to about 1960 when two of the SCA's founders, Ken de Maiffe/Duke Fulk de Wyvern and David Thewlis/Duke Siegfried von Höflichkeit met while attending language school in the military. Both were posted to Germany and began to study and to teach themselves about sword combat. When they returned to the United States they began experiments in medieval combat, making leather helmets, shields, and wooden swords with which to practice. About this time they met Paxson, who was studying medieval history.[4] Since Thewlis and de Maiffe were already attempting recreations of medieval combat and practicing in Paxson's backyard, she decided to throw a theme party, "a tournament of chivalry" inspired by the famous "Last Tournament" at Eglinton, Scotland in 1839.[5] The Eglinton tournament was one of the first organized re-creation events in modern times. Inspired by the novels of Sir

Walter Scott, a group of British nobles decided to hold an elaborate tournament of chivalry. They had armor made, got horses, made costumes, and prepared to joust just as in *Ivanhoe*. This event was made famous in Ian Anstruther's *The Knight and the Umbrella,* according to whom it was a disaster: it rained, the mud grew thick, the costumes were ruined, and the 100,000 in attendance left without seeing a show (in fact the Eglinton tourney was only postponed until the following Wednesday, when it went off successfully, but very few of the spectators stuck around to see it).

Paxson's tourney was not so elaborate. It was announced as a "Tournament of Chivalry," the winner of which was to have the honor of declaring his lady the "fairest." All the fighting was to be done afoot (since they were college students most of them could not afford a horse). Instead of being announced by invitation, this and other early SCA events were announced by fliers that were posted at college dormitories as well as along streets such as Telegraph Avenue in Berkeley, which advertised the event and invited "all knights" to come and fight. Fliers were posted in the dormitories of San Francisco State, Mills College, and the San Francisco and Berkeley Theological Seminaries, as well as all over the city of Berkeley. Guests were encouraged to "wear the dress of some age of Christendom, Outre-Mer, or Faerie in which swords were used."[6] According to Paxson, people came from all over the Bay Area. The day included fighting, dancing, and music, and as it was Berkeley and it was 1966, it ended with a march up Telegraph Avenue, protesting the twentieth century.[7]

From the very beginning, the performance of medievalism in the SCA was done in a tongue-in-cheek fashion, combining period elements with a modern sense of irony. The knights and their ladies entered into the lists to a processional from *The Play of Herod* (Paxson doesn't say which play of Herod), and they were blessed by a mock bishop who recited the first sentence from *Winnie the Pooh* in Latin ("Ecce Edvardus Ursus. . . ."). Some people came as medieval knights but others as fantasy characters. There was even a Napoleonic officer, a Roman, and a hobbit.[8]

The centerpiece of the party was a tournament, which was fought using a variety of weapons. Some people used broadswords or axes made of wood; others used modern fencing gear. The Roman fought with a net and trident. Although Thewlis and de Maiffe had been experimenting with making armor, and some of the participants had built their own reconstructions, the equipment used by early SCA members was very ad hoc, and often owed more to pop culture than to a study of history. One early fighter fought in a motorcycle helmet and black leather armor. Another fighter competed as a cavalier. The visual image most SCA fighters wanted to project was what they themselves recognized as historical, and this led them to adopt an aesthetic taken from comic books, children's novels, movies, and fantasy art. One early SCA warrior, taking his cue from the sword and sandal epics of the 1950s, fought as a Spartan, wearing simply greaves, a Greek style helmet, and a loin cloth, an image more appropriate to movies like *Troy* or *Alexander*. Although not authentic in the sense of being an accurate representation of history, this tolerance of variety allowed members of the SCA to have experiences that were emotionally authentic, as they employed those faux medieval (and in this case classical) tropes they brought with them. This is also typical of the SCA's organic development. If a single body of authority had formed the SCA, established standards of authenticity, and dictated what areas and time periods were to be studied, these links to popular culture would be much fewer and weaker. Because the SCA was a group of amateurs trying to live out their personal fantasies of the Middle Ages, it became a combination of many different Middle Ages from many sources.

Fencing bouts at the first tourney were scored by modern rules. Fights with medieval weapons were scored by a group of judges plus all other fighters in the lists. When someone was struck the group had to decide what would have happened if the blade had been real. They decided that a person who was struck on a limb couldn't use that limb any longer. Therefore, a person who was hit in the leg had to continue from his (there were no women fighters in the first tournament) knees or stand on one leg. Likewise, a person hit on the sword arm had to fight with his other hand. A fighter had lost "when he was considered to have been completely chopped up."[9] At the end of the day David Breen/ David the Herald, who was later known as Ardral Argo ver Kaeysc, was knighted for his chivalry on the field (all the others had fought using the title "sir," as though they were already knights). Several conventions of the SCA were thus established, including the creation of an SCA name, the practice of fighting from one's knees if struck on the leg, and the SCA order of knighthood, of which David the Herald is the principal member.

It was supposed to be a one-time costume party, but it wasn't. According to Paxson, the fighters had so much fun they wanted to do it again, and so another tournament was scheduled for the following Midsummer's Eve; then another in the fall, and another that next spring. The name of the group was coined by Bradley. When reserving a city park for the SCA's second tournament that summer she was asked the name of the group and she just made one up on the spot. The SCA quickly developed into a series of tournaments held on regular dates throughout the year, gatherings in which men fought in a faux medieval style to honor their ladies. To some these tournaments were simple fantasy, informed as much by the works of Tolkien as by the *Chronicles* of Froissart. To others they were an attempt to create a Pre-Raphaelite utopia. Still others, viewing them in the context of the antiwar movement, saw them as exercises in honorable combat, the type of "just war" that many found in Tolkien's *Lord of the Rings*. Early SCA members agreed that they were attempting to re-create a medieval-style tournament culture, but they weren't exactly clear about what that meant, and what they actually created was a culture unique unto itself.

According to Thewlis, two events occurred in 1968 that were pivotal in the transition of the SCA from a collection of theme parties into an international organization of medievalists.[10] The first was the World Conference of Science Fiction and Fantasy that September. The second was the incorporation of the SCA, which took place that October. However, two equally important events from 1968 were the founding of the East Kingdom that July and establishment of the SCA court structure and the orders of peerage at the SCA's second Twelfth Night celebration in January of that year.

In 1968 Bradley moved to New York City and founded a new branch of the SCA. That July the New York branch held a tournament on Staten Island to choose its own king. Breen was present as an emissary from the king in Berkeley. He knighted the victor, Bruce of Cloves, who was then crowned king. From then on the Berkeley chapter was known as the Kingdom of the West and the New York chapter was the Kingdom of the East. This is yet another bow to Tolkien: the West, name of the first kingdom of the SCA, is also one of the names for the first kingdom of men in *Lord of the Rings*, and Aragorn is referred to as "The King of the West."

The World Conference of Science Fiction and Fantasy took place that September (1968) at the Claremont Hotel in Berkeley. At this science fiction convention the SCA held a tournament and released a book, *A Handbook for the (Current) Middle Ages,* which was included in the registration packet for attendees. Several people went back to their homes to found local SCA chapters. Bruce of Cloves, the first King of the East, also attended. According to those who were there, Bruce of Cloves was convinced that the East needed "guidance," and he reportedly asked the King of the West to take the East under his kingdom's wing. This essentially put the East under the West, and greatly upset the East's founders.[11]

In October of 1968 the SCA incorporated as a not for profit corporation in California. The SCA's incorporation was the start of an ongoing controversy because, according to Hilda Powers/Viscountess Hilary of Serendip, a former society steward, the existing membership of the group was not polled to see whether or not they wanted to incorporate, or who the directors should be. The decision to incorporate was made by a small group of people headed by Don Studebaker/Jon DeCles, Ms. Paxson's husband, and for years the three member SCA board included Paxson, Studebaker, and a third person whom they chose. Because under the California laws governing this type of corporation only the directors have to vote on board members, the membership of the SCA has never had a direct say as to who governs the group.

The SCA's official documents describe it as "a non-profit educational organization dedicated to the study of the Middle Ages and Renaissance." *The Corpora and By-laws of the SCA* and *The Handbook for the (Current) Middle Ages* became the foundation for most of the SCA groups founded after 1968, particularly those in the Midwest, while in the West Kingdom and, to a lesser extent, in the East, SCA performance was based on an oral tradition tracing back to people who attended the first tournament. This is central to an ongoing conflict over the idea of primacy. The SCA's governing documents state that the primary authority in the SCA is the board of directors of the corporation, but tradition within the East and the West holds that the primary authority is the king.

Why they incorporated is a matter of debate, but the result is more or less agreed upon. Incorporation allowed the SCA to grow and prosper and created an almost constant state of conflict between the board of directors and the other, medieval side of the SCA, especially the crowns. The SCA board of directors, as the official legal authority of the SCA, has the right to set policy for and govern the SCA, but the romantic paradigm under which many people in the SCA perform their roles often places authority in the crown. At any given time, the board is usually involved in a tug of war with one set of crowns or another.

The third kingdom of the SCA, the Middle Kingdom or Midrealm, was founded around Chicago in 1969 by science fiction fans who had attended WorldCon in Berkeley the previous year. There were actually two SCA groups chartered in Chicago in 1969. The Board of Directors in Berkeley chartered the first, while the East Kingdom, which gave the area the name "The Barony Under the Mountain," chartered the second group. Writes an early SCA member:

> [All part of the competition between East and West as to who had the right to charter branches]. Berkeley, in the person of Jon DeCles, wanted a centralized operation in Berkeley, while the Easterners, led by Walter and Marion, were looking for a kind of decentralized operation where any kingdom could establish a branch.[12]

This conflict between East and West went on for several years. The two competing groups in Chicago quickly merged and a crown tournament was held that was won by David Friedman/Duke Cariadoc of the Bow, who was knighted by the King of the West upon his victory.

Phase Two: Regionality and the SCA

The founding of the Middle Kingdom ends the first phase of the history of the SCA. Expansion of the group into regions that were differentiated by contemporary regional attitudes, as well as the consolidation of authority in the SCA's board of directors, marks the second phase. After the formation of the Middle Kingdom the SCA board of directors established the process by which new kingdoms would be formed. Any future branch must begin as a part of an existing kingdom. When a group of local branches (which have to be contiguous unless they are overseas) wishes to form a kingdom, they petition to become a principality. A principality in the SCA is an area within a kingdom that is preparing to split off and become a separate kingdom, though some principalities (the Mists, in the San Francisco Bay Area, being the best example) are not intended to become kingdoms but are instead a way to have a regional figurehead without the responsibilities or power of a king, and also to have another royal tourney for the fighters to play in. The prince of a principality is chosen by a tournament in the same way SCA kings are chosen. The principality would establish its own officer and civil service structure and, eventually, could petition the board to become a kingdom.

The fourth kingdom, Atenveldt, was formed around Phoenix, Arizona, but it was not allowed to become a kingdom immediately. In November 1969 it became a barony of the Kingdom of the West and then, the following April, was declared the SCA's first principality. Some people in Atenveldt, which did not become a kingdom until 1974, resented going through a set of hoops that neither the East nor the Middle had to jump through. All of the subsequent kingdoms have begun as regions of an existing kingdom, and each traces its origins to one of the original three. The kingdoms in the Great Lakes and Farm Belt areas all broke off from the Middle Kingdom: Calontir (Missouri, Arkansas, Kansas, Iowa, and Nebraska), Ealdormere (Ontario, Canada, except for Windsor), and Northshield (Wisconsin and Minnesota). Atlantia (the Mid-Atlantic states from Georgia to Maryland), Drachenwald (Europe, the Middle East, and Africa), and Æthelmaerc (Western Pennsylvania, West Virginia, and western New York) were principalities of the East. The rest of the kingdoms eventually trace their origins back to the West: An Tir (the Pacific Northwest and western Canada), Lochac (Australia and New Zealand), CAID (Southern California and Hawaii), and (through Atenveldt) Artemisia (the western Rocky Mountain states, Utah, and Idaho), Outlands (the eastern Rocky Mountain states of New Mexico, Colorado, Wyoming, and Montana, plus El Paso, Texas), Ansteorra (the rest of Texas plus Oklahoma), Meridies (Alabama, parts of Tennessee, Georgia, and Kentucky, and the Florida panhandle), Gleann Abhann (Mississippi, Louisiana, most of Arkansas, and Memphis, Tennessee), and Trimaris (the rest of Florida). Mexico is disputed. It is claimed by the Outlands by virtue of a few members who live in Juarez, across the border from El Paso, but the few members who live in Tijuana and Ensenada claim allegiance to CAID.

The names of SCA kingdoms are obviously constructions. An Tir is Celtic for "The Land." CAID is an anagram for the initials of the four baronies that founded the principality: Calafia, Angels, Isles, and Dreiburgen, which are, naturally, San Diego, Los Angeles, Santa Barbara—for the channel islands—and San Bernardino, the name meaning "dry town" since it is out in the Mojave desert. SCA place names are often jokes. Fettburg, a group in central California, means either "party town," or else is a very poor translation of "Fat City" (referring to the small town of Manteca, California, where Fettburg is located, the name of which in English means "lard"), depending on which resident you talk to. Cynagua, a principality in the West, is a bastardization of the Spanish words "sin agua," referring to the California water wars.

The power struggle between the East Kingdom and the SCA Inc. lasted a long time and, although Easterners cast it as a conflict between East and West, the board of directors soon got into a similar power struggle with the Kingdom of the West as well. The nature of the conflict was that the board, as the legal authority of the SCA Inc., insisted on maintaining control over the group in nearly all matters, including monies. One of the first results of the incorporation of the SCA was that the Kingdom of the West no longer received the subscription fees ($1.50 per person) from the SCA newsletter, and had no funds for some time after incorporation.[13]

This struggle came to a head in 1971 (AS VI) during the first reign of Jim Early/Duke James Greyhelm as King of the West. The kingdom newsletter, *The*

Page, was at the time edited by Dorothy Heydt/Dorothea of Caer Myrddin. She had printed an editorial critical of the SCA board of directors, which upset Studebaker, who was still the chairman of the board. At that time *The Page* was printed on an old hand cranked mimeograph machine. Studebaker demanded that Heydt be removed from her office and, when that didn't happen, ordered her to hand over the means of production—the mimeograph machine. He was refused. One night he attempted to seize the means of production by showing up at Dorothea's apartment door in Berkeley and demanding that, since it was SCA property, she must hand over the mimeograph machine. She refused and called the king, who lived across town. James strapped on his sword (the real one, the one made of steel), jumped on his motorcycle and raced across town. When he got to Dorothea's apartment he found her clinging to the mimeograph machine as Jon DeCles was dragging it and her out the door.

"What are you doing?" demanded the king.

"I'm confiscating this mimeograph machine," replied Jon.

"On what authority?"

"I'm the chairman of the SCA. This mimeograph machine is SCA property and I'm taking it."

At this point King James drew his sword, placed the tip at Jon's throat and said "I'm the King of the West and that's my mimeograph machine!"

Jon prudently let go of the mimeograph machine and left.[14]

This is one of the most important tales of early SCA history. Not only does it illustrate how the early conflicts between the SCA and the Board developed, but it also illustrates how much the SCA was entwined with people's everyday lives. These three people, dressed in contemporary clothes and arguing over a contemporary piece of technology, were nonetheless acting out their SCA roles, and although Jon's role had authority under modern law, James's authority came from two sources: 1) his subjects' (represented by Dorothea) recognition of his authority as king and 2) his sword. If this story is accurate, then what James did was felony assault with a deadly weapon, but within the context of the SCA he was exercising his authority as King of the West and making sure that Jon understood it in the clearest way possible.

The second phase of the SCA's history is also marked by the development of kingdoms on a regional basis, each of which had its own unique culture incorporating the popular attitudes of the region it encompassed. Gillian Overing and Marijane Osborn, discussing Jim Wayne Miller's work on regionality, write in *Landscape of Desire* that regions "function as arenas for self definition via rejection and inclusion of the places and spaces of others."[15] Regionality in the SCA actually functions on two different planes. Each of the kingdoms in the SCA is designated as a region for administrative purposes by the corporation, and officers of the kingdom are given official, contemporary titles, so that the seneschal is the "regional president" and the king and queen the "regional cochairs." This is yet another example of the SCA corporation trying to take something that developed on its own based on a pseudomedieval model and forcing it into a modern structure.

Overing and Osborn look on place as not only an inspiration but also as character in regional myths. In this light it is worth noting that Berkeley provided a perfect backdrop for the SCA, and not just because of its position as a center of the counterculture, free speech, and science fiction fandom movements. It also provided a physical backdrop. The San Francisco Bay Area, and the Berkeley/Oakland hills in particular, were at the epicenter of the Arts and Crafts Movement in California.[16] Berkeley, once home to the architect Bernard Maybeck, is set on steep hillsides studded with eucalyptus, redwood, and oak trees. A local arboreal symbolism made its way into SCA heraldry. The winners of crown tournaments in the West are crowned with "laurel" wreaths, which are actually made of local eucalyptus leaves, and the laurel wreath is the symbol of the SCA. Likewise, the crown of the West is made of silver oak leaves and studded with acorns, the oak tree being the symbol of the West Kingdom. The original thrones of the West were made of redwood.

Writing of the California Arts and Crafts Movement in 1904, Gustav Stickley compared California to the Italian Riviera, and proclaimed that in California, "The Golden Age of the poets then becomes . . . a realized dream."[17] Berkeley and Oakland, which it borders, were the preferred home of architects in the Bay Area at that time, and the hills are thick with Arts and Crafts houses in a myriad of styles—bungalow, Spanish colonial, Neo-Tudor, French provincial, Gothic, and English country cottage—many designed by such architects as Maybeck and his one-time assistant Julia Morgan (the creator of Hearst Castle at San Simeon). However, unlike the grander scale of Arts and Crafts houses in Southern California, these houses were built primarily for the university community and for business people commuting by ferry to San Francisco. They were smaller, and came out of an intellectual and artistic aesthetic inspired by William Morris and the Pre-Raphaelites. Drawings inspired by Tolkien's "Hobbit Holes" share this aesthetic, and often look like the Arts and Crafts bungalows that can be found throughout Berkeley. The Berkeley hills are a Pre-Raphaelite paradise.

The first SCA event was held in the backyard of a Victorian house in Berkeley. The first SCA Twelfth Nights took place in Morgan's mission style great hall at Mills College in Oakland. Early events were held in oak groves at local Berkeley parks, or else across the bay at the castle like San Francisco Theological Seminary, in Marin County. The arts and crafts the SCA began to re-create in 1966, such as manuscript illumination, blacksmithing, armoring, brewing, medieval dance, medieval furniture making—the list is endless—dovetailed nicely into the aesthetic of the town and into the Morris philosophy. In addition to being part of the Berkeley counterculture, the SCA can and should be looked on as a rediscovery of the Arts and Crafts Movement.

Each new kingdom quickly developed its own traditions, customs, ideals, and modes of performing and playing the SCA king game. Kingdoms are often divided into "regions" themselves, and these regions as well develop their own unique characteristics and, usually, will form a principality and petition to become a separate kingdom, marking themselves as decidedly different from the region that spawned them. This regionality was apparent from the time the

Kingdom of the East was founded. Very quickly it differentiated itself from the West as each of the branches developed different ideas about how the SCA game should be played. Although the major difference between the two groups is cultural and stems from the differences in culture between New York City and San Francisco, it is influenced by the weather, and centers around the types of events they hold. Californians tend to camp more then New Yorkers. On the West Coast SCA events are held primarily out of doors. The camping season runs from March to November in Northern California and year round in Southern California. Around New York, outdoor activities run basically from Memorial Day to Labor Day, the days the outdoor public pools are open in New York City. Although camping does at times occur in May or September, there is both a cultural bias and a practical argument against it. Furthermore, most of the campgrounds on the East Coast provide cabins, whereas in California most camping is done in tents.

In May of 1969 the SCA in Berkeley began holding some of its events as overnight camping events,[18] and this became the normal mode of tourneying for the SCA west of the Mississippi. People arrive on Friday night, hold a tournament on Saturday, have parties (at first mostly campfire singing) on Saturday night, and then some more fighting or dancing or games on Sunday before everybody drives home.

On the East Coast most of the year the weather is not amenable to camping. Instead, one-day events are held throughout the year. These events have two separate and distinct focal points to them: a daytime activity, a tournament, and an evening activity, a feast. As a result, two sites are needed for an event, or else one site with multiple facilities: a field for fighting and a hall with a kitchen for cooking and eating. In severe weather fighting is often indoors as well, in a gymnasium or a National Guard armory. On the other hand, the East Kingdom makes up for its truncated camping season by holding the Pennsic War, getting nearly all of its camping out of the way in a two-week period.

The result has been the development of two very different cultures, a "feast culture" and a "camping culture." The entertainments at a feast are different from the entertainments at a campout. A feast lends itself more to court dancing and theatricals, whereas a campout lends itself to country dancing and to campfire singing. This split is demonstrated in the high number of people in the East relative to the West who have received membership in the Order of the Laurel for their skills at medieval-style cooking, and to a lesser extent, the high number of people in the West relative to the East who received their laurels for poetry and songwriting.

It is not that on the West Coast they don't have feasts or cooks or masques, or that on the East Coast they do not camp or sing: the difference lies in the prominence one style of tourneying takes over the other in the cultures of the two kingdoms. "Feasting Season" on the West Coast is very short, an extended holiday season from the middle of November to the end of January—or Thanksgiving weekend to Superbowl weekend. When I was Prince of the Mists the winter of 1990-1991 I gained about fifteen pounds: from my investiture in November through the investiture of the Prince of Cynagua the last week of January—including family gatherings at Thanksgiving and Christmas. I had a feast (sometimes two) to attend every weekend, all of which were centered around either a harvest theme, Yule, or Twelfth Night. This is why royalty in the West call this "the fat season."

At most Western events, feasting is not combined with fighting, and there are rarely tourneys at Western feasts. They are viewed as different activities and two completely different types of events, for which you pack different clothes and different equipment. When, after several years, two "Eastern style" events were imported to the West, they were seen as a novelty. One of these, called the "White Shield Tourney," indicates how this split is viewed by the locals. It is the only major event in the West that combines a feast with a traditional SCA tournament. Held each year in early March at the beginning of the fighting season, it marks a transition from the feasting period to the fighting period by combining both activities.

By 1980 the SCA was divided into eight kingdoms in which regional differences were firmly entrenched. A map of the SCA from that time greatly resembles the map created by Joel Garreau in his 1981 book *The Nine Nations of North America*. Although not at all an exact correlation, Garreau's map might help explain some of the regional differences among SCA kingdoms. Garreau identifies nine regions in North America which, independent of national and state boundaries, represent nine unique economies, identities, and paradigms, which he calls nations: Ecotopia in the Pacific Northwest from Point Conception to Anchorage, Alaska; the Empty Quarter, the mineral rich areas encompassed by the Sierra Nevada mountains on the West and the Rockies on the East, running all the way north to the Arctic; Mexamerica in the Southwest from Texas to Southern California and including all of Mexico; the Breadbasket in the Great Plains area of the United States and Canada; the Foundry in the industrial sections of the Ohio, Delaware, Hudson, and Chesapeake river valleys; Quebec; New England, including the Maritime provinces of Canada; Dixie, the Deep South; the Islands, a Caribbean region with its capital at Miami. As Garreau says, "Each nation has its own list of desires. Each nation knows how it plans to get what it wants from whoever's got it. Most important, each nation has a distinct prism through which it views the world."[19] They are separate and distinct, and the cultures of each of these regions influence the cultures of the SCA groups located in them.

Garreau's regional boundaries don't exactly correspond with those on the SCA map, but Garreau himself notes that the borders are fluid. Although in some of its sparsely populated areas the West Kingdom circa 1981 juts out into the Empty Quarter, it was almost an exact match to Ecotopia otherwise—certainly in its population centers, which were concentrated along the Pacific coast, the I-5 corridor, and the Inland Passage. The Kingdom of Atenveldt, although it included chunks of Mexamerica in Arizona and New Mexico, was in 1980 made up mostly of the Empty Quarter, its borders at the time running from Denver to somewhere between Salt Lake City and Reno. The Breadbasket is in the Middle Kingdom, the region known then as "The Plains (now the Kingdom) of Calontir."

The border along which Garreau divides California is the same as the border between the West and CAID. Says Garreau, "The two Pacific nations that divide California . . . are openly antagonistic. They are as antithetical as sunshine and rain."[20] The same could be said of the two kingdoms that occupy those regions. Colorado is also divided between two nations: ". . . the eastern half, which is flat, fertile agricultural land, and the western half, which rises dramatically in the suburbs of Denver to become the Rocky Mountains."[21] This is also the border between Calontir and the Outlands which, in 1980, were regions of the kingdoms of the Midrealm and Atenveldt, respectively, but are now kingdoms in their own right.

The SCA's kingdoms were influenced by the general population of the areas in which they were located, and also by the interests and attitudes of the people who founded them. A friend of mine who moved around a lot said: "When I lived in Atenveldt it was like 'we are the holy Christian knights on crusade in the desert,' when I moved to the West the attitude was 'we are the sacred land where time began,' and when I got to An Tir it was 'Hi! Welcome to Celtic World! Have a beer!'"

Christopher Scott/Master Korwyn Ariannaid has been in the SCA for thirty-five years and lived in six different kingdoms. He points out that each kingdom's character can be traced to contemporary regional attitudes. He cites the example of Calontir, which includes the capital of the Breadbasket, Kansas City, and which is famous for its communal attitude toward the SCA. It has been called a kingdom that runs like a household. Their army, instead of being dominated by units from local groups or large households, is a single cohesive unit. Everyone wears the kingdom livery and they fight in a huge shield wall. Instead of everyone driving to the war in their own vehicles the kingdom has two large buses, which they use to transport people and gear. As they march into battle they sing in harmony. Some people deride their methods as being part of a "high school football mentality," but Scott insists that the source of this attitude can be found by looking at life on the plains, where in order to survive people had to have very strong communities, where they often formed farmers' cooperatives to reduce the cost of seed and equipment to the individual farmer, and where they have to occasionally dig themselves out from floods or tornadoes as a group. Garreau also notes this collectivism in his chapter on the Breadbasket, saying:

[T]hese are virtues that are perceived as being linked to fresh memories of rural life. On the farm, you can't call in sick or go on strike or demand time and a half. By the same token, as long as you never *expect* people to look out for you when you're down on your luck, you can frequently assume that they will. . . This "we're all in it together" ethic extends itself socially and politically.[22]

This regional attitude, born of the Breadbasket, obviously has an effect on how Calontirans perform their brand of medievalism. At the Estrella War one year I happened, for the first time, to wander into the Calontir royal pavilion late on a Sunday night. Royal Pavilions are a stage set for the royalty. They are usually rectangular marquees. The thrones of the king and queen, as well as those of any royal guests, are placed under the pavilions facing out toward the populace. The pavilion provides a kind of proscenium for the rituals of the SCA court. The Calontir royal pavilion is completely different. It is a huge circle.[23] The thrones are placed at the back of the pavilion, and the performance of royalty is directed not out but inward. During court as many of the populace as can fit stand *inside* the pavilion, so that the performance becomes even more communal.

In discussing the Calontir pavilion with other SCA members at this event, I heard one of them describe it by saying that at night it looked as if a great knock out gas bomb had gone off. Another described it as the "Calontir living room." The night I was there the king, queen, crown prince, and crown princess all sat on their thrones against the back wall. The crown prince held a child on his lap. People were sprawled everywhere, lying across one another, either sleeping or conversing. Someone was always standing, facing the royalty, and singing. When one singer finished another stood and took his place. A few people listened, most did not, but the singers didn't seem to care. It struck me that this was probably a better representation of a medieval hall (product of an older communal agrarian society) than anything else in the SCA.

Former SCA board member William Rolls/Duke William of Houghton used to say that you can tell the history of each kingdom in its kingdom laws because, since each subsequent king has the ability to make new law, they often are made in reaction to what the previous king has done. For instance: an early king of the East was at the same time the kingdom seneschal, and he apparently liked being king, so he kept putting off the crown tournament to choose his successor and ended up reigning for most of a year. In response the SCA directors created a policy that a seneschal could not reign as king, and the East Kingdom created several policies to limit this situation, the most important being that the first duty of the new king is to choose his successor. The next crown tourney is scheduled before the king takes the throne, and is held within four weeks of coronation, making it difficult for the new king to reschedule. This has the further effect of making every king a lame duck for most of his reign.

In an article for the British journal *Geographical*, Rupert Isaacson describes how the SCA's made-up map of the world subverts contemporary geopolitics in favor of a utopian fantasy:

> By recreating the xenophobia and aggression of the medieval world, but at the same time taking the suffering out, the SCA has unwillingly created an international subculture of tolerance, communication and play. Real geography is transcended. The real world, "Mundania," is put on hold.[24]

Benjamin Nugent in *American Nerd: The Story of My People* suggests that the SCA's creation of an alternative world with its own rules and hierarchies is quintessentially American, "The original American Dream, for the pilgrims, for the immigrant hordes, was to construct a new country that gave them the respect and possibility the old one couldn't. Isn't that what the SCA is doing?"[25] As Nugent points out, while there are SCA branches in Europe and Asia, it is in America, which does not have its own medieval history, where the SCA flourishes.

This second phase of the SCA, in the 1970s, was further influenced by popular culture. As Lenehan mentioned, the SCA was part of a "taste group" that also included computer programmers, science fiction fans, and war gamers. Fantasy role playing games such as Dungeons and Dragons developed in the 1970s as part of the same fantasy, escapist aesthetic that informed the SCA, and many SCA members were involved in Dungeons and Dragons from the very beginning. The popularity of the game later helped fuel a growth in the SCA as people came to the group hoping to live out some of their D&D fantasies. Today there are live action role playing games, or LARPs, which serve the same function.

An equally important influence was the explosion in popularity of fantasy literature that followed on the heels of the *Lord of the Rings*. As authors, Bradley, Paxson, Anderson, and Zimmer provided a link between this realm of fantasy and the SCA; other authors such as Katherine Kurtz, Robert Lynn Asprin, Jerry Pournelle, and Mercedes Lackey soon joined the group. Some books such as *Murder at the War* by Mary Monica Pulver, a murder mystery set at the Pennsic War, and *The Warlock In Spite of Himself,* by Peter Stasheff, in which an SCA branch forms a colony on another planet, were obviously influenced by authors' experiences in the SCA. These books in turn influenced the SCA by recording some SCA myths in a mass communications format. This produced a symbiotic relationship between the SCA and popular literature.

One important aspect of this is the influence upon the SCA of two sets of fantasy novels and, even more importantly, of fantasy art. The first is the work of Robert E. Howard, a Texas roughneck who wrote in the 1930s, at the same time that Tolkien was creating his Middle Earth. A writer of pulp fiction, Howard created a very different brand of fantasy from that of Tolkien, more warlike and heroic, less concerned with the actual Middle Ages or with the weighty questions of the twentieth century. His heroes, mostly based on the Texas oil workers that he knew, were violent men—characters like the puritan adventurer Solomon Kane, the Pictish warrior Bran Mak Morn, and the king of Atlantis, Kull the Conqueror. By far his most popular and lasting hero was Conan the Barbarian who, like Tolkien's characters, lived in a prehistoric Europe peopled with magical creatures. Like Tolkien's works, Howard's are about the passing of a magical age and the dawn of an age ruled by nonmagical men, but whereas Tolkien is mourning the passing of the elves and their magic, the primary theme that runs through Howard's stories is that of man's eventual triumph over magic and superstition. The *Gor* novels by John Norman are inheritors of Howard's legacy. They are sword and sandal epics in which warriors fight over scantily clad slave girls. They were written around the misogynistic theme that all women secretly want to be dominated by men, and became very popular in S&M circles.

The aesthetic presented by these two series and others like them had a profound impact on how the SCA performed its fantasy medievalism, particularly in the 1970s, and presented a challenge to the SCA paradigm. Several large "barbarian" households formed in order to give people a chance to portray not medieval knights but barbarian mercenaries inspired by these works of pulp fiction. Some of these groups used historical tropes such as Vikings, Mongols, or Picts, but many of them were pure fantasy. Women in these households were neither the demure princesses of Victorian fantasy nor the powerful noblewomen of the actual Middle Ages, but slaves. They wore Hollywood slave girl outfits or rabbit fur bikinis and, sometimes, chains, manacles, and slave collars (since banned by the SCA's board of directors). These groups are also primarily responsible for the popularity of belly dancing in the SCA, one of the group's main nocturnal activities, though today it is no longer associated with fantasy barbarians, and is instead part of a Middle Eastern subculture that flourishes in the SCA.

Two of the largest barbarian households, Rolling Thunder and The Crimson Company, were centered around the Barony of al-Barran, the SCA branch in Albuquerque, New Mexico. Rolling Thunder took its aesthetic from Conan, while Crimson Company was based on a Gorean mercenary unit. These two groups represented a challenge to the SCA paradigm different from that of Mongols or Aztecs, who could at least claim a historical precedent for their existence. They were pure fantasy groups, and as fighting units they brought to the field a set of ideals adapted from barbarian heroic fantasy that had no use for the chivalry and pageantry of the SCA king game.

By far the most controversial of these barbarian groups is the Tuchux. Based on a group of nomadic barbarian slave traders in the *Gor* series, they operate as a separate group from the SCA, participating mostly at Pennsic, where they camp on the edge of the event, keeping to themselves. The Tuchux often perform a master/slave social structure. Many of the women in their group dress more like attendees at a rock concert or a biker rally than an SCA event. They are often seen on the battlefield bringing water to the Tuchux and wearing leather bikinis or else t-shirts with the Tuchux emblem, slave collars and cowboy hats. The Tuchux have been involved in numerous incidents over the years, such as lobbing urine filled balloons into the camp next door or duct taping someone to their "tree of woe." One of them famously jumped out of a tree on top of another fighter during a woods battle. In spite of these unwelcome behaviors they field the largest mercenary force at Pennsic, so the kings of the East and the Middle are always trying to hire them for their side. They also host a charity tournament at Pennsic.

As each of these examples demonstrates, during this second phase of its development the SCA grew and spread across North America and eventually to other continents, evolving and changing as it did so to meet the communal and cultural needs and desires of members in different areas of the world.

Phase Three: The Major Wars

The third and current phase of the SCA is marked by a coming together of the various regions in large interkingdom events. These events have been going on since early in the SCA's history, but by the 1990s enough of them had been founded that the SCA calendar began to revolve not around local and kingdom events but around the major wars and gatherings, leading to a homogenization of the SCA. Advances in communications facilitated this. The rise of the internet in the nineties allowed people in every kingdom of the SCA to communicate on a daily basis with one another. There are numerous SCA mailing lists, including an SCA wide mailing list, rec.sca.org. In addition, every kingdom has its own mailing list, and there is a list for each of the peerage orders. There are also SCA wide lists, most of them at Yahoogroups, devoted to interests such as costuming, rapier, archery, lady fighters, and brewing, just to name a few, as well as various support groups.

The oldest and largest of the major events is the Pennsic War between the East and Middle kingdoms, which is held for two weeks in August. Estrella War, held in Arizona in February, was originally a war between Atenveldt and the West, but is now a conflict among four kingdoms: Atenveldt, CAID, Outlands, and Artemisia. Gulf Wars in March involves the kingdoms of Trimaris, Ansteorra, Gleann Abhann, and Meridies, while Lilies War in Calontir is a themed war that is not based on interkingdom conflict, but instead the sides are determined by that year's theme (for instance, one year it was the two nonfighting peerages, the Laurels vs. the Pelicans, and their allies).[26] The fifth largest event is the Great Western War held in October in CAID. There are other wars in the SCA, but these five are more than just regional conflicts. They are festivals intended to attract people from all kingdoms.

One function of these events is to break down regional biases in favor of a more homogenized version of the SCA. As kingdom cultures mix and become diluted, attitudes and customs universal to the SCA become more prominent. This hybridization/cross contact has led to several arguments, mostly carried out over internet mailing lists, as to what the SCA's function is. Is the SCA primarily a social group in which people simply attend large costume parties on a regular basis, or is it an educational group that attempts to accurately reenact medieval culture? This argument has existed since the beginning of the SCA, but it has gained impetus both because of the internet and because of the interkingdom communication at the large regional events. Another way to frame the question rarely comes up: Is the SCA an antimodern counterculture set up in resistance to contemporary society?

[1] Carey Lenehan, "Postmodern Medievalism: A Sociological Study of the Society for Creative Anachronism" (BA Honors Thesis, University of Tasmania, 1994), 31.
[2] So too were a lot of other things which had no relation to the SCA: the Hell's Angels, the Black Panthers, the remnants of the Beatniks, the hippies, the free speech movement, the summer of love, and, as discussed below, the Church of Satan. See, for instance, the Mark Kitchell documentary film *Berkeley in the '60s* (First Run Features, 2002). Also during that time period, Oakland was even the center of the sports world, as the baseball A's, the basketball Warriors, and the football Raiders all won championships while publicly presenting a counterculture image; see *Rebels of Oakland: the A's, the Raiders, the Seventies* (HBO Films 2003). At a lecture I attended in Berkeley in 1986, Hunter S. Thompson—who lived in and wrote about the area in the sixties and seventies—said that the Hell's Angels, the Black Panthers, and the Oakland Raiders were all basically the same thing. The Bay Area in the late sixties was a locus of counterculture activity, of which the SCA was only a small part.
[3] In SCA documents it is stated as "Anno Societatis I" meaning the first year of the society. The SCA new year begins on May 1.
[4] David Thewlis, "A Brief Look at the Past," in *The Known World Handbook*, ed. Hillary Powers (Milpitas, CA: The Society for Creative Anachronism, 1992), 26-27.
[5] Diana Paxson, "The Last Tournament," in *The Known World Handbook*, ed. Hillary Powers (Milpitas, CA: The Society for Creative Anachronism, 1992), 24.
[6] Flier for the first SCA event, in Keyes.
[7] Paxson, "The Last Tournament," 24-25.
[8] Ibid.
[9] Ibid., 25.
[10] Thewlis, 27.
[11] Keyes.
[12] Stephan de Lorraine, quoted in "The Formation of the SCA Inc." Ibid.
[13] Sir Robert of Dunharrow quoted Ibid.
[14] Dorothy Heydt, "SCA History," a panel discussion at Collegium Occidentalis, Kensington, CA, 19 October 1996. This is the story as Heydt tells it. Early insists that, although he had his sword with him, he only drew it halfway out of the scabbard and never put it to Jon's throat.
[15] Gillian Overing and Marijane Osborn, *Landscape of Desire: Partial Stories of the Medieval Scandinavian World* (Minneapolis, MN: University of Minnesota Press, 1994), 42.
[16] See Kenneth R. Trapp, ed., *The Arts and Crafts Movement in California: Living the Good Life* (New York: Abbeville Press Publishers, 1993).
[17] Richard Guy Wilson, "Devine Excellence: The Arts and Crafts Life in California," in *The Arts and Crafts Movement in California: Living the Good Life*, ed. Kenneth R. Trapp (New York: Abbeville Press Publishers, 1993), 13.
[18] Keyes.
[19] Joel Garreau, *The Nine Nations of North America* (New York: Houghton Mifflin, 1981), 2.
[20] Ibid., 3.
[21] Ibid.
[22] Ibid., 350.
[23] This is also true of the Outlands royal pavilion, which was copied from the Calontir design but is not used in quite the same way.
[24] Rupert Isaacson, "Knights of Passion," *Geographical* (January 2000): 63.

[25] Benjamin Nugent, *American Nerd: The Story of My People* (New York: Scribner, 2008), 180.
[26] See "Lilies War" at Kingdom of Calontir (accessed 12 May 2004); available from www.calontir.org.

2

CREATIVE MEDIEVALISM

From time to time in Western society the medieval makes a resurgence. There is more to this than simply a fascination with a bygone era. Like ancient Rome and (in the United States) the cowboy era, the Middle Ages occupy a mythic status in Western history. Beowulf, King Arthur, Robin Hood, the Crusades, William Wallace, Abelard and Heloise, the castles, the cathedrals, and above all the knight in shining armor are archetypes of a world both beautiful and exotic. And it is a world that we look to again and again in movies, literature, and in groups like the SCA.

The SCA is a fringe organization, one that is easy to mock as a bunch of nerds and losers who have lost (or never had) contact with reality. *Maxim* Magazine said in August 2003:

> Founded in 1966 by Tolkien fans in Berkeley, CA, the SCA boasts 24,000 members worldwide for whom geekdom *is* a contact sport. Gatherings offer a variety of seminars in which tunic-clad campers are schooled in the use of "heavy weapons," with the ensuing mock battles lasting until *Xena* comes on. Too cowardly to fight? Learn how to make puddings and homemade mead instead, you knave. The SCA's premier event is held August 1–17, when 10,000 virgins leave their mothers' basements for the 32nd annual Pennsic War in ye olde Slippery Rock, Pennsylvania. Saddle up your noble steed and have at thee![1]

However, in the web journal *Disinformation* Ken Mondschein notes:

> The Society, after all, was more than a physical outlet for the creative energies and unfulfilled ideations of a generation of young misfits: It was also a way to impress chicks with one's physical prowess, the perfect antidote to the stereotype of the bespectacled, Spock-grokking sci-fi nerd.[2]

Ineed, a hallmark of the SCA is the dichotomy between the perception of SCA members as losers, nerds and (in what is obviously meant as an insult by *Maxim*) virgins, and the facts that SCA fighting is a vigorous and violent physical activity and that the SCA is for many of its members a sexual playground. While many older members of the SCA are married and involved in usually monogamous relationships, for others the SCA acts as one of the worlds biggest hookup parties.

Shannon McSmith/Lady Christeanne Regan MacNab has opined that the SCA is basically like high school for people who never grew up: you've got your jocks (the fighters), your cheerleaders (their consorts), your student government nerds (the Pelicans), and your weird artsy types (the Laurels). You have your in crowds and your out crowds and any number of cliques, the politics is brutal, and everybody's favorite topic of conversation is who's sleeping with whom. This is a perceptive observation. However, much of this would be true of other clearly defined groups. Fraternal organizations, business associations, theatre companies, and churches, just to name a few, have the same tendencies toward politics, cliquishness, and gossip.

For most members, the SCA becomes what Victor Turner refers to as a "star group," which he defines as

> groups to which we owe the greatest personal loyalty and whose fate is for us of the greatest personal concern . . . . A star group is the one with which a person identifies most deeply and in which he finds fulfillment of his major social and personal strivings and desires.[3]

SCA members are passionate about the SCA. The group provides them with a sense of accomplishment and power over their lives, a community of like-minded individuals, and an escape from contemporary life. In the real world they have little of the extraordinary in their lives. In the "known world" of the SCA they can be kings, knights, poets, heroes, barbarian warriors, desert sheiks, or samurai. People who stay in the SCA for a long time find that it makes up the vast majority of their nonwork social interaction, and that their closest friends and usually their significant others are also members.

Some of the issues Grossman identifies in his *Time* article reflect not just on the fans of medieval fantasy, or on those out on the fringe like the SCA, but on society as a whole. As Grossman points out, today's world shares something with the sixties, the last era (according to Grossman) in which fantasy in general and Tolkien in particular saw a rise in popularity: these are troubling times. America is fighting wars in two different Middle Eastern countries. Terrorists target American soldiers, citizens, and even buildings. Corporate globalization is reorganizing the world economy, displacing workers in both industrialized and third world nations. To many, these events seem driven and controlled by shadowy forces beyond the control or comprehension of everyday folk. In troubling times the future looks a bit more bleak and it is comforting to look back on a fantasy world where villains were clearly villains, where virtue was rewarded, and where magic and honor could provide hope. Writes Grossman:

> Tolkien, a veteran of the British nightmare of the Somme in World War I, is a poet of war, and we are in need of a good war story right now. At a time when Americans are wandering deeper into a nebulous conflict against a faceless enemy, Tolkien gives us a conflict we wish we could fight: a struggle with a foe whose face we can see, who fights out on the open battlefield, far removed from innocent civilians. In Middle-Earth, unlike the Middle East, you can tell an evildoer because he or she looks evil.[4]

It should be noted that this statement is not at all accurate in regards to Tolkien's books. Sauron, the villain in *The Lord of the Rings,* is certainly a "faceless enemy." He has no face, no body even, and is represented only by one large malevolent eye, and much of the evil he does takes place in secret not on the battlefield. Tolkien's work also has a closer association with the Middle East then Grossman realizes. It has been argued by many scholars that the inspiration for the conflict between the good peoples of the West and the dark powers of the East in Tolkien was the Turkish encroachment on Europe in the fifteenth century and, in particular, the fall of Constantinople in 1453, and that Tolkien's Sauron is at least partially inspired by the Ottoman emperor Mohamed II. But Grossman has correctly identified a major part of the appeal of medievalism: the oversimplification that in the medieval world you knew who your enemies were.

Such fantasies are, obviously, not just a matter of fairies and hobbits and hopeful outcomes. The word "medieval," originally a pejorative referring to a backward age coming between and interrupting two ages of high civilization, has taken on a variety of meanings in contemporary society, many of them negative. Medieval (occasionally in pop culture misrepresented as "Mid-Evil") continues to raise images of violence, mayhem, and barbarism. Ken Follett's novel *Pillars of the Earth* and Michael Crichton's time travel novel *Timeline* are good examples from popular culture of a violent Middle Ages where the oppressed peasants are basically waiting for the enlightenment to come along and save them. This is the Middle Ages of inquisitions and torture racks and institutionalized genocide against non-Christians. Everybody knows what it means to "get medieval" toward someone.

The Lord of the Rings and many of its medieval precursors—Thomas Malory's *Le Morte d'Arthur,* the anonymous *Beowulf,* and *The Song of Roland,* just to name a few—are extremely dark tales. They are uplifting because they are about heroes who triumph over evil, but each of them also tells of a great sacrifice made for a common good, and if we are to identify with the heroes in these medieval fantasies we must accept that in the end they either die or, in the case of Frodo at least, suffer exile from the very place they struggled to save.

This fascination with the medieval has been with us before. Umberto Eco points out that Western society has been periodically rediscovering the Middle Ages ever since the moment they ended (which he places, conveniently, in 1492).[5] In the early nineteenth century, as industrialization and enclosure were forcing the descendants of peasant farmers off the land and into the streets, slums, and (if they were lucky) factories of London, romantic novelists such as Sir Walter Scott, as well as the Pre-Raphaelite painters and followers of the Arts and Crafts Movement, looked to the Middle Ages for both inspiration and subject matter. Notes Andrew Taylor, "For nineteenth-century Europe, the Middle

Ages evoked a simpler time free from the complexities of industrial and secular society, a time symbolized by the simple but courageous knight."[6]

During the anxious times between the world wars, with the horrors of the trenches fresh in people's memories, and with a darkening shadow gathering in Germany (much like the darkening shadow that gathers in Tolkien's Mordor), the Middle Ages made a comeback. Perhaps just as important as fantasy's portrayal of good triumphing over evil is its portrayal of an agrarian society built on honor and loyalty. Another medieval fantasy from the same era as *The Lord of the Rings*, T.H. White's *The Once and Future King* (which was made into two very different films, both of which affected the formation of the SCA: *Camelot*, and Disney's *The Sword in the Stone*), also portrays a happy, peaceful agrarian world about to be ripped apart by sinister forces from outside. White was twelve years younger then Tolkien and did not fight in WWI, but both of their works, begun between the world wars and completed during the Cold War, reflect the same anxieties about the world and the same longing for a heroic age. To these two can also be added the theology and fantasy authors C.S. Lewis and Charles Williams who, along with Tolkien, formed the core of a literary circle at Oxford University known as "The Inklings."

When the SCA began, during the upheaval of the free speech movement and Vietnam war protests, many people looked to these Victorian pastoral utopias, to the Middle Ages, and to Tolkien's Middle Earth as places where right and wrong were clearly defined, war could be just, and the enemy, although shadowy, was both knowable and defeatable. Tolkien's books, just recently published in the U.S., found an enthusiastic following in the counterculture movement. At the same time the musical and cartoon versions of White's book were immensely popular. *The Sword in the Stone* was released in 1963. *Camelot* ran on Broadway from 1960 to '63 and was produced as a movie in 1967, capping a long run of popularity for medieval costume epics in Hollywood. As Eco writes:

> We are dreaming the Middle Ages, some say. But in fact both Americans and Europeans are inheritors of the Western legacy, and all the problems of the Western world emerged in the Middle Ages: Modern languages, merchant cities, capitalist economy (along with banks, checks and prime rate) are inventions of medieval society.[7]

To Eco, then, the Middle Ages do not represent a simpler time that we yearn for in times of trouble (although he considers the Middle Ages to be the infancy of modern Western society). Instead, in Eco's view, we look to the Middle Ages to understand the problems that beset us today, as a doctor looks to a patient's childhood as part of his diagnosis.

Of all these popular culture phenomena it was Tolkien who had the most impact on the counterculture and on the SCA. Grossman points out that early

SCA members were searching for the romantic ideals of honor, chivalry, and courtesy, which they found lacking in contemporary society. Wrote Paxson:

> The first Anachronists came from the leading edge of the Baby Boom. We grew up in the fifties, that triumph of plastic suburban culture, and we hated it. For the most part, no matter how hard we tried, or our parents pushed, we could not bring ourselves to truly conform. But in the sixties, the Civil Rights movement and the "New Society" heralded the possibility of change. When we gathered for the first Tournament, a catalytic reaction occurred. The moment was magic, and no one wanted it to end. And suddenly we realized that it did not have to—if we did not like the world we had been born into, we had the power to change it and create one of our own.[8]

As Andrew Rodwell notes, Paxson links the SCA's founding in Berkeley to the protest movements that were taking place on campus at the same time.[9] Thus the SCA was born out of a discontent with technology and with contemporary society, which not only places it squarely within the counterculture of the 1960s but also links it to the Arts and Crafts Movement and the Pre-Raphaelite movement of the nineteenth century.

Nostalgia and the SCA

One of the principal differences between the SCA approach and the renaissance faire approach to history is that when the SCA mocks people they are more often than not mocking themselves. Renaissance faires are farcical in the purest sense. Structurally, a farce is a genre in which people leave their home, enter a comically chaotic world, and then return home again. At renaissance faires patrons enter a comically chaotic world from a past time, in which the participants—peasantry, nobility, and merchant class—are all mocked in some way, both high and low. At the oldest renaissance faire in America, that which was put on by the Living History Center in Marin County (and which had links to the early SCA), washerwomen are portrayed as comic prostitutes, puritans as hypocritical pedants, merchants as greedy misers, and courtiers as obsequious sycophants. All of these images exist in renaissance drama; many of them are taken from Shakespearean comedy. For most of the paying customers of the faire, they provide an alternate world of greed, corruption, and comedy to contrast with the bland normalcy of contemporary society (some customers pay to get inside to dress in costume and be part of the show, not the audience—an important distinction when looking at the SCA).

The SCA, on the other hand, is nostalgic, not farcical. To many SCA members it is the contemporary world that is twisted and strange, and contemporary ideals and tendencies that are to be mocked. This is the exact opposite of the way the premodern is portrayed at most renaissance faires. The SCA is nostalgic for the Middle Ages. It is this nostalgia, the sense that somehow the Middle Ages were a better time than the present, that is the most prominent feature of the SCA. Rodwell, in the title to his thesis, referred to the SCA as antimodern performance. Wendy Erisman, too, notes that "[a]ntimodernism has, in fact, been a part of the SCA's ideology since its founding."[10] This antimodernism is also postmodern. As Jameson pointed out the two are linked: "One can, for example, salute the arrival of postmodernism from an essentially antimodernist standpoint."[11] It is also an important part of the utopianism of the counterculture. In *Science Fiction and the Real World,* Norman Spinrad writes that the counterculture is characterized by "its antitechnological ideology, the neoludditism, the suspicion of the works of science and technology, the bucolic mysticism, the back to the soil movement, the ecological awareness, the whole tiedyed ball of candle wax."[12]

In addition to pastiche, another dominant feature of postmodernism according to Jameson is what he calls the nostalgia mode: "in a world in which stylistic innovation is no longer possible, all that is left is to imitate dead styles, to speak through the masks and with the voices of the styles in the imaginary museum."[13] This is how the SCA approaches the medieval. The SCA is not the real Middle Ages, nor is it an accurate picture of the real Middle Ages. It is a pastiche, a collection of ideas about the Middle Ages, often, but not always, frankly romantic and highly nostalgic.

Nostalgia, "a wistful or excessively sentimental yearning for return to or of some past period or irrecoverable condition,"[14] is an important element of SCA culture. Nostalgia, "an antidote to what is new and unsettling,"[15] is also an important element of American culture. Grossman points toward new and unsettling times as an impetus for the revival of fantasy in America and the popularity of the SCA. Fred Davis, in *Yearning for Yesterday: a Sociology of Nostalgia,* writes, "The nostalgic evocation of some past state of affairs always occurs in the context of present fears, discontents, anxieties or uncertainties."[16] Taken in this context the nostalgic revival of fantasy in general and the romantic medievalism of the SCA in particular can and should be seen as reflective of contemporary anxieties of the 1960s. (It should be noted that Davis insists that nostalgia can only exist for a period within living memory, and that a yearning for an earlier age must be distinguished from nostalgia. Jameson makes no such distinction.)

The SCA actually employs a dual nostalgia. SCA members long first and foremost for a romantic medieval past that never existed, but they also dream about the early days of the SCA. The SCA creates its own myths and legends, which are told in songs and stories SCA members create. Often there is a sense that as the SCA has grown from a small gathering in someone's backyard to an international organization, many of the values that drew the original members of the SCA together have been lost. "People just aren't as chivalrous as they used to be" is a common complaint. This is interesting when compared to *The Lord of the Rings,* because that too is a nostalgic book. Not only is it nostalgic for a simpler pastoral time in England, but the conclusion of the *Lord of the Rings* represents the passing of an era. The Elves leave Middle Earth and sail away into the heavens, and when they go magic leaves the world as well. The people of Middle Earth are always longing for a past they cannot recapture, just as the people of the SCA are.

Nostalgia, although comforting, can get in the way of life. "Nostalgia can be dangerous," says Davis, "It can drain the juices from one's encounters with what is new and should be exciting."[17] Members of the SCA also run the risk of becoming like the subject of Edward Arlington Robinson's poem "Miniver Cheevy," who longs so much for a medieval world that he can't function in the contemporary one.[18] Miniver Cheevy is lost in his dreams about the Middle Ages because he cannot act them out. He is a Don Quixote without the courage to act out his fantasies. SCA members, on the other hand, are able to act out their medieval fantasies, to become the things they dream about.

Nick Kaye, in *Postmodernism and Performance,* sums up neatly a postmodern approach to history:

> [T]he postmodern self-consciously "replays" images of a past that cannot be known, but that can only be constructed and reconstructed through a play of entirely contemporary references to the idea of the past.[19]

SCA performance is built around interplay among ideas about the past that are consciously contemporary. Although some in the SCA clearly seek to "know" the past through interpretation, which is the project of living history, they usually recognize the attainment of this kind of knowledge as an impossibility. In looking at the SCA an image that represents not one but several ideas of the past emerges, incorporating all the various filters through which the past is viewed in popular culture and the academy. At any particular SCA event one might see a woman in painstakingly reconstructed Elizabethan gown, living historians attempting a highly detailed impression of a sixteenth-century German mercenary unit, a person wearing Danskin tights and elf ears, a knight and squire trying hard to accurately re-create the relationship between a knight and squire in the thirteenth century while fighting alongside a knight and squire who are trying to re-create the relationship between a knight and squire in Conan Doyle's story *Sir Nigel,* and any number of other medieval tropes. And everywhere you see images lifted out of Hollywood costume dramas.

A group in which contemporary people adopt romantic, fantasy, or even somewhat realistic personas based on an idea of history, be that idea scholarly or one taken from pop culture, not for the purpose of performing for an audience but instead for the purpose of interacting with likeminded people within a socially constructed faux medieval framework, fits well into theories of postmodernism. Linda Hutcheon in *A Poetics of Postmodernism* notes that, "[t]here seems to be a new desire to think historically, and to think historically these days is to think critically and contextually."[20] She goes on to say:

> What the postmodern writing of both history and literature has taught us is that both history and fiction are discourses, that both constitute systems of significa-tion by which we make sense of the past . . . . In other words, the meaning and shape are not *in the events,* but *in the systems* which make those past "events" into present historical "facts."[21]

Most members of the SCA are not this metacritical. Nonetheless for most SCA members the SCA helps to make sense not only of the past but of the present as well—or at least it sheds light on certain versions of the past and of the present filtered through their experiences within the group.

Carey Lenehan in a thesis titled "Postmodern Medievalism" argues that the SCA as a leisure activity cannot be explained using any of the standard theories of leisure. Only through theories of postmodernism can the SCA be understood, he writes, noting: "The SCA is a group where, despite appearances, purely mimetic violence is enacted within the purview of a 'sub-culture' constructed from a post-modern mélange of images, a reality that is modeled from a series of real and fictional images."[22]

This is different from the ways reenactment and living history groups stage performances of the past. The differences among the terms reenactment, re-creation, and living history are important to discuss. Reenactment is a genre in which a specific event is performed in as much detail and with as much "histori-cal accuracy" as possible. The most common of these are battle reenactments, such as the annual reenactments of Civil War battles. Living history is a genre in which an era, not an event, is performed, also with a great emphasis on historical accuracy, in order to convey a sense of time and place. Examples of this would be Colonial Williamsburg and Plimoth Plantation, where visitors are immersed in a supposedly accurate historical setting. Re-creation (the play on "recreation" is intentional) is a make-believe activity in which various aspects of a particular time period or periods are performed as a contemporary creation coded with period details, often romantic and nonhistorical. Although reenactments and living history usually have an audience, re-creation events are nearly always performed as gatherings in which an outside audience is not present, and the performance is staged solely for the participants. In other words, it's a big game of make-believe.

SCA people often participate in other forms of make-believe performance: renaissance faires, American Civil War reenactment, Sealed Knot Society (English Civil War), Victorian fancy dress balls, Victorian Christmas fairs, Steampunk, Cowboy Action Shooting, Buckskinning, Revolutionary War, and (especially) science fiction fandom. The SCA's particular brand of incomplete history clearly demonstrates the tension between product and process, which is another element of postmodern theory. SCA members take elements of medieval history, various theories about medieval culture, movies, books, and fantasies about the Middle Ages, period romances, and Victorian melodramas and combine them into their own personal performance of medievalism. The SCA was created not from the top down but organically, and participants' performances are based on the knowledge, beliefs, and fantasies they bring with them to the group. In a sense, the SCA is a postmodern construction of a Hollywood version of a Victorian image of a romantic Middle Ages that never actually existed. In *The Courtesy Book,* a guide for new members of the SCA, the author (who writes under his persona name, Orlando Ambrosius) writes, "The SCA incorporates aspects of living history but remains a rather formless, anarchistic sort of living history, owing more to the Victorian idea of medieval culture than to actual medieval culture."[23]

The SCA is strongly tied to fantasy and historical literature. The first SCA event was a party thrown by Paxson, and was attended by the fantasy writers Paul Edwin Zimmer and Marion Zimmer Bradley, as well as the family of the author Poul Anderson (who could not attend that day himself but was heavily involved thereafter). Science fiction and fantasy fandom—particularly to the works of J.R.R. Tolkien—provided a context and inspiration for early SCA events, as well as a community of fans to draw upon for new members. The early SCA was made up of members of what Tolkien ruefully referred to as his "deplorable cultus."[24]

Hollander often lists what he refers to as "roots literature," meaning literary works that had a great influence on the SCA. Included in this list are Tolkien's books, *Sir Nigel, The Chronicles of Narnia* by C.S. Lewis, *The Once and Future King* by T.H. White, and several other works of fantasy and romance. His list also includes primary sources such as *Le Morte d'Arthur* and the tales of Sir Parsifal, but it is made up mostly of contemporary sources, and all of them are literary works.[25] It is these works that, according to Hollander, informed the SCA's version of medievalism (though he is quick to point out that everyone in the SCA has his or her own list of sources that inspire them). To many in the SCA, literature informs history and vice versa. Serious reenactors both within and without the SCA criticize some members' use of literary and filmic tropes in constructing their SCA performances, but this is also in keeping with postmodernism. As Hutcheon points out:

... [I]t is this very separation of the literary and the historical that is n̶o̶... challenged in postmodern theory and art, and recent critical readings of both history and fiction have focused more on what the two modes of writing share than on how they differ. They have both been seen to derive their force more from verisimilitude than from any objective truth; they are both identified as linguistic constructs, highly conventionalized in their narrative forms, and not at all transparent either in terms of language or structure; and they appear to be equally intertextual, deploying the texts of the past within their own complex textuality.[26]

This statement applies very well to SCA practice. The SCA uses a fiction (persona, their created world, images from literature and film) in order to explore aspects of the historical Middle Ages, while at the same time employing the texts of historians, fantasists, and medieval authors of both chronicle and romance in the performance of their game.

Schechner links all types of historical performance (which he terms "historical restoration") to filmic images of the past, and places them firmly within the context of postmodernism and performance:

These exist only for those who study them, either in books or through restorations/re-creations. Restorations are increasing. Maybe this is because films seem to bring us genuine experiences of earlier times in ways more fleshed out and genuine than archaeological or written accounts do . . . . For the historical restoration is actually a version of the postmodern. It assumes that spectators, and restorers, can shift temporal channels. Moving through a restored environment involves swift adjustments of frame and accurate processing of multiplex signals.[27]

This type of restoration, this shifting of temporal frames, was a major goal of Paxson's when she threw the party which became the first SCA event.

The SCA was hardly unique. It is one of several groups that started at the time, many of them in the San Francisco Bay Area, linked to the counterculture and to each other in their desires to reject the banality of modern society. In his internet article in *Disinformation,* Mondschein notes that the Church of Satan was officially founded at midnight on the same day as the SCA, just across the bay in San Francisco. The Church of Satan was a nonconformist, anti-Christian group set up in protest of the strictures that existed in American society at the time. Church of Satan founder Anton LeVay said:

We established a *Church* of Satan—something that would smash all concepts of what a 'church' was supposed to be. This was a temple of indulgence to openly defy the temples of abstinence that had been built up until then. We didn't want it to be an unforgiving, unwelcoming place, but a place where you could go to have fun.[28]

As Mondschein points out:

> Though the two groups, at first glance, would seem to be nothing alike, in fact, they share much common ground: A sense of profound alienation from the banality of twentieth-century American culture, the embrace of a romantic alternative ethos held to be more "true" than that adhered to by the vast herd of humanity, and the creation of an alternative space in which this ethos could be translated into real life.[29]

A year earlier, in 1965, another nonconformist group was founded in San Francisco that has a similar social structure to that of the SCA. The International Imperial Court system is a society of drag queens that now has branches all over the world. Their main function is to hold an annual charity ball and coronation in which an elected emperor and empress are crowned. Their court structure, with not only empresses, but also princesses, duchesses, and baronesses, is very similar to that of the SCA.[30] Another branch of science fiction fandom (in the early days this is how many participants looked at the SCA) that started about this same time is the Trekkies, fans of the television show "Star Trek" who stage their own type of performative escape by holding conventions where they can trade memorabilia, meet people involved with the production of the show, and even dress up and pretend to be Star Trek characters. All of these groups demonstrate something about the late sixties and early seventies: a desire to escape, resist, and even subvert contemporary society. Eco suggests a strong relationship between the new Satanism, Tolkien, *Excalibur*, the Avalon sagas, Jacques Le Goff, and *Star Wars*. "Indeed," he says, "it seems that people like the Middle Ages."[31]

The SCA has a bad reputation among medieval scholars, much of it well deserved, because, although most of the group's activities are social and recreational, not scholarly, many SCA members think that because they go out to fight in armor or practice medieval arts and crafts they know more about the Middle Ages than medieval scholars do. They learn by doing, but this has led to tensions with academics—for instance, according to Pamela Sheingorn of the Department of Art History at the City University of New York, the SCA was at one time asked not to participate in the International Congress of Medieval Studies, which is held annually in Kalamazoo, Michigan. However, SCA activity actually ranges from the purely recreational to the stringently academic, and the SCA has produced a number of accomplished medieval scholars who have earned their Ph.D.s doing research that they began as part of their participation in the SCA. Many of these scholars present at conferences, including Kalamazoo, on a regular basis, often keeping their membership in the SCA closeted, so to speak. This also depends on the discipline in which they work. For instance, although cultural historians may not make their participation in the SCA well known, it is not considered a bad thing among scholars of material culture. Susan Carroll- Clark, editor of the SCA's quarterly magazine, notes:

> Each year I attend [the Kalamazoo conference], I meet more and more members of the Society who are presenting their research in the form of conference papers, often to considerable acclaim by professional and amateur scholars alike. In certain fields—particularly costume studies, cookery, and research into medieval martial arts—the contributions of scholars whose interest was first piqued as members of the Society are beginning to receive the recognition they deserve.[32]

Critics from both inside and outside the SCA think of SCA events as large make-believe parties with lots of drinking, flirting, and hitting people with sticks as the main activities. The tension that these positions create within the group is played out in participants' performances. However, the SCA is also a pop culture phenomenon. I prefer to look at the SCA as an ongoing, roving work of performance art in which people perform fantasy relationships that become, for them, very real (I was pleased to find in the course of my research that someone else had made this analogy in a publication called *Thinkwell*, referring to the SCA as "performance art by committee"[33]).

The ways in which SCA members play their parts, both as members of a contemporary educational corporation and as part of a make-believe romantic kingdom, make up a pattern of resistance. The conflict between living history and recreation/re-creation as paradigms, between lingering regional differences and homogenization of values, and between the current SCA and a nostalgic longing for a past SCA, all contribute to tension within the group, but all stem from a rejection of contemporary society in favor of a self-created postmodern fantasy.

Speaking of nostalgia in *The Lord of the Rings,* Hanna Edwards/Lady Gracia Vasquez de Trillo said:

> In one way Lord of the Rings is very depressing because this era of intense camaraderie and heroic deeds has come to an end, and you almost wish the evil was still around so that great deeds can still be done. The great evil of Sauron was what necessitated and permitted the great beauty of the elves, and the sorrow and nostalgia are for that beauty. When Sauron's magic left the world the elves' magic left as well.[34]

A lost heroic age, whether inspired by medieval history, Victorian romance, or contemporary fantasy, is what many SCA members are trying to recapture. Notes Evreinov, "Although chivalry became in the epoch of its decline (that is to say, at the dawn of the Renaissance) a synonym of violence and banditry, it survives in our memory as a synonym of honesty and noble-mindedness."[35] Evreinov was writing in Russia in 1917, but this idea of chivalry remains with us to-day in popular culture.

Communal Medievalism

To frame their performances and give themselves a stage to act upon, SCA members collectively create their own world and culture, separate and different from that of contemporary society. Turner identifies this type of creation as an important byproduct of leisure in *From Ritual to Performance:*

> Leisure is freedom from work. . . . Leisure is also: (1) freedom to enter, even to generate, new symbolic worlds of entertainment, sports, games, diversions of all kinds. It is, furthermore, (2) freedom to transcend social structural limita-tions, freedom to play . . . with ideas, with fantasies, with words (from Rabelais to Joyce and Samuel Beckett) with paint (from the Impressionists to Action Painting to Art Nouveau), and with social relationships.[36]

This is clearly what SCA members do: generate a new symbolic world of play wherein they create new and different social relationships based upon a romantic medieval model and rooted in faux-medieval combat and faux-medieval ritual—the realms of the Winter and Summer king in medieval folk festival. The rituals of the SCA are very rigidly established: courts, ceremonies, litanies, feudal contracts, fighting, flirting, etc. All of these activities have agreed-upon conventions, forms, and conditions that accompany them within the SCA's faux-medieval frame. According to Erving Goffman, the frame is the major enabling device allowing the fictive world of "play" to take place. Serious acts become playful by being presented in a different "key": that is to say, the action is changed in some obvious way to make it less serious and therefore "play."[37] SCA members frame their activities using the Middle Ages, but the idea of the Middle Ages they use is in a constant state of flux—as is, indeed, the idea of any historical era.

The Middle Ages is a communal invention. The very idea of the medieval was invented in the Renaissance by scholars who wanted to distinguish their own time from what they saw as a dark and backward age that came immedi-ately before, in order to draw a connection between their era and that of classical antiquity. So, in a sense, the scholars of the Renaissance invented the dark side of the medieval, what Norman Cantor refers to as

> a Middle Age of barbarism, ignorance, and superstition that allegedly consti-tuted a period of persistent decline between the twin peaks of classical Rome and the Italian Renaissance at the end of the fifteenth century. This was the negative view of medieval culture that had been invented by the fifteenth cen-

tury Renaissance Italian humanists themselves as the historical theory to ac-company and give narrative depth to their claim that they were engaged in the salutary post medieval revival of ancient learning and classical Latinity.[38]

This is the "medieval" as adjective in the phrase "get medieval," the Middle Ages that is full of iron maidens and racks and torture and witch burning, a su-perstitious time of extreme violence. This is a common view of the Middle Ages, and one that SCA members may joke about and play with: Question: How do you get a Saxon poacher out of a tree? Answer: Cut the rope; Question: What were Edward II's last words? Answer: "You guys are early—is it poker night already?"; Question: How many peasants does it take to dig a moat? Answer: All of them, three days a week as is my right!

In spite of these jokes, this violent Middle Ages is not the version that SCA members are trying to re-create. They seek a second, equally popular image of the Middle Ages, of which Cantor writes, "The romantics of the early nineteenth century replaced this negative view of the Middle Ages with the shining image of a Gothic culture steeped in idealism, spirituality and adoration of women."[39] The Middle Ages sought by most members of the SCA was the invention of the Victorian romantics—a Middle Ages of knights in shining armor, beautiful maidens, and heroic deeds done by the former in honor of the latter. The build-ing blocks for this version of the medieval existed in the period in the form of aristocratic romances: all the Victorians (and SCA members) had to do was ig-nore the brutal realities of medieval life and, where the Quattrocento humanists concentrated on violence and ignorance, look instead on the medieval achieve-ments in art, spirituality, and, especially, romance.

Umberto Eco goes much farther. Eco establishes ten separate versions of the Middle Ages "to warn readers that every time one speaks of a dream of the Middle Ages, one should first ask which Middle Ages one is dreaming of."[40] His "Ten Little Middle Ages" are the Middle Ages as pretext, ironical revisitation, barbaric age, romanticism, *philosophia perennis* of neo-Thomism, national iden-tities, decadentism, philosophical reconstruction, tradition, and "the expectation of the Millennium" which, in Eco's view, means an expectation of the Apoca-lypse.[41] All ten of these versions can be found in the SCA.

Cantor argues that "the Middle Ages are the invention of the twentieth cen-tury,"[42] and that "the Middle Ages as we see them are the creation of an interac-tive cultural process."[43] In Cantor's view, scholars of the twentieth century took the two dominant versions of the Middle Ages created by the Renaissance scholars and the Victorians and altered them with their own personal views, agendas, and experiences to create the contemporary Middle Ages. It is a proc-ess that the SCA feeds upon and contributes to. The arbitrary thousand-year pe-riod known as the Middle Ages encompasses a great range of history, cultural attitudes, artistic development, and philosophy (Cantor notes that only in English is "Middle Ages" plural; in all other languages it is singular: "the Middle Age"). By grouping such disparate eras and geographies together into a single monolithic whole, Renaissance scholars delegitimized a thousand years of change. Those who have had to respond to them have been somewhat trapped by this problem: contemporary scholars examine the complexities of the Middle Ages but are still more or less bound by the periodization established in the Renaissance.

As Cantor points out, the Victorians thought no less monolithically, and their simplistic, romantic view of the Middle Ages was colored both by the Renaissance view and by their own penchant for categorization and generalization. Even the Renaissance, which falls into the SCA's time period, is a matter of great debate. Some scholars, C. S. Lewis among them, see the Renaissance as medieval, as the culmination of medieval culture, not as a separate era. However, in current academic usage, the transitional period popularly known as the Renaissance is folded into the longer period called "early modern," linking it not to the Middle Ages but to that which came later.

Cantor is an academic and is writing mostly about academic interpretations of the Middle Ages. He is only occasionally interested in popular culture interpretations of the Middle Ages, and he concentrates on those that have the stamp of academic approval, such as Umberto Eco's *The Name of the Rose* and Barbara Tuchman's *A Distant Mirror*. For the SCA, however, pop culture images and ideas of the Middle Ages are highly influential, as much if not more so than academic ideas. Most people who come to the SCA are not academics, and the ideas they have of the Middle Ages come to them from contemporary mass media. Later, through their participation in the SCA and their own research, they might gain more historical knowledge and exposure to academic sources and thus alter their performance, but they might not. Many are content to simply recreate what they've seen in the movies or read about in novels.

Fantasy literature has already been discussed as a primary influence on the SCA's reinvention of the Middle Ages, but filmic images are also central to many people's interest in the medieval. "We can't ignore how important those costume epics of the fifties were,"[44] says Forgue. It is too early to know how much of an effect Peter Jackson's films of *The Lord of the Rings* will have on the SCA, whether the popularity of the trilogy will have an effect on SCA membership, but in the past movies and television have certainly been an integral part of SCA culture. One of the SCA's founders, Henrik Olsgaard/Duke Henrik of Havn, bears as his arms the arms of Prince Valiant with the colors changed. After the TV miniseries *Shogun* there was a rise in popularity of Japanese culture in the SCA; *Troy* and *Gladiator* have resulted in a bump for classical cultures, and people dressing in Roman or Greek garb, or fighting in Roman or Greek armor, are increasingly more common.

One area of popular culture that Cantor does take an interest in is that promulgated by the Inklings. Of Tolkien and C.S. Lewis, Cantor says:

> In terms of shaping of the Middle Ages in the popular culture of the twentieth century, Tolkien and Lewis have had an incalculable effect, and the story is far from ended. Their fictional fantasies cannot be separated from their scholarly writing. Their work in each case should be seen as a whole and as communicating an image of the Middle Ages that has entered profoundly and indelibly into world culture.[45]

As Cantor writes, Lewis and Tolkien created "fantasy literature for a mass audience that communicated the sensibility of medieval epic and romance."[46] He goes on:

> Both men were deeply affected by a nostalgia and a love for a rapidly disappearing England graced by the middle-class, highly literate Christian culture into which they had been born. . . . Lewis and Tolkien wanted not only to preserve but to revitalize through their writing and teaching this Anglo-Edwardian retromedieval culture.[47]

Cantor believes that Tolkien's impact on both academic studies and popular culture is likely to be more important and longer lasting than Lewis's, and he was writing a decade before Peter Jackson's films came out. Lewis should not be overlooked, however. His Christian-inspired fantasy series *The Chronicles of Narnia* was so widely read in America, particularly in the 1950s, that it had a huge impact on the founders of the SCA in their childhoods. Cantor quotes a passage from Lewis's *The Silver Chair,* one which shows the kindred spirit between the Inklings and the SCA's founders:

> Thus, in *The Silver Chair* (1953), the witch tries to stop goodness by denying the possibility of putting a romantic shine on the mundane world: "Look how you can put nothing into your make-believe without copying it from the real world, this work of mine, which is the only world." But comes the response: "We're just four babies making up a game, if you're right. But four babies [Inklings?] playing a game can make a play-world which licks your real world hollow."[48]

The Inklings were making up play-worlds that they considered better than the real world, and so were the early members of the SCA, inspired by Tolkien and Lewis.

Cantor's use of the phrase "add a romantic shine to the mundane world" is also interesting in an SCA context. The "Mundane World," "Mundanity," or "Mundania" is how SCA members refer to everything in the contemporary world that is not part of the SCA. Mundane can be either a noun or an adjective.

Non-SCA members are "mundanes." The police are often referred to as "the mundane authorities." Contemporary clothes are spoken of in either fashion: they can be "mundane clothes" or simply "mundanes" as in "I'm slipping into some mundanes to go off site." The term originally appeared in the *Xanth* series, a series of fantasy novels by Piers Anthony, in which it is used to describe everything outside the magical world of Xanth, much like the word "muggle" in the Harry Potter series. Notes *The Courtesy Book*, an SCA primer: "If one accepts the SCA as a 'magical' environment (in whatever sense of the word one prefers), then Anthony's usage is particularly appropriate."[49] Clearly what the SCA is trying to do is to put a romantic shine on the mundane world, much as were Lewis and the Inklings.

Reconciling a Victorian romantic view of the Middle Ages and Tolkien's darker view is not particularly easy. To Cantor, *The Lord of the Rings* is a "counterromance, 'telling it like it really was,' not like the court poets told it to flatter their lords."[50] The darkness of *The Lord of the Rings* Cantor interprets as being nonromantic. Others see this as an element of style Tolkien borrows from Icelandic saga and early Germanic poetry. The links between Tolkien and *Beowulf*, for example, are numerous, as in *The Hobbit*, where the theft of the cup that rouses Smaug from his lair, leading to his death at the hands of the hero (and soon to be king) Bard of Lake Town, is borrowed directly from the last section of *Beowulf*.

Cantor also notes that several of Tolkien's critics, particularly Robert Giddings, Roger King, and Nigel Walmsley, interpret Tolkien as an example of the commodification and privatization of cultural consumption, and link him to studio recordings, computer games, and psychedelic drugs. They also connect him to the urban environmentalism that inspires people to move to communes in remote places—part of a different escapist culture that promotes isolation and a detachment from the problems of the world. Highly critical of Tolkien and his world, they see his commercial success as encouraging fantasy, which prompts people to avoid taking part in social struggles—as Timothy Leary said, "tune in, turn on, and drop out."[51] Of course, to Leary, drugs were the answer, not mass media, but to Walmsley they were all the same. Cantor quotes Walmsley as saying, "*The Lord of the Rings* provided the alternative course of cerebral atavism for those in Britain and America who did not want to stray beyond the end of the block."[52]

Walmsley's criticism applies to the SCA as well. As a group, members of the SCA are rarely political. Although the founders of the SCA were part of the sixties counterculture, it is possible to argue that their SCA participation muted their political activism in much the same way that the music scene in the Haight Ashbury muted the activism of many others. George Liptsitz writes that, in spite of its rejection of middle-class values, the counterculture was apolitical. The counterculture value of "dropping out"—that is to say a rejection of society, its structure and its politics—doomed any politicization of the counterculture to failure. Those in the counterculture simply did not care enough to actually change the world, they only wanted to escape: "the counterculture did too little to interrogate the axes of power in society—the systematic racism, class domination, sexism, and homophobia that constrained individual choices."[53]

The SCA's mild form of protest at the first event, the march up Telegraph Avenue protesting the twentieth century, should be seen as a happening, a performance piece designed to point up the absurdities of modern life, but it was obviously being done in a very tongue-in-cheek fashion. Its closest relatives in performance are the antics of the San Francisco Suicide Club and its later incarnation, the Cacophony Society, which stages events such as a nude cable car ride or a tea party on the Golden Gate Bridge, the goal of which is primarily to shock and amuse by being (once again) different.

The idea of Tolkien's works as thematically and structurally medieval has also been recently challenged. Varlyn Fliegler of the University of Maryland, arguing for a postmodern reading of Tolkien, suggests that while the elements in *Lord of the Rings* and the *Silmarillion* that are obviously inspired by medieval literature are stressed in most critical analysis, the elements that are not medieval are often ignored, yet these modern elements are woven together with the medieval ones in a complex literary pattern. At a paper presented to the International Congress of Medieval Studies in 2004, Yvette Kisor likens Tolkien's interlacing themes, styles, and storylines to interlace in Celtic art (she notes that the same is true of *Beowulf* as well).[54] The hobbits and Hobbiton are clearly Victorian (or Edwardian, as Cantor suggests, see above). Although Tolkien denied that the ring was meant as an allegory for the A-bomb, and noted that he began writing the stories long before the bomb was invented, still it is, in Tolkien's words, an allegory for absolute power. Like William Morris, Tolkien was obviously concerned about the dehumanizing effect of machines and the machine age, a nineteenth-century anxiety that became even more pronounced in the course of the twentieth century. The environmental message in Tolkien, latched onto by many of his fans in the 1970s, is also a concern of the early twenty-first century. Many other scholars find echoes of Tolkien's experience in the Somme in the way he writes about war and battle. This interweaving of medieval storytelling methods with twentieth-century concerns helps to explain not only why Tolkien's work resonates so strongly today, but also why his particular brand of medievalism would have been so influential for the SCA's founders, who were frightened by the bomb and disillusioned by modern society.

The communal medieval world they have created, informed by images from both academia and popular culture, gives SCA members a canvas on which to paint their fantasies. While SCA members study medieval history, often intently, nonetheless their concepts of the medieval are contemporary, informed by the many different Middle Ages that Eco and Cantor identify. The SCA represents a type of medievalism unto itself, one in which the Middle Ages are not only the backdrop and the frame of their performance, but both subject and object (or objective?) as well.

Class and the SCA

Miriam Rainbird of the University of Notre Dame links the rise of interest in the Middle Ages among the middle class to an increase in leisure time and disposable income in nineteenth-century England, as well as their nostalgia for a simpler past. As she puts it, "An age of piety is comforting in the face of perceived world decline."[55] This has obvious implications for both the popularity of Lewis in the 1950s, as described by Cantor, and also for the attitudes of the early members of the SCA. At the height of the Cold War, in the midst of the Free Speech Movement and Vietnam protests, the SCA's founders sought out a more comforting, recognizable, just, and sane world in a fantasy, reinventing the Middle Ages not as they were but as SCA members thought they should have been. Rainbird's position fits in well with Erisman's analysis of the SCA. Erisman's work is primarily class-based, contrasting the SCA, which she considers a bourgeois activity, with the proletarian activities of Buckskinners. However, class distinctions in the United States are not so clear-cut.

Carey Lenehan's thesis includes demographic analysis of SCA groups in Australia and California based on interviews and surveys. He writes, "One of the most distinctive features of the interviewees is their firm background in the 'new classes' and professions."[56] Educational capital is high: at the time of Lenehan's analysis 52.4% of SCA members had college degrees and 40.4% were still studying. According to his research, 33.7% of SCA members were in the professions, while 22.2% worked in a clerical field. Clearly, the SCA represents an escape for the desk-bound. Another revealing statistic is that although 18% of members' parents were self-employed, only 0.4% of members were self-employed themselves. Lenehan postulates that this may be because the SCA is a very time-consuming hobby, but he notes that this, as well as the large clerical population, could be due to the fact that a large number of SCA members are either in college or just beginning their careers.[57] It should also be noted that by limiting his sample to Northern California and Western Australia, he may have skewed his results.

The SCA is by and large a suburban hobby, and this is not solely because most people in the United States live in the suburbs. It is a matter of time, space, and money. Having a nine-to-five job makes SCA participation easier because SCA events are held on weekends and practices and meetings on weeknights. Owning a vehicle also helps. A newcomer attending his first fighter practice in

Oakland, California, noting the vehicle of choice for everyone there, and seeing the amount of armor, weapons, and shields people brought with them, said, "Wow. You really need a truck to play this game, don't you?" That is an over-statement, but not much of one. To fully participate in the SCA a person needs a way to haul a lot of gear to events. Furniture, armor, pavilions, ice chests, stoves, and clothes made out of heavy wool have to be transported, and SUVs, light trucks, vans, and station wagons are considered necessities by many SCA members. Space is also important. It helps to have a shop/studio/sewing room/brewery in which to repair armor, build furniture, make clothes, paint, or brew mead. Even someone who purchases all of the props used in his or her SCA performance has to have a place to store them all. SCA members often say they have enough possessions for two people, their mundane self and their persona.

This is not to say that persons of low income never participate in the SCA, nor that there are not SCA branches in rural or urban areas, simply that they are limited in their performances. Away from the economic centers on the East and West coasts the SCA includes many rural participants in lower income brackets. At large SCA events you are likely to encounter carpenters, truck drivers, movers, handymen, and janitors as well as teachers and computer programmers. One segment of the population, which tends not to have high incomes or large vehicles but that continues to be an important part of the SCA, is college students. Friedman teaches workshops on how to construct the bare essentials for SCA performance in as much space as you'll find in a college dorm room: a wooden box, chair, and small table on the one hand and boiled leather armor on the other. Many who live in cities such as San Francisco, Chicago, and Manhattan do not have much space and often do not own a car but do make do by keeping most of their participation local. But these areas are far less active and have fewer members than the suburbs surrounding them, despite the obvious difference in population.

People in rural areas face a different set of problems. They may have plenty of space to build and store SCA gear, but the SCA also works best when a large number of members live in a relatively small area. If the nearest fighter practice is two hours away and most events are a five-hour drive, it is difficult to maintain a high level of activity.

As for people of wealth, although there are a number of people in the SCA with high incomes, it is not a hobby of the rich. One possible reason for this is that the rich have other ways to gain prestige. In the SCA, people who have little prestige in contemporary society are able to gain power and fame within a small group of like-minded people. This conveys a sense of self-worth and accomplishment though, as I've noted elsewhere, this accomplishment and fame do not carry into the larger world outside the SCA. Wealthy people who have attained prestige and power in the world at large have no need for the pretend power and prestige available in the SCA (though they can be equally theatrical in their display of prestige—even more so through the act of conspicuous consumption).

In light of Lenehan's statistical analysis, although the SCA is clearly not an activity enjoyed by the upper classes, it is problematic to state, as Erisman does, that the SCA represents a bourgeois ideal. Clearly, in terms of leisure time, educational capital and disposable income, the SCA can be seen as an activity of the middle class, but this is belied by the large number of people in the SCA who do not fit neatly into one class category or another. This makes postmodernism, as Lenehan noted, an excellent tool to analyze SCA activity: since breaking down hierarchies is a function of postmodernism, one of the hierarchies it necessarily breaks down is class. In *Nobrow: the Culture of Marketing and the Marketing of Culture,* John Seabrook argues that leisure activities and entertainments, long divided into taste categories based on class, can no longer be categorized in this way because these taste divisions do not exist in contemporary society. Postmodern consumerism has created a space where there is no such thing as taste, a space that Seabrook called Nobrow, the exact midpoint at which culture and market converge.[58] The SCA, though not a mass marketed consumable, is nonetheless a nobrow activity, one which exists outside the modernist hierarchies of taste and class.

Lenehan notes that there are more women in the SCA than men—83.3 men to every 100 women in the California survey. This is surprising, since the SCA's most visible activity is decidedly masculine: fighting. However, fighters make up only a small percentage of the total SCA population, and although many women are there in relation to the fighting, either as consort to a fighter or as a fighter themselves, there are numerous other activities involved. The SCA creates its medieval frame not only through action but also by the re-creation of material culture. SCA members do more than just fight. Much of the SCA is dedicated to learning about other, in most cases more authentic, medieval activities, which the SCA groups under the heading of "the arts and sciences." Among these are brewing, woodworking, calligraphy, and illumination, as well as performance genres such as music, dance, and poetry.

However, it is important to note here that the purpose of these activities is to set the stage for SCA performance. For example, although more than 10,000 people attend Pennsic, only about 2,000 fight. The rest are there to party, to shop, and to attend the more than 1,200 classes offered during the course of the event. Although at the first tourney fighting was the *raison d'être* for the event, there were other activities surrounding the fighting, such as dancing and music. As the SCA has grown, participation in these activities has far outstripped the growth of SCA fighting. This has changed the face of the SCA somewhat and contributes to a tension between those people who see the SCA as reenactment and those who see it as a social group.

Race and Ethnicity in the SCA

The SCA supposedly re-creates pre-seventeenth-century Europe, but this is not always a hard and fast rule. The only body that has any governance at all over the roles played by SCA members is the SCA College of Arms, which is responsible for regulating and registering the SCA's names, heraldry, and insignias of rank, and what little influence they have over persona is through the approval and registration of SCA names. In spite of the SCA's official Eurocentricity, the rules allow for someone to register a name that could be found in any culture with which Europeans came into contact prior to 1600. This includes just about everything outside of Australia. There are personas that are Japanese, Chinese, Native American, Mongol, African, and Indian. Furthermore, although the term "Middle Ages" appears in the SCA's governing documents, there is no beginning date for the SCA. As a result, while most SCA members perform roles that are recognizably medieval, based in Western Europe between the years 1066 and 1500, some members choose to portray decidedly nonmedieval personas: Romans, Gauls, Picts, etc. Most members who want to see the SCA as living history disapprove of this, arguing that Japanese or Romans or even Vikings have no place in a chivalric tournament culture, and view these types of persona as only a step above elves, hobbits, and Klingons, which are officially not allowed but still show up at Pennsic.

This situation makes the place of race in the SCA very fluid. It is not a much bigger step to dress up as a samurai than it is to dress up as a Norman knight. Both are elite warriors from a historical feudal period when the sword was a weapon of the warrior class. The vast majority of SCA members are white and so are the vast majority of SCA samurai, Saracens, Mongols, and Aztecs. Likewise, the performance of race by many of the SCA's few people of color becomes foregrounded by their choice of persona. Many black SCA members choose to portray Moors, but many do not. Few of the SCA's Asian members portray Asians, instead adopting medieval European white personas. Their position is transgressive. A person of color who portrays a Moor fighting with the Europeans is one thing, but a person of color who portrays a person who must have been white calls race as a signifier into question in the same way drag challenges the notion of gender.

According to Kwame Anthony Appiah, racialism, the modern idea of race—that physical characteristics and parentage determine social characteristics—dates from the same Victorian romantic period that gave rise to the SCA's version of medievalism.[59] Indeed, he and other scholars consider *Ivanhoe*, with its promotion of Anglo-Saxonism, to be a central text in the building of a theory of the races and of the inherent racial superiority of Germanic peoples.[60] Ideas of race in the Middle Ages were much less determinate. The supposed inherent inferiority of Othello and Shylock, according to Appiah, should be attributed not to the inherited characteristics of their race but in their status as non-Christian.[61] The SCA structures race as part of a performance, not something that is inherent. This postmodern view of racial identity is very much in line with concepts of race in Shakespeare (*The Tempest* aside) as interpreted by Appiah.

Race in the SCA is a form of drag—it is something you can shed or change at will. Indeed it is the clothes someone wears, not the color of one's skin, that determines what race he or she is portraying in the SCA. A white man in a kimono is Japanese and an Asian man in a kilt is Scottish. While in other circumstances a white man in a kimono can be seen as someone from an imperialist society appropriating the culture of its colonial subjects, in the SCA the appropriation is more temporal than it is cultural. SCA members appropriate images out of time, regardless of culture. In this way not only is the hegemony of the SCA's Eurocentricity undermined, so is the idea of race as a whole.

Eric Gardner is a black man in the SCA who formerly went by the name Eric of Huntington. As a squire to Steve Beck/Duke Stephen of Beckenham, Gardner portrayed a European squire of the late fifteenth and early sixteenth centuries at all times until he was knighted. In the West Kingdom knighting ceremony there is a place immediately before the dubbing, appropriate for a rite of passage, where the candidate is asked, "By what name do you wish to be knighted?"[62] Nearly everyone uses the name he or she has always used. However, some people surprise the heralds by announcing a new name (which then needs to be researched and registered before it can appear on the writ that accompanies their knighting). When asked this question Gardner replied, "Eric Ibraheim Mozarabe." The king was Chris Ayers/Duke Christian du Glaive, whose persona is a Norman crusader. A strong proponent of acting "in persona" and maintaining a medieval attitude at all times, he was clearly bothered by Gardner's declaration. He had no problem knighting a black man, but for this crusader knighting a Muslim created an issue. As a compromise he continued the ceremony using both names, saying, "Eric Ibraheim Mozarabe, also known as Eric of Huntington, I dub thee. . . ." What Ayers did not know is that Ibraheim Mozarabe is a Christian name. Ayers had assumed that because it was Arabic that the name must have been Muslim, indicating that Gardner had a Muslim persona. According to Gardner, Ibraheim means "child of God," and "Mozarabe" refers to a population of Christians living under Moorish rule in Spain after the eighth century.[63]

Gardner had clearly made this a part of his persona story. He had been inspired to do so by the story of St. Maurice, the Catholic saint who is often depicted as a black Moor and a knight. Upon reaching knighthood and becoming his own (and the King's) man, Gardner, in persona, decided to call himself by his true name. In doing so Gardner made an issue not only of his own race but of his persona's race as well. Up until this time there were two possibilities regarding Gardner's persona: he could be seen as simply himself with a made-up medieval name, or he could be seen as a black man who had a white persona. Since it would be nearly unheard of for a young black man to be a squire to a knight in fifteenth-century England, many people assumed that Eric was portraying a white squire. Now however, Gardner's race became part of his persona. He could no longer be looked on as a European squire. Now he was portraying a black Moor who had been knighted. There is nothing wrong with this from a historical perspective. St. Maurice is often represented as a Moorish knight. Othello was a captain, possibly a knight (and Gardner, a tall, handsome black man with a deep bass-baritone voice, enjoys referencing Othello in his SCA performance). But from an SCA perspective Gardner was forcing people to acknowledge his race when before they had not had to do so.

A similar situation occurred with Tonessa West Crowe/Duchess Isabella of York, a black woman from New York City and an expert costumer. Crowe's persona is that of an Elizabethan noblewoman. Of course, when she took the throne, she wore reconstructions of gowns from portraits of Elizabeth I (her coronation dress weighed 87 pounds).[64] Her gown for her second coronation was a reconstruction of the famous "phoenix dress." Her referencing of Elizabeth as part of her performance became even more distinct when, during her second reign, her king, a Marine Corps reservist, was called up to active duty in Iraq and she finished the reign by herself as a sovereign queen. Elizabeth I was famous for painting her face white, stressing her race and her purity as the "virgin queen." As a black woman with a white persona, reigning as queen without a king and referencing Elizabeth I, Isabella pointed up the racial hegemony of both the SCA and the Middle Ages, while at the same time calling that hegemony into question.

These examples illustrate how the SCA undermines the contemporary notions of race by making it a part of performance. Race in the SCA is a mask, and wearing that mask challenges the notion of race as a signifier. However, just as drag accentuates gender while calling it into question, the SCA construct of race does the same. A blond, blue-eyed samurai stands out because he is blond, as does a black man in a kilt because he is black. Gradner and Crowe illustrate the dual nature of such transformative performances: crossing cultures in their dress highlights their own race and challenges the very notion of race at the same time.

Death and the SCA

About 1500 people died at the Pennsic War in 2004, many of them several times over. Two of them died for real. Both died of natural causes after long illnesses, and just happened to be at Pennsic when they were struck down. One of them was a member of the SCA, the other a member of the Cooper family, which owns and operates the campground.

In a society built on fantasy, in which death is a game, real death comes as an even greater intrusion, because real death is a part of "real life," and the intrusion of real life undermines the fantasy. The SCA has often been described as a worldly version of Valhalla, the ancient hall of the Viking gods, in which heroes gathered to drink and revel at night, and in the daytime battled one another to the death, only to be resurrected to return to Odin's banquet. In the SCA mock warriors fight and "die" during the day and revel through the night. In such an atmosphere a real death has little or no cultural place. Not only does it remove someone from the people's presence, it shatters the illusion of the SCA world.

The death of an SCA member creates several areas of conflict within the culture of the group. Most SCA members know each other only within their SCA performances. Often, they don't know each other's mundane names. To many in the SCA the person who has died is a medieval persona, or at least an SCA identity. They are far removed from the mundane world in which the person spent most of his or her life. Often, they do not even know the family of the deceased and will not attend the funeral, and yet they have suffered a severe loss and must find some way to express their grief. It is in this moment that the SCA member is most clearly divided into his or her mundane and SCA selves, but it is in the grieving of SCA members that this division is most clearly erased.

The performance of a memorial service in the SCA will usually include many medieval or faux-medieval elements, the most common of which will be praise poems written in honor of the deceased. Much of this can be illustrated by examining the memorials for Lawrence White/Sir Kylson Skyfyre, the first Prince of Oertha (Alaska), who suffered a heart attack while walking off the field after winning a tournament on June 19, 2004. Because he died in armor at an SCA event the death of his persona was more immediate than usual. His death was obviously a "Viking Death"—that is, dying as a result of battle—and this made it both more poignant and more medieval. This, and the fact that he was an important figure in the history of the SCA, prompted an enormous outpouring of grief. Three memorials were held for SCA members, one in Alaska, one in California, and one in Virginia. At each of these bards performed poems and songs, many written for the occasion, others written by or for White during his lifetime. A memorial page was set up for White on the West Kingdom website. On these sites contemporary and medieval performances of grief intersect, as digital pictures of the deceased have been posted along with eulogies and medieval-style poetry.

At each Pennsic a ritual is held to memorialize everyone in the SCA who has died in the previous year. A four-foot model of a Viking ship is built and shields painted with the arms of SCA members who have died since the last war are placed in it. On the last night of Pennsic the boat is set on fire and pushed out onto Cooper's Lake (aided by a battery powered motor which will shut off once the fire has reached the waterline). It takes about an hour for the ship to burn, and as it does so the crowd of people standing on the shore call out the names of those who have died, to which the others reply, "Wassail." Intermixed with this will be other expressions of grief, songs, and prayers to several different deities. The year I attended, "Danny Boy," "Amazing Grace," several SCA songs, and "Something Wonderful" by Rodgers and Hammerstein were sung, along with recitations of the Lord's Prayer, the Kaddish, and prayers to the Goddess, Odin, Bast, and Ra. It is unstructured and improvisational, a communal rite that does not employ the hierarchical structures that are a part of most SCA rituals.

The memorial service is a performance of grief, but it is grief for a fantasy persona. The memories that are shared will be memories of deeds performed within the context of the SCA. Other memories—stories from a person's youth, accomplishments in jobs or sports, relationships with people not in the SCA—all parts of the person's life, will be unknown to most SCA members and not remembered in the SCA memorial. However, all the things he or she did in the SCA, awards received, battles won, deeds of skill or prowess or courage, although part of a fantasy, will be real acts as remembered by those who were there to witness them, and their grief will be real as well. This is the final expression of the postmodern fragmentation of identity which people in the SCA experience, and affirms the breakdown of the dichotomy between real vs. imaginary, which Carlson says is ultimately not useful.

Subculture, Counterculture, Medieval Culture

In literature and in song, the SCA often refers to itself as "the Current Middle Ages," establishing itself as a medievally coded counterculture, a communally created space rooted in the now but in which various fantasies about the Middle Ages can be acted out. This creates problems for members who want the SCA to function as a serious reenactment of the actual Middle Ages, and the conflict of ideas between the SCA as contemporary subculture and the SCA as scholarly reenactment group is at the heart of all SCA arguments over authenticity. Forgue, who has served on the SCA's board of directors and also as society seneschal, tries to draw a middle ground, saying, "It's a counterculture informed by historical research. Without either part it wouldn't be the same activity."[65] In Forgue's view the SCA offers a contemporary alternative to the dominant culture, one that does not pretend to be medieval but is framed by medieval imagery. Although this may be an accurate description, it ignores the fact that such a situation must create conflict. Those who are content with a historically informed counterculture will be happy in the SCA. Forgue, and most SCA members, are perfectly willing to acknowledge within their performance that it is all a game. However, while there may be room in Forgue's counterculture for reenactors, there is no room for Forgue's counterculture version of the SCA in a true reenactment. Forgue's position implicitly acknowledges the contemporary world, which a true reenactor cannot do since that would break the illusion.

A different challenge to the idea of SCA as counterculture arises from the fact that, as the SCA has matured, it has become more conservative. People who have joined the SCA since the 1960s do not necessarily share the utopian counterculture views of the SCA's founders. There are many more Republicans in the SCA than there once were, and many more who see themselves as patriotic. Although the SCA originally presented itself as an alternative to modern society, and particularly to modern politics and war, many current SCA members have no real desire to escape to a better place, only to vacation there on the weekends. The SCA is very popular in the US military. There are branches on military bases (called "strongholds") and even on a couple of naval vessels. It was primarily through the military that the SCA spread to Asia. For instance, activities in Japan, known as the Stronghold of Vale de Draco, center on Camp Zama, a military base south of Tokyo where many members of the Stronghold are stationed.[66] Many SCA members have engaged in combat in Iraq and Afghanistan, and many others are involved in support groups for SCA members stationed overseas.[67] To some SCA members serving in the Middle East, President George W. Bush's references to the Iraq war as a "Crusade," as well as Osama Bin Laden's pejorative reference to American troops as "crusaders," were marks of pride. For example, one Marine Corps officer who is also an SCA knight said he considered himself a liberator as opposed to a crusader; he did, however, fly his household banner, which has a crusader cross on it, as his command post flag. He did it because the Marines had been ordered not to fly the American flag so as not to antagonize Iraqis. His tongue-in-cheek solution was to fly a flag with a crusader cross instead.[68]

William Fisher/Lord Haarek Stormraven, an SCA member and avowed conservative Christian Republican, writes a conservative political blog that he calls "The Crusader," which he began because of

> a resurgent, but spirtually [sic] and intellectually bankrupt Islam, that would like to set the clock back to the Eighth Century A.D. These forces are fighting a war of terror as part of a political and religious strategy to conquer the Christian West. Most Westerners thought this war was won at the gates of Vienna and shattered walls of Granada. Islam lost the initiative then, but unlike us, they are not so naive as to discount hundreds of years of history.[69]

SCA members are accustomed to contextualizing both themselves and the world in reference to the Middle Ages.

But mundane politics is often trumped by romantic medievalism, as the examples of Hollander and Margaret Silvestri (below) point out. Their desire for an antimodern fantasy based on medieval heroism comes from two very different political perspectives.

As Hollander sees it, the SCA is about romantic heroism: "To me that's what it's all about, is being a hero."[70] According to Hollander there are several types of heroes and different hero tales, but in his view everyone in the SCA seeks to be some kind of hero.

> [P]eople are obviously working to be heroes, heroes being a generic term for people who fulfill a heroic archetype of one sort or another. We all have different heroes but if you read the hero tales, and it's not just modern fantasy, but there are many, many hero tales. . . . Very few people will go out and specifically design themselves to be villains.[71]

Hollander has taken this theme further. At a panel discussion that I moderated in 1996 titled "The History and Culture of the SCA," another longtime SCA member objected to the heroic paradigm, stating that he had no interest in being a hero, that he was more of a reenactor, he was a craftsman and his enjoyment in the SCA came from reconstructing the material culture of the actual Middle Ages. Hollander was unfazed, saying, "That is a kind of heroism as well. You are the person who makes the sword with which the hero slays the dragon, or the person who feeds him when he is hungry, and that makes you no less a hero."[72]

Margaret Silvestri/Duchess Megan nic Alister of Thornwood notes that her desire for romantic heroism arose out of a dissatisfaction with popular culture. She describes herself as a political conservative who had no use for the counterculture of the sixties when she was growing up, and her objection to certain elements of the counterculture ethos in film is what prompted her to join the SCA.

> Heroes are very important in my perception of what the SCA is all about. I grew up in a time when the anti-hero was starting to become popular, and the bad guys won, and I grew up wanting to find heroes, the good guys who won. I have a very strong sense of right and wrong and fair play, and for me the SCA provided that outlook of justice and fairness, and that heroes were the good guys and at the end of the day the hero wins and evil fails.[73]

So Hollander, a self-described "old hippie freak," and Silvestri, a self-described conservative, both base their SCA performance on a romantic desire for heroism, which they came to from entirely different political perspectives. In both cases they demonstrate an alienation from contemporary society, a desire to find something better, which they identify as the heroic ideal. What was missing from the contemporary world for both Hollander and Silvestri was heroism, a clear sense of right and wrong and the ability on someone's part to right the wrongs, to (metaphorically) slay the dragon.

David Townsend, in "Ironic Intertextuality and the Reader's Resistance to Heroic Masculinity in the *Waltharius*," argues that intertextual irony was often used to undermine assumptions of heroic ideology in medieval literature. Although heroic ideals of masculinity are normally considered to be a universally accepted ideology, close reading of medieval heroic texts shows them to be anything but.[74] Such heroic ideology is also supposedly universally accepted in the SCA as well. However, as with the poems Townsend is critiquing, the SCA is full of ironic references that undermine that heroic ideal, and the arguments about the purpose of the SCA, often framed in terms of historical accuracy, can also be seen as a central hegemonic ideal—the "Dream" mentioned by Lenehan, and Rodwell—being challenged and subverted by groups who do not share the romantic knight as a reference point or as source material for their performance. Some, such as archers, promote a much more peasant-oriented ideal of the SCA. Merchants represent the rise of the middle class, which was the most serious threat to the nobility and the romantic ideals they purported to embody. And, of course, the chivalric ideal is challenged by various barbarian subcultures, whether historical or fantasy-based. In a way, fencers, archers, siege engineers, peasants, Tuchux, and non-European personas form a culture of resistance to the hegemony of the high medieval, chivalric combat monolith.

Obviously, although it is a communally constructed fantasy, there are many SCAs. While the SCA is clearly a subculture, its status as a counterculture is contested by a view of the SCA as reconstructing medieval culture. There are various competing cultures and views within the SCA, and while the romantic heroism ideal dominates the group it is contested by both authenticists and competing fantasies.

Carolyn Dinshaw examines the phrase "get medieval" in detail in her book *Getting Medieval: Sexualities and Communities, Pre- and Postmodern,* and states that, although it is normally used to mean "undertaking brutal private vengeance in a triumphal and unregulated bloodbath," she intends the phrase to mean "using ideas of the past, creating relationships with the past, touching in this way the past in an effort to build selves and communities now and into the future."[75] In a very real sense, this is what the SCA does—it takes images of and ideas about the Middle Ages, reworks them, adds to them, changes them through performance, and uses them to create communities and selves in which the medieval and modern intersect in a very postmodern way.

NOTES

[1] Grit, "Summer Knights 10/1/2003," *Maxim*, August 2003.

[2] Ken Mondschein, *The Society for Creative Anachronism* (Disinformation, 2002, accessed 8 February 2002); available from http://www.disinfo.com/site/ displayarticle2028.html.

[3] Turner, 69.

[4] Grossman, 92.

[5] Umberto Eco, "Dreaming of the Middle Ages," in *Travels in Hyperreality* (New York: Harcourt Brace Jovanovich, 1986), 65-66.

[6] Andrew Taylor, "Chivalric Conversation and the Denial of Male Fear," in *Conflicted Identities and Multiple Masculinities: Men in the Medieval West*, ed. Jacqueline Murray (New York: Garland Publishing, 1999), 182.

[7] Eco, 64.

[8] Diana Paxson, *The Seed and the Tree* (accessed 15 December 2003); available from http://www.currentmiddleages.org/3yc/seed.html.

[9] Andrew Rodwell, "Anti-Modern Performance in the Society for Creative Anachronism" (M.A. Thesis, University of Western Ontario, 1998), 38.

[10] Erisman, 89.

[11] Fredric Jameson, "Theories of the Postmodern," in *Cultural Turn*, ed. Fredric Jameson (New York: Verso, 1998), 22.

[12] Norman Spinrad, *Science Fiction in the Real World* (Carbondale, IL: Southern Illinois University Press, 1990), 113.

[13] Jameson, "Postmodernism and Consumer Society," 7.

[14] Webster's New College Dictionary, rev. ed. (2001), s.v. "Nostalgia."

[15] Reese Cleghorn, "Of Hounds, Turtles and Old Flags," *American Journalism Review.* September 1997: 4.

[16] Fred Davis, *Yearning for Yesterday* (New York: The Free Press, 1979), 34.

[17] Ibid.

[18] Edwin Arlington Robinson, "Miniver Cheevy," (1907), in Lewis G. and Marcus Konick Sterner, ed., *Tales in Verse* (New York: Globe Book Co., 1963), 322-323.

[19] Nick Kaye, *Postmodernism and Performance* (New York: St. Martin's Press, 1994), 20.

[20] Linda Hutcheon, *A Poetics of Postmodernism* (New York: Routledge, 1998), 88.

[21] Ibid., 89.

[22] Carey Lenehan, "Postmodern Medievalism: A Sociological Study of the Society for Creative Anachronism" (B.A. Honors Thesis, University of Tasmania, 1994), 8.

[23] Orlando Ambrosius, *The Courtesy Book*, 3rd ed. (Urbana, IL: Folump Enterprises, 1989), 9.

[24] Grossman, 92.

[25] Frederick Hollander, interview by author, 15 February 2004, video recording, Phoenix, AZ.

[26] Hutcheon, 105.

[27] Schechner, 106.

[28] Blanche Barton, *The Church of Satan: A Brief History* (The Church of Satan, 2003, accessed 27 November 2004); available from www.churchofsatan.com.

[29] Mondschein.

[30] Empress Milo, *An Introduction to the ICS* (Imperial Court Internet Services, accessed 23 March 2005); available from www.impcourt.org/icis/about/intro.html.

[31] Eco, 61.

[32] Susan Carol Clark, "A Missive from the Editor," *Tournaments Illuminated*, no. 147 (2003): 3.

[33] Sir Needham Bledsoe, *Thinkwell*, no. 16.

[34] Hanna Edwards, interview by author, 6 May 2004, from notes, New York, NY.

[35] Nikolas Evreinov, *The Theatre in Life*, trans. Alexander Nazaroff (New York: Brentanos, 1927), 84.

[36] Turner, 35-36.

[37] Erving Goffman, *Frame Analysis* (Cambridge, MA: Harvard University Press, 1974), 43.

[38] Norman Cantor, *Inventing the Middle Ages* (New York: Quill, 1991), 28-29.

[39] Ibid.

[40] Eco, 68.

[41] Ibid., 68-72.

[42] Cantor, 36.

[43] Ibid., 38.

[44] Lee Forgue, "S.C.A. History," a panel discussion at Collegium Occidentalis, Kensington, CA, 19 October 1996.

[45] Cantor, 208.

[46] Ibid.

[47] Ibid., 209.

[48] Ibid., 221. Quoting C. S. Lewis, *The Silver Chair*, The Chronicles of Narnia, vol. 6 (New York: Harper Collins, 1994).

[49] Ambrosius, 56.

[50] Cantor, 229.

[51] Timothy Leary, *The Politics of Ecstasy,* quoted in Robert Andrews, *The Columbia World of Quotations* (Columbia University Press, 1996, accessed 24 March 2005); available from http://www.bartleby.com/66/86/35186.html.

[52] Nigel Walmsley, quoted in Cantor, 223.

[53] George Lipsitz, "Who'll Stop the Rain: Youth Culture, Rock 'n' Roll, and Social Crises," in David Farber, ed., *The Sixties: From Memory to History* (Chapel Hill: University of North Carolina Press, 1994), 223.

[54] Yvette Kisor, "Weaving the Web of the Story: Tolkien's Use of Interlace in *The Lord of the Rings*," seminar at *the 39th International Congress on Medieval Studies* (Kalamazoo, MI: 2004).

[55] Miriam Rainbird, "The Medievalization of Middleclass Taste," seminar at *the 39th International Congress on Medieval Studies* (Kalamazoo, MI: 2004).

[56] Lenehan, 18.

[57] Ibid., 19-21.

[58] John Seabrook, *Nobrow: The Culture of Marketing, the Marketing of Culture* (New York: Vintage Books, 2001), 213.

[59] Kwame Anthony Appiah, "Race," in *Critical Terms for Literary Study*, ed. Frank Lentrichia and Thomas McLaughlin (Chicago: University of Chicago Press, 1995), 274.

[60] Ibid., 279-82.

[61] Ibid., 278.

[62] West Kingdom College of Heralds, *West Kingdom Ceremony Book* (Berkeley: Free Trumpet Press, 1991), 82.

[63] Eric Gardner, to the author, 5 May 2008.

[64] O'Donnell, 47.

[65] Lee Forgue, interview by author, 14 March 2004, video recording, Davis, California.

[66] Victoria James, *Let's Fight* (The Japan Times Online, 2003, accessed 27 March 2005); available from http://www.japantimes.co.jp/cgi-bin/makeprfy.pl5?fl20030504a1.htm.

[67] There is currently a Yahoo discussion group set up for SCA members serving in Iraq: SCAsandbox2003@yahoogroups.com.

[68] Andre Sinou to author, 18 April 2005.

[69] William Fisher, *The Crusader* (Blogger, 2004, accessed 24 March 2005); available from http://christian-patriot.blogspot.com/.

[70] Frederick Hollander, quoted in Tina Cardinale and Christopher Burns, *In Service to the Dream* DVD. Dir. Christopher Burns (Los Angeles: Mythos Productions, 2001).

[71] Hollander.

[72] Frederick Hollander, "The History and Culture of the SCA," panel discussion at *The Thirty Year Celebration* 12 June 1996, St. Helena, Washington.

[73] Margaret Silvestri, interview by author, 14 March 2004, video recording, Davis, California.

[74] See David Townsend, "Ironic Intertextuality and the Reader's Resistance to Heroic Masculinity in the *Waltharius*," in *Becoming Male in the Middle Ages*, ed. Jeffrey Jerome Cohen and Bonnie Wheeler (New York: Garland Reference Library of the Humanities, 1997), 67-86.

[75] Carolyn Dinshaw, *Getting Medieval: Sexualities and Communities, Pre- and Postmodern* (Durham: Duke University Press, 1999), 206.

3

INTERPERSONAL PERFORMANCE

The SCA is about transformation, about transforming both oneself and one's world, but like adopting a character for the stage, that transformation is a process. It take a bit of time.

It is the first day of the Pennsic War, the SCA's largest annual event, which is held for fifteen days each year in Slippery Rock, Pennsylvania.[1] I am sitting on the steps in front of the camp store with some friends watching people arrive and begin the transformation from modern to faux-medieval people. The area in front of the camp store is essentially the town square of Pennsic. Most of the attendees pass in front of the store the first day they arrive, and we are sitting there watching them pass and drinking the famous Pennsic chocolate milk, a concoction so delicious, so addictive, it is known to SCA members as "Pennsic Crack."

We are wearing more or less identical uniforms: shorts, t-shirts, and tennis shoes. With me are Charlie and Mitch, with whom I drove out from Brooklyn, and Chris, a friend from Vermont. We are watching folks arrive at the camp. Some, like us, are dressed more or less like normal people; others, maybe half, are dressed in medieval or fantasy garb. The first guy we notice is sort of in between. He is short, a bit stooped, in his early twenties, with coke-bottle-thick glasses and brillo-pad hair. He is wearing the same thing we are—shorts, t-shirt, and tennis shoes—but this guy has gone the extra mile. He is also wearing a hand-stitched leather satchel the size of a briefcase and a long medieval-style belt, so long that the tip of the belt hangs below his knees as in paintings of twelfth-century knights. A huge dagger in a sheath hangs on the belt.

"Look at this f#&@ing guy," says Charlie. "Briefcase man: he gets here and the first thing he does is put on his knife, like now he's in garb."

A pickup truck pulls up and out of the bed jump a whole bunch of young goths. Their leader seems to be a tall thin guy wearing camouflage pants in hunter safety orange. His hair is dyed the same shade of orange as his pants.

"Target Boy," says Chris. "We don't have people that look like him in Vermont: can't hide. The hunters would shoot him dead."

"Check it out," says Charlie, "Goat whore."

"Huh?" I say. Then I see her, a young woman wearing an eye-catching t-shirt. It is black, of course, and has a pentagram with a goat's head silk-screened onto it, above which is the word "Göatwhore," complete with the umlaut over the first "o" (obviously the name of a band).

That's when I spit out my milk.

Göatwhore makes a beeline for Target Boy, gives him a big hug and hooks her arm through his as they wander off together. This is when Mitch sees her and also spits out his milk. We decide they are made for each other.

In *The Theatre in Life,* Nikolas Evreinov writes:

> Man has one instinct about which, in spite of its inexhaustible vitality, neither history nor psychology nor aesthetics have so far said a single word. I have in mind the instinct of transformation, the instinct of opposing to images received from without images arbitrarily created from within, the instinct of transmuting appearances found in nature into something else, an instinct which clearly reveals its essential character in the conception of what I call theatricality.[2]

Evreinov's theory is that, instead of descending from rhetorical debate or religious ceremony or poetic recitation, theatre is descended from play. To Evreinov, dressing up and pretending you are someone else is natural, a game children play instinctively, and it is natural for adults to play elaborate versions of this childhood game, whether in the form of Mardi Gras or a Broadway musical or painting your body in team colors when attending a football game.

The SCA is playful performance. People in the SCA seek to transform themselves through dress, name, and action. Even the people we are watching in front of the store, who have not yet changed into an attempt at medieval dress, are in costume and performing transgressive roles. By dyeing hair safety orange, by donning a shirt that says Göatwhore, and by wearing medieval accessories with modern clothes, the three people we saw outside the Cooper's store were already engaged in the type of transformative role-playing that takes place at SCA events. Having decided that "normal" is too normal for them they are determined to act pointedly abnormal in an effort to protest and subvert normality. When they arrived at Pennsic they were subverting not only the normality of modern society but SCA normality as well. They would be doing the same thing once they don the medieval or (more likely) fantasy garb they will wear for the two weeks of Pennsic. And the four of us who were sitting there laughing at them, who passed most of a fortnight as three Vikings and a Khazar, would be subverting real-world normality while reinscribing SCA normality.

This chapter is about interpersonal performance. I derive the term from interpersonal communication, which is commonly used to describe communication between two people. It is a way of describing how performance is used in direct communication, what Evreinov calls "The Theatre in Life." I intend to show in this chapter ways in which SCA performance is highly theatrical, and suggest that, contrary to current divisions amongst critics, "performativity" and "theatricality" need not be mutually exclusive.

Theatricality has numerous meanings, which make it problematic as a critical concept.[3] As Janelle Reinelt has pointed out, Western and particularly Anglo-American critical theory has, from Plato onwards, associated theatricality with deception and trickery.[4] The term has been primarily used as part of an antitheatrical discourse, in which "theatrical" is a negative term describing falseness: the attempt and subsequent failure of theatre to re-create reality.

Twentieth-century criticism has tended to favor the term performance over the-atricality, seeing more truth and spontaneity in the former. Schechner, among others, favors the immediacy of performance over what he considers to be the untruths of theatrical make-believe.[5] This sets up an opposition between the two terms: performance reveals truth whereas the theatrical revels in falsehood. Carlson links the decline of the term theatricality to the rise in popularity of per-formance as a concept: "In some cases its decline can, I think, be almost directly correlated to the success of performance, where the two have been posited as rhetorically opposite terms."[6] Carlson argues for a resurrection of theatricality as a critical concept and suggests that the terms can, in fact, compliment one an-other. Moving beyond Carlson's formulation, postmodernism allows us to take up the concepts equally and apply either or both as we will. A principle of post-modernism is that there can be no truth: or rather, there can be more than one truth. If, indeed, performance is the primary expressive form of postmodernism, it must be for some other reason than the fact that it reveals the truth. Those postmodernists like Schechner who favor performance over theatricality are setting up a rather modernist hierarchy.

This conflict creates some problems when using the theatrical in reference to the SCA. Following current trends in critical thinking, people who write about reenactment and re-creation in general tend to favor the concept of performance. Typical is Rodwell, who writes that, "[a]bove all, the SCA is a site of extensive performative activity."[7] However, he struggles to fit SCA performance into per-formance theory:

> I need to bridge the gap between theories of ritual/entertainment and theories of interpersonal interaction in everyday life; I need a middle ground of theory which addresses both the group and the individual at interstices of cognition and interaction . . . this is a slippery business in the SCA as there are both for-mal and informal spaces of performance (e.g. events and practices): ritual and everyday life.[8]

Lenehan in his earlier work had essentially solved this problem through post-modernism, and Erisman did so by using theories of class and created commu-nity. While both these approaches proved useful, the application of theatricality, of people's desire to be different, is ultimately more so. Thomas Postlewait and Tracy Davis in their book *Theatricality* note that a more positive view of theatri-cality has emerged as scholars have sought to reclaim the term: "[T]hey desig-nated it a descriptive term that could be used to identify the essential perform-ance qualities of any dramatic performance at any time and place."[9] Carlson in his attempt to rehabilitate performance writes that theatricality "can still be rec-ognized as an essential element in the continued vitality and enjoyment of both theater and performance[.]"[10] Theatricality and performance need not be mutu-ally exclusive concepts, and thus they can be applied to the SCA together.

Evreinov's ideas about theatricality, which come out of the avant-garde theatre of early twentieth-century Russia, are, though somewhat old fashioned, nonetheless the most useful version of theatricality for examining SCA activity. As Silvija Jestrovic notes, Evreinov views the notion of self as a metatheatrical phenomenon: "[T]he intrinsic theatricality of *I* is played out through transformation. By doing so, one deliberately transforms *I* into *other*, turning the familiar, supposedly intrinsic self into his/her own stranger."[11] This formulation has serious implications for the way in which SCA members construct identities for themselves within the setting of the SCA game. Many SCA members see themselves as living multiple lives (modern and medieval) while others see themselves as revealing different aspects of the same life through performance.

Evreinov has an even more direct connection to the types of game the SCA plays. Evreinov was very interested in performance reconstruction and historical reenactment, especially medieval reenactment, and was a strong proponent of a search for historical authenticity. He went so far as to suggest that audience members be dressed in period costumes as a way to gain insight into the social and intellectual conditions in which a performance took place.[12] This idea, which would be later echoed by Robert Sarlos in his work on performance reconstruction,[13] can also be applied to theatrical performances in the SCA. Evreinov believes that the instinct to be different and to experience things different from the commonplace is fundamental.[14]

This instinct to be different is one of the central elements of the SCA. It is a clear way to separate oneself from the mundane, to reject normalcy. Every SCA member senses that something is lacking in contemporary society and, as with other escapist subcultures, from hippie communes, to Burning Man, to science fiction fandom, seeks to differentiate him or herself from the normal. It is not just a matter of running to the Middle Ages or away from modern times; it is also a desire to be different. The quote from Maxim above accused SCA members of being geeks, but the more accurate term would likely be "nerds." Webster defines "nerd" as "a dull, ineffectual or unattractive person," or "someone engaged in an unsocial pursuit." Popular usage expands the second definition to include people who perform an activity out of the norm, one which most people in society find boring or useless or weird. Nerds are people who find the normal boring, who enjoy arcane knowledge, and who revel in being different. Many activities mocked as being nerdish in popular culture, such as Star Trek fandom, Dungeons and Dragons, and renaissance faires, are also theatrical, in that participants are using costume and/or action to transform themselves in some way, rejecting the mundane for the purposes of play.

Through the theatricality of costume and role-playing, SCA members perform their rejection of the mundane. Many SCA people speak not only of lost values and a lack of chivalry and honor in contemporary society, but also of their opinion that contemporary society is uninteresting. The things that most people enjoy are rejected precisely because most people enjoy them. Like the typical nerd, SCA members seem to be in on a private joke—they understand how banal most people's lives are. They revel in being different. Maxim's jokes about the SCA were not that inaccurate, but as Evreinov says, "It goes without saying that if you are a businesslike Sancho Panza you will never understand why Don Quixote indulges in Don-Quixotism."[15] Evreinov coins the idea of "Theatre for oneself," the performance of fantasy, the theatre of Don Quixote and Robinson Crusoe. Both of these famous literary characters fantasize about feudal societies, and Evreinov maintains that these fantasies are universal. We are all, according to Evreinov, Don Quixotes, joyfully repudiating the modern world with its "Unimaginative matter-of-factness."[16]

In a way, the SCA is what happens when a thousand or more Don Quixotes get together. Don Quixote's isolation is ended. He is suddenly among his own kind and they can begin to build the fantasy communally. He finds like-minded people who begin to see the barber's basin the way he does as soon as he describes it to them. As Nugent notes, "It's easy to ignore the signs of the real world when you're nestled in an army of true believers."[17] The theatre for oneself has become a theatre for themselves. There is still no outside audience to passively observe the performance, but the fantasy has become a group activity, and this moves it from the isolated delusions of a madman to a kind of game. But the SCA is full of Robinson Crusoes as well as Don Quixotes, people who recognize the absurdity of what they do and take time once in a while to laugh at it. They alternate between taking the SCA very seriously and making fun of it. Irony is not, regardless of what Rodwell says, eschewed in the SCA; it is embraced.

Serious Play

If there is a performative aspect to everything people do—that is to say, if every action a human being takes is intentional and enacted to create a specific effect—then it is no great revelation to say that the SCA is performance. In the SCA, however, performance is highlighted through theatricality. SCA members dress up and play roles different from those they play at other times. This is also true when I put on a swimsuit and go to the beach. There I am playing the role of bather, but most people wouldn't recognize that as a role. It is too normal. SCA roles are different because they are so far outside the norm of everyday activity, and tunics are as weird almost anywhere as a bathing suit would be in a bank. People outside the SCA recognize people in medieval clothes as different, as involved in some kind of role-playing. SCA members, on the other hand, often do not see themselves as playing a role at SCA events. To members of the SCA, dressing up in medieval clothes for a weekend is normal and therefore not performative, even though it is obviously play—and play that they take very seriously.

Irving Goffman in *Frame Analysis* proposes that play activities cannot be serious as they do not affect life and death. His distinction between "serious" and "unserious" activities is problematic because it establishes a hierarchy of behavior that does not exist in a postmodern society. The seriousness of any activity depends more on how the people performing that activity feel about it than any on outside observation. However, SCA activity is obviously play. A.D. Putter, writing after Goffman, notes:

> The tournament, with its fixed rules, places, and duration, creates what anthropologists call a "play-world": a world in which actions take place at one remove from reality and have a certain license, because the play-world frames them as unreal or unserious.[18]

Most SCA events are faux-medieval tournaments, and the SCA clearly creates a type of play—world in which people are playing not only with social roles but also with time. A great deal of license exists at SCA events. Conflicts are played out, politics are performed, romantic trysts take place, and people act out various fantasies of power and enfranchisement. However, in spite of Goffman's and Putter's hierarchy, the people involved in these activities often see them as very serious. Like other subcultures built around leisure—surfing, for instance—the SCA becomes for many of its members both their primary social interaction and the focal activity of their lives. To some, the job is just what they do in between events to pay for their medieval habit.

The libertarian philosopher Karl Hess would not agree with Goffman's hierarchy. Hess said that if you want to know how people view themselves you should look at their hobbies. "You can tell what a person really wants to do by their hobbies. Most people want to be gardeners or musicians. Nobody's hobby is insurance."[19] Hess didn't pay much attention to the fact that everything we do is a role that we play. His point was that society divides us into economic categories by identifying us as our occupation ("I'm a doctor," "I'm a teacher")— echoing Goffman's favoring of serious activity. Most people, according to Hess, would rather be identified with the things they do for fun and recreation ("I'm a golfer," "I'm a skier"). Hess maintains that most people, given a choice, would rather pursue a hobby than work, and that the job, in a modern society where so few resources are actually spent on subsistence, is primarily a means of accruing the wealth necessary to perform those activities we wish to perform, not just in consuming goods but, in Hess's view, becoming the person we envision ourselves to be.

Willis Harman in *Creative Work* suggests that, as most tasks are no longer needed for survival, work needs to become a place of personal fulfillment as opposed to one where people earn their survival.[20] Hess took a different view. He eschewed wage work all together. To sustain himself he grew his own food, farmed fish in a basement, and bartered with people for goods. Hess sought personal identity and fulfillment outside of normal "work." Many SCA members approach their game in the same way, as a means of fulfillment and of personal identification. Many of them identify more closely with their SCA roles than they do with their roles in contemporary society. Dr. Dana Kramer-Rolls/Viscountess Maythen Gervaise was once doing a demo for a group of Boy Scouts, when one of them asked, "You don't actually think you're a real knight, do you?" She replied, "Do you think you're a real Eagle Scout?"[21] This is a very practical view of SCA knighthood. Like Eagle Scout status, knighthood is an award given by a group that only has meaning within the group itself (a lot of knights are, in fact, also Eagle Scouts). But it also says a great deal about self-identification. Maythen is a knight not only because the king has recognized her as such but also because she sees herself as such. It is an important part of her personal identity. As Hess implied, this type of self-identification is transgressive because in a market-based economy the most important identifier for people is their value to the economy: their monetary value, the ways in which they contribute to the economy, their purchasing power, etc. Identifying oneself with a hobby subverts this.

As Lenehan states,

> The hyper-differentiation of a society associated by Crook, Pakulski and Waters (1992) with the move out of "modernity" and an increasing intermingling of cultures give impetus into the proliferation of taste cultures that lie behind the process of postmodernization. Each member of a post-modern culture is "free" to draw upon the palette of experience that has been collected by their society and in an attitude of "do-it-yourself," construct the lifestyle that suits their tastes.[22]

Postmodern theory resists the type of economic pigeonholing that prompts people to identify with their professions, thereby breaking down Goffman's categorization of activity into that which is serious and that which is not. If old hierarchies and categories are broken down by postmodern theory, and people are allowed to create their own systems of value independent of broader society, then there is nothing unusual with people identifying themselves in terms of what a small group of people think.

Goffman identifies five categories of framing, three of which overlap to frame the SCA. First of all, SCA activity is clearly a form of make-believe. Second, it includes both contests and ceremonials. It can also be said to include practice and rehearsal, Goffman's fourth category. About make-believe Goffman writes:

> Make-believe: By this term I mean to refer to activity that participants treat as an avowed, ostensible imitation or running through of less transformed activity, this being done with the knowledge that nothing practical will come of the doing. The "reason" for engaging in such fantasies is said to come from the immediate satisfaction that the doing offers. A "pastime" or "entertainment" is provided. Further, the engrossment of the participants in the dramatic discourse of the activity [the innermost plane of being] is required, else the whole enterprise falls flat and becomes unstable.[23]

Engrossment is a key element. SCA members become very dedicated to their SCA lives. They often take the politics, rewards, and relationships built within the game very seriously and transfer them to their mundane lives. The game sometimes borders on reality. E. F. Morril/Viscount Sir Edward Zifran the Bastard of Gendy, in his Art of Being class, sums it up nicely: "This is make-believe," he says, "but we create a very real world."[24]

Are SCA roles make-believe? Are they our true selves? A part of our true selves? How we'd like to see ourselves? Or, as my best friend would say, is it just a way to get babes? My own identity in the SCA is emblematic of how SCA members engage in what Patrick O'Donnell called "controlled multiple personality disorder."[25] I play a lot of different roles in life: actor, scholar, teacher, filmmaker, each of these roles growing out of my interaction with a specific professional or artistic culture. However, in all of them I use the same name. In the SCA I don't. In the SCA I am called Valgard Stonecleaver, a name I chose myself. Valgard, the name of a character in *Njal's Saga*, I selected from a list of Viking names when I first joined, because my introduction to the group came through a "Viking household." Stonecleaver, which sounds like an occupational surname for a mason, I chose because the first person I ever "killed" in battle was a knight belonging to House Stonecroft. In the SCA I play a lot of different roles as well. I am a knight (an award for fighters), a viscount (an ex-prince), and a count (a one-time king), though in lieu of count I use the Scandinavian title "jarl." I am also a marshal, a bard, and a herald. SCA members are constantly performing various roles based on their interactions within the SCA culture. These roles give me status and position within the SCA and convey nothing in broader society.

The term "make-believe" which Goffman employs is a conflicted notion. It implies a nontruth. But to make is to construct, and to construct a belief is not necessarily the same thing as to pretend. Some SCA members are pretending to be people living in another time period. Their SCA selves are an identity they put on with a costume. Most SCA members see themselves differently, as just being their natural selves in a more desirable setting. The members of the SCA have constructed a reality, they have "made a belief" and a belief system through medievally coded ritual and performance. It is a utopian reality, a clear alternative to contemporary society, in which the roles they have created for themselves give them status and power within the play realm they have established.

Persona

An important element of this dichotomy between those who pretend they are in the Middle Ages and those whose performance is rooted in the here and now of the SCA is the concept of persona. Most introductory SCA literature addresses the concept. Persona for society members is "the person they would have liked to have been had they lived in the Middle Ages."[26] Both Erisman and Rodwell place a great deal of emphasis on persona in their analysis of the SCA. Erisman in particular believes that persona stories are an important method by which SCA members construct identity through a "personal narrative." Rodwell writes that "[m]edieval personae are the most important adjuncts to the re-creations Scadians perform."[27] ("Scadian" is a common term for people in the SCA).

In fact persona is a highly contested concept in the SCA. Erisman acknowledges that persona stories are mostly private and play an ambiguous role in constructing the SCA community.[28] O'Donnell in *The Knights Next Door* noted of SCA members "In practice, the majority treats their persona like a crazy aunt they left home in the attic. They shop for it, make things for it, refer to it in the third person, but never bring it out into public. They certainly don't act like it, talk like it or live like it."[29] Some members don't "play persona" at all. *The Courtesy Book* says, "Sometimes a persona is nothing more than a name and a nationality, sometimes it is even less. And sometimes a persona is a highly detailed, researched and organic biography."[30]

Many people, especially when new to the SCA, write elaborate persona stories that are romanticized and allow them to incorporate many different regions and elements into their story: "I am a Welsh princess born in 1345 and kidnapped by gypsies at age two . . ." etc. At other times the persona story is more general: "I'm a fifteenth-century French knight." This gives people a time period to research and an established set of props and costumes to pick from as part of their performance but does not include details of a life that was never actually lived. Those who are seeking a living-history experience in the SCA often develop a very detailed persona, with complete biographies and personality profiles, but one which is more realistic than the stereotypical "Welsh princess" persona story. They will stick to dates, times, and historical events in which their persona participated, but not try to make themselves sound like the hero of a romance novel or an adventure story. At the other extreme are people who don't have a persona at all other than their name. These are the people who believe that in the SCA they are able to be their "true selves," as Rodwell puts it.

If we look at these two extremes of performance and examine them in terms of theatricality we can see a clear dichotomy. The first version of persona, in which the SCA member is portraying a person from the historical Middle Ages, can be related to mimetic performance. These SCA members have constructed and are portraying detailed, well-defined characters (whether or not their personas are well-researched or realistic). Like a method actor, they seek to re-create reality, to form as real an impression as possible of a medieval person. In contrast to this, SCA members with no persona other than their identities in the "Current Middle Ages" are using persona in a way akin to some performance art. By adopting made-up names within a postmodern fantasy world they foreground the contemporary and reveal attitudes and beliefs that are hidden in the course of their everyday lives. They are bringing aspects of themselves, buried by contemporary society and contemporary strictures, to the surface.

Hollander, eschewing the more common terms "SCA name" or "persona name," refers to "Frederick of Holland" as his "chosen name" (which doesn't have much import when you realize that "Frederick of Holland" and "Fred Hollander" are essentially the same name), implying that this is his true identity. One SCA knight jokingly describes his persona as "a guy from the Middle Ages who fights," with no more elaboration. Bill Jouris/Count William the Lucky, a long-time member and past president of the SCA Inc., when asked for his persona's biography for the contributor's section of an SCA publication, wrote that "Count William the Lucky never figured out what a persona was or what he would do with one."[31] These people each insist that they are not pretending to be someone else—who they are in the SCA is simply who they are. They do not erect a wall between their contemporary and medieval selves.

Hollander, like Jouris, does not use persona in the common SCA sense because he does not see his participation in the SCA as mimetic:

> Some people enjoy making up detailed tales of who they would have been in the original Middle Ages, and fulfilling them with greater or lesser authenticity. In that sense persona is an artificial construct designed to help them study the Middle Ages. In a larger sense, persona is the attitudes and reality I bring to the SCA, which is different in some small manner than the attitudes I bring to the 20th century. . . . My persona in the SCA is my history in the SCA. I am a laurel, a pelican, a herald, a champion to my queen, I fight on the battlefield for my king. I fight on the tournament field those who will come against me. All of this is part of my persona, and all of these things are things I do not do in the 21st century. So, in essence, persona is the things we do in the SCA that we don't do in modern times.[32]

Of course, Hollander is doing these things in the 20th century. His categorization, and the phrase "original Middle Ages," (as opposed to the SCA's "current Middle Ages"), reveals how temporal categorization is a social construct. Hollander is not speaking of time as a scientific phenomenon but of people's use of time to categorize.

Reconciling these two views of persona is difficult, and understanding them important to any analysis of the SCA. The fact that some members of the group do not portray a person from another time is one of the things that separate the SCA from historical reenactment. It also moves the activity into the realm of ritual and ceremony. Notes Goffman,

> Finally, observe that in plays a performer appears as a character other than himself; in ceremonials, on the other hand, the performer takes on the task of representing and epitomizing himself in some way one of his central social roles: parent, spouse, national, and so forth. (In everyday life the individual is himself, too, but not in so clearly a self-symbolizing way.) [33]

Add to this list "knight, duke, hero," and SCA activity might also be seen as an activity in which people epitomize a social role.

Forgue is suspicious of the concept of persona. She said in our interview:

> I am very dubious of people who join the society and it's their third event and they have a story that is eight pages thick that they think is their persona. How-

ever, many of the people who've been in the SCA for very many years have a functional persona. They know a lot about sometimes one, sometimes a variety of cultures, they are familiar with the history, the material culture, all the things that go into representing a person from a particular era. They don't go around saying "I am the daughter of the prince of Wales who was kidnapped by gypsies and taken to Byzantium," but they know what a person who was born in Wales at approximately the time period they're interested in would have worn and ate [sic] and how they would have lived. Is that a persona? I don't know. Is the "kidnapped by gypsies" a persona? I don't care.[34]

The SCA's use of a large and loosely defined time period is an example of pastiche in the construction of postmodern leisure.[35] It also presents an obvious stumbling block for any type of reenactment. When walking through any SCA event you are likely to meet Vikings, twelfth-century crusaders, fourteenth-century knights, fifteenth-century Venetian ladies, and sixteenth-century mercenaries, and probably a samurai or two. This makes it impossible to behave and react the way a person of a specific class from a specific time period would have reacted. In staging an interpersonal performance between a Saxon warrior of the tenth century and a master goldsmith from fifteenth-century Amsterdam, where would you begin? Says Shannon McSmith:

> My opinion of persona is that it's a really good idea; the problem is that the way the SCA is built up it's almost impossible to do. Since the SCA covers roughly from 600 to 1600 it's really hard to go to an event and be strictly in persona for the entire time. I can dress in my persona, which is a late 16th century Scottish woman. I can dress in my persona, I can eat the things that she would have eaten, I can indulge and do the hobbies she would have done, I can indulge and flirt the way she would have flirted, I can do all of those things but I'm still going to have to deal with a Viking or somebody from the 14th century or somebody from the Middle East who I never would have come in contact with.[36]

McSmith is a reenactor who would like to see the SCA reflect less fantasy and more of the realities of medieval or renaissance life, but the only way to do this would be to narrow the SCA's time frame.

McSmith's partner, Thomas Moore/Sir Thomas Logan, complained to me:

> As I learn more and more through my own research about how people in the Middle Ages and Renaissance actually lived I find myself frustrated at the way some people interpret it in the SCA. There's also a lot to be said for being involved in a reenactment group where everybody is playing the same culture and the same time period because you have a sense of community that is much easier to build than it is in the SCA. You almost have to build a mundane community with your SCA friends and then extend that into the SCA milieu, because we're all dressed from different cultures and different time periods; we wouldn't have ever met one another.[37]

Erisman's thesis, of course, directly disputes this. To her the inclusive nature of the SCA, its shared history and ritual, are what builds community within the SCA, and the quest for historical authenticity is something that threatens that community. However, reenactors in the SCA are seeking a shared experience of living in and reenacting a specific time and place, and the broad scope of the SCA prohibits that kind of performance experience.

One interesting take on persona, designed to get around the problems created because the SCA includes just about anything that existed prior to 1601, comes from Chris Rolls/Duke Christopher of Houghton, who lists his persona as "an Elizabethan Noble who belongs to a group that recreates the Middle Ages."[38] In other words, his persona takes part in a period version of the SCA. Such re-creations were an important part of the Renaissance masquing tradition, and this allows him to maintain the conceit of persona while interacting with personas from earlier cultures.

None of these people, whether they see persona as a character they play or as an extension of themselves, are being themselves by contemporary standards. The SCA name still constitutes a persona, it is still a mask. In *Drama and Resistance: Bodies, Goods and Theatricality in Late Medieval England,* Claire Sponsler, examining the medieval Robin Hood game, argues that a primary function of festive misrule was as a means for people to resist the modes of discipline imposed on them by society, which Robin Hood does not only through robbery but also through cross dressing, changing both his gender and his class. Looking at the ballads "Robin Hood and the Bishop" and "Robin Hood and Sir Guy of Guisborne," Sponsler argues "[t]he Robin Hood who appears in these two ballads is an antidisciplinary figure whose salient characteristic is a refusal to recognize the authority of cultural categories or the rule of acceptable codes of behavior."[39]

The SCA resists contemporary disciplining forces in a number of ways. One way in which contemporary persons are disciplined is through identity. As far as contemporary society is concerned each of us has an official identity in the form of a name, registered on an official document called a birth certificate and recorded in various other places like school, medical, and legal records. If we want to change our name we have to appear before a judge and have the change approved and duly recorded. The only exception to this is when a last name is changed as a result of a marriage ceremony, but this change must still be legally recorded by a county clerk when the marriage license is filed. The idea that people might operate under assumed identities is seen with suspicion in those bodies of government concerned with the disciplining of the populace, the police and the courts. If you adopt a new name it is assumed that you are trying to hide something.

In the SCA this form of discipline is clearly resisted. SCA members have close relationships, often lasting several years, without even knowing each other's "mundane" names. In the SCA, a culture with a large oral as well as written tradition, stories are told, songs are sung, and gossip is spread about people using only their SCA names. This separation of identity is often blurred, as O'Donnell has noted: SCA names and mundane names sometimes become interchangeable. A person might be called by his mundane name at an SCA event, and is even more likely to be called by his SCA name in a social gathering of SCA members, even at a purely contemporary activity like dinner at a restaurant or going out to a movie.[40] Sometimes coworkers and family members not involved in the SCA will come to know and use a person's SCA name, further breaking down the borders between SCA activity and the rest of the world. In this way SCA members break down the borders between fantasy and reality and resist the disciplining rules of broader society.

Evreinov said, "The main thing for us is not to be ourselves. This is the theatrical imperative of our souls."[41] This type of transformative make-believe is present in both extremes of persona, but it is performed in different ways. People who create a character as their persona separate their SCA/medieval roles from their mundane selves. Some even take this to the point of "persona death," when a person kills off one persona in order to adopt a different one. This view of persona is close to that found in live action role-playing games. Those who see their SCA roles as extensions of their contemporary selves, or as their "true selves" also take part in transformative make-believe through what Evreinov calls "Don Quixotism." He says:

> The "theatre for oneself" to which Don Quixote has dared to surrender is the most logical, the most uncompromising and the most complete expression of man's will to the theatre. If you are fascinated by a fairy-tale, you naturally wish to see it materialized.[42]

The separation implied by persona between a medieval self and a contemporary self reveals the type of subject/object relationship common in mimetic performance. A reenactor in the SCA seeks to know the Middle Ages by becoming someone else—a medieval person. The desire in this case is not merely to escape the contemporary but to be absorbed into the past. The objectified medieval self is never aware that it is the puppet of the contemporary subject, but the subject is always aware of its own existence, ruining the illusion of time travel. The ideal is for the subject to be consumed by the object, to become the medieval person and to be unaware of the contemporary, but this is for the most part a temporal impossibility. If people actually started to believe they were in the Middle Ages, or if they believed it for more than a fleeting moment, they would no longer be able to function in a contemporary world.

This dichotomy is not unique to SCA members and their personas. Raghnild Tronstad points out that Thomas Hobbes considered expressing one's personality and playing a role to be the same thing. Hobbes noted that the word "person" is derived from persona, and that it originally meant "mask."

> *Persona* in Latin signifies the *disguise,* or *outward appearance* of a man. . . . So that a *Person* is the same as an *Actor* is, both on the Stage and in common Conversation; and to *Personate* is to *Act,* or *Represent* himself, or another.[43]

The idea of having a separate identity within the SCA, even if it is simply a made-up name, is one of the group's most carnivalesque qualities, and is a link to medieval carnival, of which Bakhtin writes:

> It could be said (with certain reservations of course) that a person of the Middle Ages lived, as it were, *two lives:* one was the *official* life, monolithically serious and gloomy, subjugated to a strict hierarchical order, full of terror, dogmatism, reverence, and piety; the other was the *life of the carnival square*, free and unrestricted, full of ambivalent laughter, blasphemy, the profanation of everything sacred, full of debasing obscenities, familiar contact with everyone and everything. Both lives were legitimate but separated by strict temporal boundaries.[44]

The carnival square life is not necessarily a false identity. It does not hide one's identity. The carnivalesque allows qualities that would otherwise be hidden to come to the surface. It is a mask that reveals.

Authenticity and "the Dream"

Lenehan, Erisman, Rodwell, and O'Donnell all note the tension created by the quest for authenticity in the SCA. Erisman goes so far as to suggest that the conflict between the "authenticity mavens" and the "fun mavens" poses a serious threat to the community, while O'Donnell notes that the central question for members of the SCA is, "How 'medieval' do I want to be?"[45] A quest for authenticity, or a type of authenticity, informs everything SCA members do within their game. But while some seek authenticity in material culture, others seek an authentic emotional experience.

Lenehan writes, "the mythos of the group (jokingly referred to as 'the dream') is that it is possible today to escape the mundane world outside and to briefly create the realm that Mallory [sic] wrote of and that John F. Kennedy dreamt of."[46] This is the frame that defines and confines SCA activity, and within this frame the contemporary often becomes faux-medieval. Goffman notes that, "All social frameworks involve rules."[47] The SCA's rules favor participation over historical accuracy (much to the chagrin of reenactors within the group). The SCA sets the framework as the Middle Ages and Renaissance, with a cutoff date of 1601 (even this is a debatable point, as some early SCA literature put the cutoff date at 1650), but there are no set standards for authenticity. Everything used at an SCA event, even modern everyday objects, are contained within the group's medievalist frame. Coleman stoves, sleeping bags, modern tents, folding chairs, etc., can all be found at an SCA event, but it is common for people who use such items to long for a more period set of props, so people who sleep in a Coleman tent may one day advance to a medieval-style pavilion, or the propane stove might be replaced by a cast iron brazier. Some of the SCA's more serious reenactors forgo the use of ice chests, even at the SCA's longest events, working weeks in advance of the event to pickle or smoke all the perishables they might need.

Those who do not have the resources to create a medieval camp will often disguise or at least code their modern objects as medieval. Rowena Porter/ Duchess Rowena d'Anjou used to teach a class called "Medieval Verisimilitude" that typifies most SCA members' approach to authenticity. In simple terms, they fake it. In her class she demonstrated how her large marquis pavilion was made not of canvas but of double knit polyester. Although not waterproof, this fabric gave the roof a very delicate curve up to the peak, without her having to sew a complicated curved seam. She recommended using wooden director's chairs (which are actually based on a period style) but disguising them with decorated seat covers and backs. For tables she would place removable screw mounted legs on 2x4 foot pieces of unfinished plywood, which she would then cover with table cloths that had medieval or renaissance patterns, a modern version of the trestle table. More such cloths would be used to cover modern items such as ice chests, especially if they were in the front of the pavilion in full view. She referred to these cloths as "medievalizers."[48]

This type of coding by disguise is common to the SCA. The SCA often appropriates items of modern culture by coding them as medieval. Erisman notes that the SCA has a junkyard culture. SCA members scour garage sales, trash bins, and flea markets for cast-off items that can be coded as medieval whether through application or by disguising them in some way (she sees this appropriation, using objects in ways they were not originally intended to be used, as a form of cultural resistance).[49] Members often look for something that can pass as medieval, especially if they have limited resources. An unusual hood ornament might make a decent finial for the top of a banner pole. The old peaked canvas Coleman tents, a design that goes back to Roman times basically unchanged, are obviously modern but will look a bit more medieval if you sew a row of simple dagging onto them. As time has passed, however, the knowledge and skill level of SCA members has increased and so have the opportunities for more serious reenactment and more accurate reconstructions. There have always been people in the SCA who did extensive research and attempted accurate reconstructions within their means, and over the course of the group's existence they have rediscovered or invented many techniques necessary to replicate medieval craftsmanship.

Bill Dawson/Master William Bjornson, one of the SCA's most accomplished medieval-style jewelers,[50] once said that the SCA lost a lot when its members got good at re-creating medieval artifacts. In his view it was in some ways better when members used their imagination, when someone sewed a few dags onto a Coleman tent and everybody would just see it as a pavilion. SCA members have always used their imaginations to block out modernity, but now, as more people engage in very elaborate and painstaking reconstructions, modernity stands out more than it used to. When there were not accurate pavilions to compare it to, it was easier to look at the Coleman tent with dags and see a pavilion off the unicorn tapestries.

Evreinov addresses this transformation through imagination, so important to the SCA, in writing about Don Quixote. He notes that at one point Don Quixote is prompted by the sound of a shepherd playing a pipe to reimagine his surroundings, transforming them from an inn to a castle. Says Evreinov, "Do you not envy this magical change of decorations that follows upon the sounds of a reed pipe? Or perhaps you would prefer to see the world as Sancho Panza, the priest and other positivists see it?"[51] With the help of music, Don Quixote is able to imagine a castle where everyone else sees a dingy tavern, just as SCA members, with the help of some simple dagging, are able to see a pavilion instead of an old tent. Although some in the SCA want to see the Coleman tent replaced with a medieval-style-pavilion, others, like Don Quixote, don't really care what other people see. This is a form of escapism, an eagerness to see the world in a different, better, more romantic light. The SCA has created an alternate world in which fantasies like Don Quixote's can be played out. Rodwell calls the SCA "an anti-modern alterity," and this is certainly how most SCA members view themselves. They are protesting contemporary society by harkening back to an era more attractive to them. They are protesting Now.

To some SCA members, this protest is not limited to using medieval-style objects. For years, in spite of the presence of canned propane, Hollander preferred to use an old hand-pumped white gas Coleman stove to cook breakfast at SCA camping events. His reasons were not financial. He could certainly afford a new stove. He said the reason he didn't switch to propane was because it was more modern than the white gas, even though both are the products of twentieth-century technology. He wanted something old. "I find it less intrusive," he says.[52]

Modernity—not in the critical sense but in the material sense—is one of the things Hollander is protesting. He carries this forward to his other equipment as well. Old things that perform the same functions around camp—heating, lighting, etc.,—even if they are not medieval, nonetheless create the proper ambiance for Hollander:

> The barn lanterns that we have hanging from the corners of the BC are not, by any stretch of the imagination, medieval: they are, however, old high tech. They're relatively primitive, and I find them acceptable because of the quality of light. If I were to have an Osberg lamp, burning tallow with a rag for a wick, it would have an orange flame, similar to the orange flame that we get from the lanterns, but the lanterns are significantly safer and more convenient. I would not have in my camp voluntarily anything that gave a white light. It doesn't work, and in terms of older technology, yes, it seems to be less intrusive.[53]

In his approach to the SCA, Hollander displays an antitechnology bias that is revealing when looked on as an escape from his contemporary life. As a professional, Dr. Hollander is a research crystallographer at the University of California at Berkeley. He uses the most advanced scientific equipment available to break down and analyze chemical compositions. In his off time he gets as far away from this world as possible. His recreational retreat into a low-tech agrarian fantasy echoes the same anxieties that have already been discussed about modern technology in relation to medievalist movements in the nineteenth and twentieth centuries.

Hollander is an important case study of the SCA, not because he is typical but because he is archetypical. Of all the people who attended the first event Hollander is the only one who has been continuously active ever since. Moreover, since about 1985 he has attended between forty and fifty SCA events a year. By his own count he has attended over 1,000 SCA events, far more than anyone else.[54] Hollander represents the extreme end of the continuum between romantic fantasy and historical reenactment. When asked if he is a reenactor he says,

> Absolutely not. I am a re-creator. That is my words. My definition is, I am trying not to reenact a specific time, place, situation, say, the battle of Agincourt or the Thirty Years War, or the fifth year of the reign of Henry the Fifth, before he went over to France but after he took the crown and got rid of his disreputable companions. I want the feelings that go through me as archetypes.[55]

To Hollander the SCA as contemporary subculture dominates his mode of performance. When asked whether the history and culture of the SCA inform his participation more than medieval history, he replied,

> Oh, yes, absolutely. My history within the SCA informs all that I do. Original history is background material which I get to work into my interaction with the SCA, for instance, over the last five or so years I have been studying more and more period forms of song and poetry and to that end have been adapting what I write, verse and song to reflect—quote—a little more accurately, what someone would have written had they been writing about the SCA, or even about historical happenings. That I use the historical as background for the SCA is a fact of life. I am a subject of the Crown of the West, not a subject of any European crown.[56]

As these examples illustrate, SCA members, like Don Quixote, reject the contemporary world through a carefully constructed fantasy.

Book Authenticity vs. Authenticity of the Heart

The word "authentic" has several meanings, the most important of which for this study are the ideas of "historical authenticity" and of "emotional authenticity." In other words, things that feel authentic to some people we know to be historically inaccurate, while things that we know to be historically authentic seem old and dead, and do not carry with them an emotional impact. It is worthwhile in this instance to look once again at Sir Walter Scott, since it is from Scott that so many contemporary concepts of the medieval originate. As mentioned in the section on race, *Ivanhoe* was part of a racialist project. Following close on the heels of the French Revolution, and against the backdrop of England's wars with France, *Ivanhoe* was in part an attempt to stress England's pre-Conquest German roots. None of this is important to our study, except that it bears on how the relationship between Saxons and Normans was expressed in *Ivanhoe* and later artistic works. In Sir Walter Scott's version of medieval history, a long, underground patriotic struggle existed between Norman invaders (who brought with them the French language and culture) and Saxon nationalists, who sought to preserve England's Saxon heritage. In *Ivanhoe*, he employs as a minor character the English folk hero Robin Hood and turns him into a figure of resistance to the Normans, a figure whom a contemporary audience would recognize as a guerilla fighter. Although the characters of Ivanhoe, Rebecca, and Brion du Bois Guilbert do not appear much outside of *Ivanhoe*, the character Scott did not create, Robin Hood, becomes in the end a kind of medieval Che Guevara, fighting not only the colonialist Norman occupiers but also fighting *for* a kind of early communism: if the feudal overlords will not share their wealth Robin will seize it through violent force and redistribute it, robbing from the rich to give to the poor.

This idea of Robin Hood as a Saxon freedom fighter did not exist in the Middle Ages. Robin Hood is more strongly associated with the reign of Edward I than with that of Richard I. He operates in Barnesdale forest, not in Sherwood. Although clearly a figure of resistance and rebellion against feudal authority, and one which can be said to have proto-communist ideals, Robin Hood is not a Saxon freedom fighter because at the time in which the ballads were written, and even in the time in which they are now set, this idea of a Saxon resistance did not exist. By the time of Richard's reign the Normans had already assimilated the Saxon nobility. The view of Robin Hood as nationalist freedom fighter is not historically authentic.

It is, however, very emotionally authentic. People in the SCA grew up with visions of Robin Hood as a popular medieval icon. The Saxon freedom fighter who lives in the forest, robs the rich and gives to the poor, fights the evil Normans and allies himself with the one good Norman, Richard, in an effort to reconcile the two warring nations—all of this we grew up with. We get it from Errol Flynn and Douglas Fairbanks and Sean Connery and even Kevin Costner. The movie and television Robin Hood touches a deep emotional chord among contemporary Americans and among members of the SCA. To contemporary people this version of Saxon/Norman relations feels authentic. The joke about getting a Saxon poacher out of a tree is just one obvious example. Most SCA members seek an emotional attachment to the Middle Ages, one that is hard to get from history books, one that is unabashedly romantic. This leads them to re-create a Middle Ages that includes many filmic and romantic images that are not authentic in the historical sense, and this creates tension both from within and without the SCA.

As is to be expected, reenactment groups are often highly critical of the SCA. The Pike and Musket Company, a seventeenth-century reenactment group from Australia commonly known as the Routiers, has been waging an ongoing battle over the internet with SCA-Australia, otherwise known as the Kingdom of Lochac, for years. On their official website, www.theroutiers.org, they used to have twelve separate web pages enumerating everything they considered to be wrong with the SCA (they now include links on their website to both the SCA website and to the SCA Australia website, under the ehading "the Stainless Steel Age"). These included quotes from debates about authenticity posted to SCA discussion lists, a critique of the SCA fighter's handbook, and pictures of some very poor SCA armor, all of which highlighted that side of the SCA that placed no value on historical reenactment. Their main objection, that the SCA has lower standards of authenticity than they do, is undeniably true. Officially the SCA has no standards of authenticity. To the Routiers, the SCA's conventions make it a fantasy organization (and a poor one at that), which masquerades as a living history group, and there are many in the SCA who would agree with them. Dr. Greg Rose/Baron Hossein ali Quomi is a professor of medieval studies and long-time member of the SCA. On the Routiers' website he is quoted as saying:

> The SCA is fundamentally a fantasy organization, and I say that as someone who has participated in SCA events for more than twenty-five years. While there are a few people in the SCA who are genuinely interested in historical re-creation, the majority are either indifferent to history or more committed to a neo-Arthurian ethos (heavily influenced by Victorian romanticism) which is commonly called "The Dream" than to any historical view of the Middle Ages. Indeed, if I had to identify what is at the core of the SCA, it would have little, if anything, to do with the Middle Ages. . . . The core values of the organization make medieval re-creation effectively impossible.[57]

Among the values Dr. Rose lists are an "intense inclusivity" and "official rejection of the principal cultural characteristic of the Middle Ages: religious practice."[58] Although he uses the term re-creation where reenactment would be more accurate, Rose is quite correct in his observation. The SCA as a contemporary society adheres to modern-day principles of fair play and secularism, often to the dismay of some of its members who seek a more accurate stage on which to perform their medievalism. The place of religious practice in the SCA is very marginal. Religious wedding ceremonies are common at larger events, and occasionally Christian, Pagan, or Jewish worship services are held, but under society rules they may not be part of the official activities of the event.

However, the quest for authenticity is often reframed in the SCA. Some people see the SCA not as an experiment in reenacting the material culture of the Middle Ages so much as reenacting medieval attitudes. Morril, for example, has a mixed philosophy with regard to SCA performance. He is not a reenactor in the usual sense. His garb is not particularly accurate and his camp less so (although it has period-style pavilions, everyone sits on nylon camp chairs). He is not interested in the design elements of SCA performance even though he is a scenic designer by profession. What he is interested in reenacting is attitude and behavior. To this end he teaches a class at Pennsic entitled "The Art of Being."

In this class Morril teaches people to play their roles as if it really were the Middle Ages. He stresses that he personally plays "Robin Hood and knights in clanky armor." The appeal of the SCA to Morril is not being in the twenty-first century. His performance is fiercely persona-based and fiercely time-based. To him, persona is like backstory to a method actor. It is 1203 (not 1522, not 1453): a time, he points out, when everybody belonged to somebody else. Even the king belonged to God. This being the case, he bases his performance on service as well as being served. "To whom much is given much is expected," he says. He has the arts and service peerages as well as the fighting peerage. Part of Morril's game is allowing himself to give over his will to someone else. He has to be willing to be ruled by kings, and kings have to be willing to rule. Most people in the SCA, operating with a modern mindset, feel uncomfortable having things done for them. Morril insists that for peers, and especially for royalty, part of their duty is to let people serve them. "If I do not let people serve I screw up the game for them because they want to believe."[59]

Morril's goal in the class is to teach people that in order to be medieval, they must be willing to be subservient to their liege and to command and rule those beneath them, in spite of the egalitarian prejudices of their twenty-first-century selves. Morril seeks an "authentic" medieval experience as does David Friedman, but while Friedman's authentic experience is rooted in the material culture of the Middle Ages, Morril's goal is to seek an emotionally authentic experience. He is, however, aware of the limitations of this. "If I was a real Norman knight," he told the class, "I probably would have burnt the tent to the ground and taken all your wallets."[60]

Echoing Evreinov, Morril sees the SCA as a game of make-believe: "If you think you're five years old it will help," he says, "because five-year-olds know how to play make-believe. You!" he yells at one student, "It's 1203! Grow a beard! Put on a dress! Be a man!"[61]

Friedman's approach is different. He is one of the most vocal advocates of living history in the SCA, and has written often arguing for the pursuit of authenticity. He views SCA events not as gatherings of twentieth-century hobbyists whose hobby is the past, but rather as a "joint fantasy" in which people become their personas at events. In the first view, he argues, persona is a way of focusing one's research, while in the second it is a character that one performs.[62]

The goal in Friedman's approach is not simply to portray the role of a medieval person but to come to believe, for just a moment, that one is actually part of the real Middle Ages. This is what one SCA member I know refers to as "the medieval moment," the moment where he or she forgets the modern mundane world. It's what hardcore Civil War reenactors call the "period rush." This moment is what many people seek when attending SCA events and, according to David Wiles, was an important part of the king game in the Middle Ages: "In a conventional king game, the real world can either be forgotten or be imitated, so that, temporarily, the real world vanishes."[63]

Friedman therefore reframes the question as being not one of authenticity but one of acceptance and belief: a person participating in the first (hobbyist) SCA can make an extremely authentic costume that he/she knows is a costume, while a person in the second (Friedman's) SCA can convince himself or herself to believe that his/her inaccurate garb is the real thing, but only if he or she doesn't have the knowledge of what was authentic in the first place. Friedman stresses research and studious reconstruction, but he feels the second person would have the more authentic experience.[64]

One result of Friedman's theories was the creation of what he called the Enchanted Ground. The Enchanted Ground is one of the most clearly defined performance spaces at any SCA event not associated with an official activity. It is a period encampment, one where not only the props (tents, fire, food, clothes, etc.) are authentic but the attitudes as well. People do not discuss modern things. Not even authenticity can be discussed, because to point out that something is inauthentic is to speak as a twentieth-century person. To get around the problem that the SCA covers a thousand-year period Friedman proposes the use of the conceit of authenticity as a solution: a person should respond to someone from another time in the same way his persona would. The assumption would be, according to Friedman, that said other time is actually another place. When someone from Celtic England encounters someone from Tudor England each should simply assume that the other is a traveler from another place and start up a conversation. Differences in attitude, knowledge, and technology can be explained away easily if you assume that they all exist at the same time, and one's persona just doesn't know about them. After all, to the Celt, a traveler from China and a traveler from Tudor London would likely seem equally as odd.

Enchanted Ground is set up every year at the Pennsic War and occasionally at other large interkingdom events. Not only do people there camp in period-style pavilions and use period-style camp furniture, many of them do not even use ice chests to store their food. Their goal is to create, both through their camp and their actions, the type of living history environment found in places such as Plimoth Plantation and Colonial Williamsburg.

Sometimes, however, the Enchanted Ground type of SCA performance points up its own absurdity. At one banquet in the East Kingdom a group of people, inspired by the Enchanted Ground, decided they would have an Enchanted Table. This is a much harder space to establish, since the boundary around a table at a feast is much more fluid than the boundary around a campground, which can be marked off with rope or ribbon or even a wall. It is easier for a person who is not part of the Enchanted Table to intrude with some modernity and ruin the conceit.

In this instance, Morril was walking by with his wife, Beth Moran/Baroness Elizabeth Talbot. The feasters invited them to the table, saying "Sir Edward, please join us. We are going to be feasting in persona."

Sir Edward politely declined. The feasters insisted: "No, join us: it will be fun." Sir Edward politely said it was a bad idea, and that he felt that they didn't really want him at their table. Again they entreated.

Several things must be noted before moving on to the next part of this story. First, none of the people sitting at the table was an SCA peer, while both Edward and his wife are. Second, in addition to being a scenic designer Ed Morril is an actor, with a deep booming voice and a keen sense of the theatrical. Third, although both Edward and the person he was speaking with, in their modern selves, are Jewish, only the person inviting Edward to the table had a Jewish persona. Edward's persona is that of a Norman knight of the twelfth century who believes that the famous twelfth-century English knight William Marshal is the font of all knightly wisdom and etiquette. Finally, Edward had just seen the Jean Reno film *The Visitors*, in which a Norman knight travels forward in time to the twentieth century and behaves in what to him is a very civilized manner but to everyone else seems barbaric, and he was inspired by this.

"First of all," Edward boomed in a terrible voice, "you would not dine with me. You would wait on me and my lady wife, for that is your place. Secondly you would not sit at my table. You will stand by and attend me, or sit on the floor, and all you will have to eat is whatever scraps I choose to throw your way. Thirdly if any of you were to speak to me unless spoken to I would have you whipped, and if you dared to speak to my lady wife I would have you killed. And finally, I would not dine with you nor with any other infidel Jew." They then walked away toward another table, leaving the Enchanted Table in a state of shock.

This is clearly in keeping with the way Morril teaches his "Art of Being" class. Dining at the Enchanted Table would have been impossible for Morril's persona. This points out an obvious problem with medieval re-creation in a social (as opposed to reenactment) setting: the Middle Ages were rigidly hierarchical whereas contemporary society is more or less egalitarian. Period mores dictated a code of behavior very different from today's. The SCA is a social game of make-believe. People bring to the game not only their concepts of the Middle Ages but also modern ideas about equality and fair play, and those who base their performances on staying "in persona" must abandon many modern principles. Of course it would be impossible for Sir Edward and his wife, in a medieval setting, to dine in public with people who were not peers. More to the point, from a medieval point of view, it was improper for a group of nonpeers to invite two peers to join them.

Ayers taught a class on how to act in persona at a conference in Berkeley, California, in 1991. Like Morril's class at Pennsic, it addressed issues raised when modern and medieval sensibilities clash. Like Morril, Ayers uses William Marshal as inspiration for his performance. He cited the story of William Marshal and the Monk, recounted in Georges Duby's *William Marshal, the Flower of Chivalry,* as an example of the difference between medieval and modern attitudes of conduct. In this tale Marshal encounters a young noblewoman and a monk who are eloping. He offers to take the woman back to her family, but she refuses to go and he does not force her. However, when he asks how they will support themselves the monk tells him that he has a purse of 48 pounds and that they plan to invest it and to live on the interest. Marshal takes the purse and sends them on their way with no means to support themselves. Later, not wanting the money for himself, he gives it to his friends so they can pay their bar tab.[65]

To Duby this story offers an insight into medieval manners. It presents a monk breaking his vows, a noblewoman eloping, and a knight who wishes to stop them but does not—all of them breaking stereotypes. As Duby points out the money bag is key to understanding the story. The reason Marshal takes the money is not just to punish the couple but to keep them from living on the interest. When Marshal finds out that this is their plan his reaction is, "Upon Usury? By God's sword you shall not."[66] It is not the elopement that he feels compelled to prevent, even though the girl is forsaking her family (Marshal knows her brother) and marrying beneath her. He objects to their living on interest. Notes Duby:

> The loathsome thing is that this tonsured fellow, who takes a noble girl to his bed, should claim to use it [the money], even as a bourgeois might do, by putting it out at interest. A man of quality does not profit in this fashion. He profits by his valour, by seizing his prey at the risk of his body, not by exploiting others' needs by lending—in particular, as he knows, to knights, to improvident knights, at usurious rates. William therefore loots the monk with a clear conscience, taking the coins, "saving" them from a wrong purpose by putting them to the only purpose that is not malodorous: for festive expenditures.[67]

It is the usury that Marshal objects to.

Ayers asked his class if Marshal's behavior was "wrong." For a long time nobody answered, afraid (I guess) of telling the Duke to his face that his hero was wrong. At last, with some prompting, somebody said, "Of course it's wrong," and Ayers agreed. By contemporary standards Marshal was nothing more than a brigand. He robbed these young lovers of their only means of support. There was nothing wrong in their behavior from a contemporary point of view. They were in love, so they eloped. So too there is nothing wrong today with loaning money or investing it to earn interest. But to a medieval Christian knight usury was a sin and, furthermore, one that often ensnared people of his own class. Instead of killing the monk with his sword he attacked the couple economically because the economic crime they were committing was far greater than the social crime. Ayers told this story to point out that one cannot behave as a medieval knight would behave in modern society because much of the behavior would be socially unacceptable and at times illegal; this is much the same point Morril was making when he walked away from the Enchanted Table.

The question of religious intolerance raised by Morril's response to that dinner invitation is even more problematic. The oppression of the Jewish people by the European aristocracy, including the Normans, is well documented. Anti-

Judaism is the defining characteristic of the relationship between Jews and Christians during the Middle Ages. Not only did Morril make the proper reply for a Norman knight, but it was completely improper for a person with a Jewish persona to invite a gentile to eat at his table because that would be against kosher law (an entirely different problem is created by the fact that the feast being served was not kosher). When he invited Edward to his table this man was speaking as a modern person and obviously hadn't thought through the implications of his invitation.

I witnessed an even more extreme example of this sort of medieval/modern conflict at the Estrella War several years ago. Estrella is the SCA's second-largest event and is held annually on Presidents' Day weekend outside Phoenix, Arizona. I was wandering the camp with Lori Taylor/Viscountess Lore de Loraine, who was at the time the SCA Board of Directors' executive assistant. Among other things, it was her job to secure insurance certificates for SCA events and to handle any insurance claims involving the SCA.

We were looking for a friend of mine, Gavin Dankar/Lord Gavin Malcour, who was camped with the Red Company, a group of reenactors from outside the SCA who occasionally participate in SCA events, and who portray a company of fifteenth-century German mercenaries. Since they mostly do living history and not the SCA, their camp is one of the most carefully crafted period encampments around. Naturally, they were placed in the Enchanted Ground, which at that event was way out at the fringes of the site. Gavin had been complaining to me about being in the Enchanted Ground earlier that day. His first complaint was that the camp was so far from everything. At the time, Enchanted Ground was often shoved way off in a corner. Supposedly this was so campers there would be less likely to encounter "mundanities" (in fact it was right next to a parking lot), but it also marks living history as an activity liminal to the SCA. The members of Gavin's group, mostly people who worked in the entertainment industry as actors and artists, were highly conscious of the theatrical nature of SCA performance, and being out on the edge of the event meant that hardly anyone got to see their work. The other thing he complained about was that the Enchanted Ground people had no sense of humor. They were *so* serious![68]

When we found the Red Company camp they were just finishing dinner. In a large pavilion they had set three tables up so that they formed an unconnected U shape. On the left were servants and some guests. On the right were some soldiers of the company, while at the center (or high) table was the head of the company, Lord Tristan Keck, his wife, Gwen, and, at each end, two honored guests, Master Giles Hill of Sweetwater and my friend Lord Gavin. Giles received his well-deserved peerage for making extremely elaborate Elizabethan costumes, while Gavin is a film actor and an artist who bears a striking resemblance to Lawrence Olivier in his performance as Henry V (a resemblance that Gavin plays upon to the point of reconstructing both costume and armor from the Olivier film). Nearby sat Gavin's man servant, Hod, who was something of a cross between Jeeves and Baldric from the Rowan Atkinson series *Black Adder*, depending on his mood. Lori and I were given a seat at the other end of the tent and we sat down to watch the performance, which was apparently the way their dinner conversation went every night.

Giles started it off, saying, "It was a lovely dinner, ma'am."

"It was indeed," Gwen replied. "I shall convey your compliments to the cook."

"I especially liked that Jewish dish," Giles went on.

"Jewish dish," she said, "I don't recall any Jewish dish. Of what are you speaking, Master Giles?"

"Why, the Rice Moil, Madam."

All this while, Gavin had been sitting at his end of the table playing with his food by poking at it with a knife. Without looking up, he said, in a voice much like that of Jack Lemon as Prince Hapnik in the movie *The Great Race*, "Is that what it was? I thought it was calamari, it was so chewy!"

At about this time Giles dropped a piece of food on the ground and a Labrador retriever, which had been hiding beneath the table cloth at the high table, quickly stuck its head out, inhaled the food, and popped back under the cloth.

"Madam," I said, "You have a ferocious beast at your feet."

"Yes," she replied, "It sucks things up off the floor. I call it my 'Hoover dog.'"

"Hoover dog?" said Gavin, "Hoover dog? I don't think I've ever heard of a Hoover dog. Pray, what kind of breed is a Hoover dog?"

Lord Tristan, master of the camp, had all this while been leaning back in his chair with a bored look on his face, carefully listening to the conversation swirl around him. Now, finally, he spoke.

"It's Dutch."

"Oh!" exclaimed Gavin, "A Hyoover Dog!" He pronounced it with a "y" sound, and a sort of umlaut, mimicking a Dutch accent, and he kept repeating it over and over, gleefully. "A Hyoover dog! I see. I need to get myself one of those Hyoover dogs!"

Tristan's provost entered the tent with a large writing desk, a quill, and inkwell, and proceeded to pay the company. Each member was paid in coins, minted by Tristan, for every event they attended. The problem was that the provost couldn't add very well (I don't think this was an act), so a long discussion ensued over how many pence make a shilling and how many shillings make a pound.

"Can I help?" asked Gavin.

"No, Master," Hod said drolly, "This is money. Remember our arrangement? You handle the fighting, I handle the money."

"Hah!" said Gavin, "If I do not handle these things once in awhile how will I know when you are cheating me? Did you think of that?"

"No, Master, it hadn't occurred to me."

"So, let's see," Gavin went on, "It's ten pence to the shilling and ten shillings to the pound . . ."

"No, Master," Hod corrected him, "it's twelve pence to the shilling and twenty shillings to the pound."

"Twenty pence to the shilling and twelve shillings to the pound?"

"No, Master: twelve pence to the shilling and twenty shillings to the pound."

"I've got it now!' Gavin declared proudly. "Twelve pence to the shilling and twenty shillings to the pound!"

"That's right master," Hod said, "and twenty-one shillings to the Guinea."

Gavin got a very confused look on his face, which morphed into worry, then back into confusion, and finally said, "Oh! Let's not go there! I hate Guinea."

Gavin now looked very pleased with himself, and continued "Well! Now I am ready for the Inns of Court! I know how many pence there are to the shilling, how many shillings there are to the pound, and I know all about exotic Dutch hunting breeds!"

At that very moment a droopy-eyed old Springer Spaniel stuck his head into the tent and began to nuzzle my left knee, so I leaned over to pet him, and asked, "Well, Lord Gavin, if you know so much about dogs, tell me: what kind of dog is this?"

Gavin got a haughty look on his face and said, "Hah! You think to trick me, sir! Everyone knows what that is! That is a Spaniard!"

Uproarious laughter.

Taylor and I got up and were thanking Gwen and Tristan for their hospitality when there was a scream from outside. Hod stood up and grabbed a crossbow which had been hanging from one of the tent poles. Gavin looked quite put out. "Hod! What are you doing?" he cried. "Those are weapons! Remember our arrangement! You handle the money, I handle the fighting!"

"Yes, Master, I'm sorry," he answered.

I just couldn't resist: borrowing my favorite line from *Black Adder II*, I said, "Hod, just who do you think you are, Wat Tyler, that you can go about brandishing weapons any time you like?"

As we went outside we found out what the commotion was. One of the soldiers was being dragged before Tristan, accused of having fallen asleep while on guard duty. Tristan grabbed the crossbow from Gavin, who had taken it from Hod, and pressed it (not drawn) to the miscreant's head.

"God have mercy on me!" He screamed.

Tristan roared back, "You had damn well better beg mercy of me!"

"I think this is our cue to leave," I said to Taylor. She was laughing so hard she could barely stand, and I nearly had to carry her out of camp.

"So long as I don't have to file the insurance report on this!" she giggled. As we left we could see the other denizens of the Enchanted Ground peeking out of their tents to stare at the goings-on in front of Tristan's camp. They had very worried looks in their eyes.

Most interpersonal performance in the SCA is not this clever. Most people in the SCA sit around camp or around the feast table discussing perfectly mundane topics such as movies, computers, and travel, etc. Sometimes they will discuss topics unique to the SCA, such as a past battle or an upcoming tournament or a particular costuming technique. Often they share gossip about other SCA members. Rarely do they speak "in persona." But in this case the people involved with the conversation were aware of their interpersonal performance *as performance*, and were foregrounding its theatrical aspects. They saw the SCA not just as social interaction but as improvisational theatre. They were not contemporary people being "themselves" at a costume party, but instead were actors portraying characters different from themselves who lived in the fifteenth century. Everyone in the camp was playing his or her role. The servants accepted that they were servants and were expected to defer to their superiors. The soldiers behaved as soldiers, even to the point of creating a dramatic situation by pretending to fall asleep on duty. Tristan's reaction, unthinkable within most contemporary or even SCA contexts, was within the confines of their performance completely acceptable. Taylor's comment that she did not want to have to deal with the insurance claim merely pointed up how far from acceptable this behavior would be in a contemporary world of corporations, lawsuits, and insurance companies.

Rodwell argued that although the SCA is intrinsically ironic, as a group the SCA eschews irony and paradox: "If we are to understand the SCA at all we must accept that irony, and to a lesser extent paradox, is that which SCA performance strives to avoid."[69] However, as this performance shows, irony is often embraced in the SCA. While the other residents of the Enchanted Ground may not have appreciated the ironic nature of the performance, most SCA members would enjoy it as Taylor and I did. So too, paradox is an important part of the SCA performance. Many SCA members, those who are not seeking a living history experience at least, gain pleasure from the paradox established by SCA participation. If indeed playing in a different time is what makes the SCA enjoyable, then that enjoyment can only come by acknowledging the contemporary and taking pleasure from the different modes of performance and theatricality that the SCA allows for.

What made the Red Company's ironic performance acceptable was that it was comical and that everyone involved was playing along. If the people at the Enchanted Table had been willing to sit on the floor eating scraps and to be whipped by Sir Edward whenever they spoke, that too could have turned into a comical performance. This use of irony is discussed by Evreinov as well. Evreinov makes one distinction between Don Quixote and the other medieval fantasist he discusses, Robinson Crusoe. Evreinov considers Crusoe to be superior to Don Quixote because Crusoe is able to step back from his fantasies, comment on them, and even laugh at them. Says Evreinov, "This new knight-errant differs from the old one in that he often looks at himself with a humorous and even skeptical eye, he is very fond of his 'theatre for himself,' but he can also laugh and ironize over this theatre."[70] This is how the Red Company approached their medieval performance, with irony. They made it funny, playing with less attractive historical tropes, i.e., mercenaries instead of knights. They showed not only that the SCA is not particularly historical, but also that history is not particularly attractive. They emphasized the game aspect of SCA participation by being both frivolous and outrageous. The people in Enchanted Ground or those who invited Sir Edward to their table are those whom Rodwell discusses. They are incapable within their interpersonal performance of being ironic, since they have to treat everything around them as real. They have to be serious, as Gavin complained. But they are a very small minority within the SCA. To use irony in their performance would be to acknowledge the contemporary world. This makes their performance in a way both more romantic and more real. Only Morril/Sir Edward was able to move between the two views, but that is because he did not stay at the Enchanted Table for very long. By pointing up the fallacies in asking a knight to join a group of peasants, Morril was using an accurate historical performance in an ironic way.

Other members of the SCA employ irony in their performances by juxtaposing the medieval and the contemporary, such as the fighter who registers a tiger wearing a helmet and grasping a sword as his arms, and then paints Garfield, the comic-strip cat, as a Viking on his shield. This type of thing is frowned upon in some circles of the SCA, but it points up the ridiculousness of the game everyone is playing. This juxtaposition of medieval and contemporary is a source of great amusement to many SCA members—particularly when they can do it outside SCA events.

Freaking the Mundanes

One way the juxtaposition of the medieval and contemporary plays out is when SCA members go "off site" and interact with mundanes. At June Crown, AS XXXVIII (2003), an event occurred that illustrates the nature of SCA performance in the presence of outsiders. Although choosing the next crown prince and princess was the most important matter of the day, another major event outside the SCA threatened to overshadow it—the release of the new Harry Potter novel. When I saw an old friend from high school later that week, who had left the SCA nearly twenty years before, the first thing he asked about Crown was, "How many copies of the new Harry Potter book did you see and were people talking about it?" The answer was six and yes.

Apparently, the novel had been released at 12:00 midnight on Saturday morning, and Forgue and some of her friends had preordered copies for pickup from a local bookstore. According to one of the women, Forgue, who is sixty, silver-haired, and very imperious, "looked like a Hogwarts headmistress as she swept into the room [at the bookstore], with her gown and the three of us trailing behind her."

This kind of activity is called "Freaking the Mundanes." Many SCA members relish going out into public in their medieval garb and inducing shocked looks. According to *The Courtesy Book*, "'Freaking the Mundanes' is a term coined to describe an arrogant attempt by members of the SCA to shock non-

members through action or appearance. The activity is demeaning to the participants and hazardous to the dignity of the SCA."[71] Nonetheless many SCA members find it amusing to see people's reaction to strangers in medieval clothes.
Most mundanes are "freaked" simply by the sight of someone in garb. The SCA
even has a filk song (filk is a song on an SCA theme set to a contemporary tune;
see Chapter 5), sung to the tune of "Waltzing Matilda" about all the strange
situations an SCA member in garb can encounter. ("You'll come a freaking the
mundanes with me . . ."). An original folk song by Heather Rose Jones/Mistress
Tangwystyl verch Morgant Glasvryn lists the many answers one can give to the
most common question SCA members hear from nonmembers: "Excuse me: are
you in a play?"

This is an ongoing joke within the group. Most people, when they encounter
someone at a convenience store dressed as a sixteenth-century German landsknecht, assume that he must either be coming from or going to a rehearsal, since
dramatic activity is the most normal activity people can think of that would require that type of costume. Goffman might say that "freaking the mundanes" is
an example of breaking the frame. SCA members are "freaky" in public because
taken out of context there's no way to explain why they are wearing medieval
clothes. The syndicated SCA cartoonist William Blackfox drew a four-panel
comic that appeared in several local newsletters, in which as a fighter gets older
his answer to this question changes from an enthusiastic description of the SCA
to more and more cynical replies. In the first frame the young fighter gives the
long litany of the SCA: "We're a non-profit education group dedicated to the re-
creation of the Middle Ages . . ." etc. In the second panel a slightly older fighter,
now a knight, says, "It's the SCA, It's like those Civil War groups." In the third
panel the now portly knight, sporting another peerage medallion and wearing a
county coronet, replies "Yeah. *Death of a Salesman.*" In the final panel an old
man wearing a ducal coronet and a t-shirt that reads "Do it in chainmail," replies
"Shoot no! I'm going to a Grateful Dead concert." Perhaps the most famous (in
the SCA) reply to this question comes from an apocryphal story about Johnny
Fulton/Duke John the Bearkiller, another past president of the SCA Inc. According to legend, he stopped off at a convenience store in Tennessee on the way to
an event and an old lady asked him if he and his friends were in a play. Johnny
smiled and said, "No, ma'am. We worship goats. Are you a virgin?"

Freaking the mundanes is one of the few activities in which the SCA interacts with nonmembers. One of the main characteristics of the SCA, which was
developed very early on, is that an SCA event is not a performance for an audience. Only rarely does the SCA put on shows, and these are small demonstra-
tions of either medieval arts and crafts or of SCA fighting, usually for children's
groups. The rest of the time they do it for themselves.

No Spectators!—The Use of Clothing in the SCA

The SCA is very ostentatious. Members wear weird and often elaborate
clothes which, in the eyes of most people, are "costumes"—hence the question,

"Are you in a play?" Garb in the SCA is ostentatious because someone constructed it and someone is wearing it to present a particular face, to aid in portraying a particular role.

SCA members prefer the term "garb" to "costume" because

> [a] costume is an artificial construct: something one wears to disguise himself. A costume is more a mask than anything else. While wearing a costume, one moves and acts in an artificial, affected manner; a costume is a dramatic convention, a prop, an artificial construct. "Garb" on the other hand is much more natural, merely a convenient shorthand for indicating that what is being referred to is medieval rather than civilian clothing, a uniform, if you will, but it is worn and recognized as natural.[72]

The "natural" vs. "artificial" dichotomy here once again supposes that SCA activities are not theatrical and are somehow more "real" than a performance could be. At one time, people going to SCA events cobbled together whatever they could to present a medieval appearance. My parents attended one of the early Twelfth Night celebrations in the West Kingdom, and my mom dressed my dad in cotton long johns dyed gray to simulate mail.

One of the SCA's oldest rules is that everyone who attends an event is required to wear some attempt at medieval garb. As it says on the Middle Kingdom history page: "From the beginning, the group was geared toward participants rather than spectators, and medieval costume was required almost from the very beginning."[73] This is a simple solution to a complex problem: if everyone present, even spectators who just happened by (there is often an officer on site in charge of loaning garb to newcomers and visitors), is dressed in medieval clothes, then no one is an outsider. Everyone is part of the performance. This state of inclusion is an important part of the carnivalesque in *Rabelais and His World,* in which Bakhtin writes, "In fact, carnival does not know footlights, in the sense that it does not acknowledge any distinction between actors and spectators."[74]

The authenticity of SCA garb, like everything else, varies greatly. Danskin tights are often worn in place of hose. Modern fabrics are common; modern shoes more so. Garb is the place where historical inconsistencies are most visible, and to reenactors in the SCA this lack of authenticity makes the organization a "laughing stock" among living history organizations. However, even among the living historian camp there is a range of opinion as to what constitutes authenticity. Are hand sewn garments required or simply garments made of natural fiber material? Some reenactors would have kit policed at every event the way the Civil War reenactors often do. However, in *Confederates in the Attic* Tony Horowitz writes about how even in Civil War reenactment tension exists between people who just want to dress up and have fun and people who are serious reenactors, those who call themselves "hardcores":

> Hardcores didn't just dress up and shoot blanks. They sought absolute fidelity to the 1860s: its homespun clothing, antique speech patterns, sparse diet and simple utensils. Adhered to properly, this fundamentalism produced a time-travel high, or what hardcores called a "period rush."[75]

This is essentially the same sort of experience Friedman talks about seeking.

Others, in both the SCA and in Civil War reenactment, simply wish to adopt "the ten feet rule," that is to say, a person's kit should look authentic from ten feet away. This allows for some modern conveniences like machine woven cloth, machine sewn outfits and even rubber-soled shoes. The ten foot rule, however, would not eliminate the debate over authenticity. Moving the acceptable limit of modernity simply moves the point of debate as to how authentic is authentic enough.

To be wholly authentic is, of course, impossible. What a member of a living history group presents to the outside world is not an authentic person but a model of an historical person created out of and by a modern person. If a person is portraying a fourteenth-century English knight and wears fourteenth-century style clothes that are machine sewn, he can improve his performance by wearing clothes that are handstitched. If they are handstitched, he can improve by making them out of hand woven wool and linen. If he wears handwoven wool and linen, he can improve even more by only wearing wool and linen from the regions of England and Flanders where an English knight of the fourteenth century would have gotten his raw materials. However, sheep have been bred over the last seven hundred years to produce a different variety of wool, so it would not be authentic after all.

The body of the performer creates the most problems for a living historian seeking authenticity, and changes to the body represent the greatest form of dedication to authentic portrayal. Horowitz describes how the hardcore Civil War reenactors try to emulate not only clothing but body type.

> Losing weight was a hardcore obsession, part of the never-ending search for authenticity. "If you look at pension records, you realize that very few Civil War soldiers weighed more than a hundred thirty-five pounds," Rob explained. Southern soldiers were especially lean. So it was every Guardsman's dream to drop a few pants' sizes and achieve the gaunt, hollow-eyed look of underfed Confederates. Eavesdropping on the chat about grooming, sewing, hip size, honed biceps I couldn't help wondering if I'd stumbled on a curious gay subculture in the Piedmont of Virginia.[76]

Hardcore Civil War reenactors go on punishing diets to achieve an authentic weight. Though Horowitz doesn't explicitly state as much, the implication is that many of these men, in pursuit of their idea of the ideal male body, engage in anorexic and/or bulimic behaviors to make weight. In this way, the dedication to an authentic physical form becomes physically dangerous to the reenactor.

This is also the pursuit of authenticity Eco seems to favor. Indeed, Eco believes that a "real" Middle Ages can be understood and, like reenactors, he is much more interested in an authentic than a romantic Middle Ages.

> Our return to the Middle Ages is a quest for our roots and, since we want to come back to the real roots, we are looking for "reliable Middle Ages," not for some romance and fantasy, though frequently this wish is misunderstood and, moved by a vague impulse, we indulge in a sort of escapism á la Tolkien.[77]

Eco would clearly not be impressed with the SCA.

Among SCA members, few go to the sort of transformative extreme that the hardcores pursue, but there are other ways in which some alter their bodies in order to present a better portrayal of their personas. Many will sport medieval hairstyles. The long hair and beard of the fourteenth century and the bowl cut of the fifteenth century are not too out of place in modern society, and many SCA members style their hair in these ways. Some members have been known to alter their hair even more, however. A person whose persona is a Norman soldier, for instance, might shave the back of his head in the Norman style for the duration of an event. Men who portray monks often shave tonsures into their hair. Such temporary alteration is common. Some people will adopt a more permanent alteration in the form of tattoos using medieval designs. In this instance, SCA members are permanently imprinting their medieval performance upon their bodies in a way that cannot be changed. In alterations to the body the line between mundane and SCA becomes completely and often permanently blurred.

It is worthwhile to return to Robin Hood for a moment as an example of how clothing is used as an expression of resistance. Sponsler argues that the Robin Hood game broke down social categories through clothing. By dressing either as a woman or as a wealthy man, Robin Hood upended the gender- or class-based sumptuary laws that were a part of medieval English society, and demonstrated that a person could move from one social station to another. Clothing is transformative. Garb codes the body as medieval. Says Morril, "The clothing we wear makes us do what we do. Clothing is a mark of station."[78] In other words, garb makes the knight. A knight is expected to dress like one. If the knight does not have a European persona, he is still expected to dress like an elite warrior of his chosen culture, be it as a samurai or as a member of the Aztec order of the Jaguar.

In a class she taught on SCA culture, Kramer-Rolls argued that garb in the SCA does not mark people as being "medieval" so much as it marks them as being in the SCA. But Kramer-Rolls takes this a step further, postulating that garb actually marks SCA members as being part of a counterculture. She notes that in the early days of the SCA a person could walk up Telegraph Avenue in Berkeley in SCA clothes and not be out of place. The dress of the counterculture—poet's shirts, vests, harem pants, t-tunics, caftans, etc.—was the dress of the SCA at the time. In addition to linking the SCA to the counterculture of the sixties, Kramer-Rolls argued that this appropriation of fashion from various time periods and cultures as "medieval" was an example of how clothing was used by SCA members to create their own culture instead of reenacting another: "When I see a fighter in a thirteenth-century surcote and fourteenth-century armor who wears a fifteenth-century shirt and a sixteenth-century flat cap, I know it's a Gryffon,"[79] she says, referring in this case to members of Gryffonsguard, a large and well-known household, and to the outfit and armor members of that group commonly wore. By employing clothing elements from several different centuries they had created their own ahistorical group identity. In a similar vein, Jouris rather pointedly wore a t-tunic to SCA events over blue jeans with engineer's boots, even when he was king. Not only were his SCA clothes "normal," but they were also pointedly modern. His tunic alone coded him as being at an SCA event. The blue jeans and engineer's boots he wore under it were inconsequential because he was not playing a character other than himself. His tunic was a uniform, not a costume or the clothing of an imaginary medieval person. In this way, as with his rejection of persona, Jouris resisted the concept of the SCA as reenactment and instead reinscribed the idea of SCA as contemporary counterculture.

To this day, the most common garb in the SCA is a variation of what Jouris wore: a simple t-tunic over pants and boots. Sometimes it is harem pants and turned-sole boots, but often it is modern pants simply tucked into the tops of engineer's boots. This is what most people wear when they first join the SCA because it is the simplest type of garb to make. However, SCA costume-construction techniques have become quite sophisticated over the years, so much so that some SCA members now find employment doing reconstruction of period garments for museums and living history centers both in the U.S. and in Europe. Textile arts are the place where SCA scholars tend to be taken most seriously outside the SCA, and within the SCA the members of the Order of the Laurel who received their peerages for their abilities as costumers commonly outnumber those who received the accolade for other pursuits.

Lenehan says, "For SCA members, like their medieval counterparts, 'conspicuous consumption of valuable goods is a means of reputability to a gentleman of leisure' (Veblen, 1994:47)."[80] Like one's camp, one's garb is an ostentatious method of pointing out dedication to the group and a conspicuous display of consumption. Wool outfits with hand embroidery, gold metal trim, or jewels (or all three) are as expensive and time consuming to construct as armor, and there are fewer people in the SCA selling period garb than there are selling armor. Although recently a few merchants have begun carrying reenactor-quality clothing, it is very expensive and almost exclusively middle class clothing from the fourteenth century. Economics of scale dictate that off the rack clothing be less elaborate and often less authentic than custom-made garb. The amount of labor that goes into making an Elizabethan outfit, for instance, would make the cost prohibitive for nearly all SCA members were they charged for it, so they have to acquire the skills and make it for themselves or else befriend someone who will build it gratis.

As a result, people who have been in the SCA longer tend to wear more elaborate clothes as they develop better sewing skills and move up within the ranks of the group. One longtime member noted that this results in a sort of "persona shift," particularly in those kingdoms where persona is not as common a device. T-tunics and basic trews or harem pants, what most members start out in, are the garb of early cultures such as Vikings and Saxons. The next place people move from there is usually to a simple shirt and a long surcote, the garb of the Normans in thirteenth-century England. The next step is often to a cote-hardie of the fourteenth century, then to a houppelande of the fifteenth century, and finally to the elaborate Italian, German, Spanish, and Elizabethan costumes of the sixteenth century. In this way, as people's incomes rise and their knowledge and skills increase, they often replicate the progression of the medieval period as a whole.

The transformative nature of clothing is what is really at the core of SCA performance. You can act like a king all you want, but if you're dressed in parachute pants and a tank top, no one will take you seriously. Clothes, more even than attitude, are what make SCA members medieval. This was demonstrated clearly at "Bake by the Lake," Purgatorio coronation in 1982, when it was so hot that the king held court in the water of Lake Berryessa. Suddenly nobody was in garb anymore. A former SCA member I know dropped out after witnessing this event because it destroyed the illusion for him. Everyone had stripped down to their underwear—mostly modern underwear. A few people were wearing swim suits, a couple more were in loin cloths. They were no longer medieval. By stripping off their clothes they had been stripped of their nobility and of the illusion of their mutual fantasy, of their "medievalness." Suddenly they did not appear so romantic or heroic anymore.

The most important point proven by this big swimming party is that it is in garb—costume—the act of coding one's body by wearing medieval or at least fantasy-medieval clothes, that the SCA exists as a transformative activity. SCA members understood this when they made the rule that everyone at an event must wear some attempt at medieval clothing. In this way everyone becomes a participant, and there are no spectators. Clearly it is garb that makes all other illusions of SCA performance possible. Garb does indeed make the knight.

Don Quixotism

As Evreinov points out, people have an innate desire to pretend, to be something else, to play make-believe. In the SCA they simply devote more energy to it than most other people do.

Everything discussed in this chapter—persona, garb, behavior, all engaged in conflict between the contemporary world and the search for an "authentic" medieval experience—forms the basis of the fragmented identity of SCA members. SCA members have several different layers of identity, all of which come together to frame their performance and create within each member a subject/object dichotomy, which is most pronounced in those SCA members who employ persona. The SCA is, obviously, a masquerade. On one level an SCA member is a twenty-first-century individual. Layered onto this is a constructed identity within the SCA subculture that is based on conflicting notions of the Middle Ages from both popular and academic culture, and layered onto this is the persona, a constructed medieval identity that should be unaware of the contemporary world in which the subject actually lives. Those who employ persona cannot escape the dual nature of their constructed identity—they cannot jump straight from their contemporary selves to their medieval selves, skipping over their SCA identities, because in order to function in the SCA they have to interact with SCA members within the culture and structure the group has created, which is faux-medieval, not truly medieval, and revolves around nonmedieval situations and signs. They therefore need an SCA identity separate from their persona. Enchanted Ground is, of course, an effort to provide a safe refuge for those seeking to remove themselves from their SCA identity, but they still must cope with their contemporary self as subject objectifying their medieval self. The search for the "medieval moment," or the "period rush," can be seen as a desire to fully and completely escape the contemporary self and to become a medieval subject, totally unaware of the contemporary and SCA selves.

As source material, Tolkien and the fantasists have faded in importance over the years as the 1960s have receded and scholarship in medieval studies has become more popular in the SCA. The group as a whole knows more about the Middle Ages than they used to, their reconstructions of medieval artifacts have gotten better, and interest in the late Middle Ages (basically the fourteenth century) has come to dominate much of the SCA game. In costume, armor, and persona, at least, many members of the SCA have replaced Tolkien and Doyle with Froissart and Malory as the base material for their performances, and the court culture they seek to recreate is that of Richard II or Gaston Phoebus. This shift, however, doesn't make the SCA any less postmodern; in fact, as Andrew Taylor writes, "Froissart's poetry participates in the elaborate play of self-reflexivity that makes French court poetry of the late Middle Ages seem almost postmodern in sensibility."[81]

And yet whatever the inspiration, be it Froissart or Malory or Tolkien or Shakespeare, SCA members are drawn to some form of idealized past as an attractive alternative to contemporary society: "[T]o flee the decivilizing influence of the mundane world . . . they consciously enter the civilizing influence of courtly graces and mimetic violence."[82] They may pattern their personal performance of the medieval on William Marshal or on Gandalf; they may have an elaborate biography for their medieval character, just a name and a period, or simply be a knight of the SCA. Whatever the case, they are engaging in a collective fantasy rooted in Evreinov's "Don Quixotism," with a disparate group of like-minded souls.

[1] The word "Pennsic" is a play on the word "Punic," using the old abbreviation for Pennsylvania.

[2] Evreinov, 23.

[3] Thomas Postlewait and Tracy C. Davis, "Theatricality: An Introduction," in *Theatricality*, ed. Thomas Postlewait (Cambridge: Cambridge University Press, 2003), 1-39.

[4] Janelle Reinelt, "The Politics of Discourse: Performativity Meets Theatricality," *Substance* 31, no. 98-99 (2002): 206.

[5] Richard Schechner, *Between Theatre and Anthropology* (Philadelphia: University of Pennsylvania Press, 1985), 36. See also Virginie Magnat, "Theatricality from the Performative Perspective," *Substance* 31, no. 98-99 (2002): 149-153.

[6] Marvin Carlson, "The Resistance to Theatricality," *Substance* 31, no. 98-99 (2002): 239.

[7] Rodwell, 27.

[8] Ibid.

[9] Postlewait and Davis, 21.

[10] Carlson, "The Resistance to Theatricality," 249.

[11] Silvija Jestovic, "Theatricality as Estrangement of Art and Life in the Russian Avant-Garde," *Substance* 31, no. 98-99 (2002): 50.

[12] Marvin Carlson, *Theories of the Theatre* (Ithaca, New York: Cornell University Press, 1984), 325-326.

[13] Sarlos, 208.

[14] Evreinov, 23.

[15] Ibid., 90.

[16] Ibid., 89.

[17] Nugent, 180.

[18] A.D. Putter, "Transvestite Knights in Medieval Life and Literature," in *Becoming Male in the Middle Ages*, ed. Jeffrey Jerome Cohen and Bonnie Wheeler (New York: Garland, 1997), 286.

[19] Karl Hess, "Interview with Karl Hess," interview by Sam Merril, *Playboy*, July, 1976, 66.

[20] See Willis Harman and John Hormann, *Creative Work* (Indianapolis, IN: Knowledge Systems, Inc., 1981).

[21] Dana Kramer-Rolls, "SCA Culture," seminar at Collegium Occidentalis, 6 March 1993, Berkeley, Calif.

[22] Lenehan, 9.

[23] Erving Goffman, *The Presentation of Self in Everyday Life* (Garden City, New Jersey: Doubleday Anchor, 1959), 48.

[24] E.F. Morril, "The Art of Being," seminar at *The Pennsic War*, 10 August 2003, Slippery Rock, Pennsylvania.

[25] Patrick O'Donnell, *The Knights Next Door* (Lincoln, NE.: iUniverse, 2004), 148.

[26] *Forward into the Past: An Introductory Guide to the S.C.A.* (Kingdom of Ansteora, accessed 31 May 2003); available from http://hospitaler.ansteorra.org/ articles/fip.htm.

[27] Rodwell, 39.

[28] Erisman, 103.

[29] O'Donnell, 149.

[30] Ambrosius, 49.

[31] Bill Jouris in Society for Creative Anachronism, *The New SCA Fighters Handbook* (Milpitas, CA: The Society for Creative Anachronism, Inc., 1993), vi.

[32] Hollander, interview.

[33] Goffman, *Frame Analysis*, 58.

[34] Forgue, interview.

[35] Lenehan, 18.

[36] Shannon McSmith, interview by author, 14 March 2004, video recording, Davis, Calif.

[37] Thomas Moore, interview by author, 14 March 2004, video recording, Davis, Calif.

[38] Chris Rolls in *The New SCA Fighters Handbook*, vi.

[39] Claire Sponsler, *Drama and Resistance: Bodies, Goods and Theatricality in Late Medieval England* (Minneapolis: University of Minnesota Press, 1997), 25.

[40] O'Donnell, 149.

[41] Evreinov, 83.

[42] Ibid., 92-93.

[43] Thomas Hobbes, *Leviathan* (Harmondsworth: Penguin Books, 1985), 217, quoted in Ragnhild Tronstad, "Could the World Become a Stage: Theatricality and Metaphorical Structures," *Substance* 31, no. 98-99 (2002): 216.

[44] Mikhail Bakhtin, *Problems of Dostoevsky's Poetics*, ed. C. Emerson, trans. C. Emerson (Manchester, UK: Manchester University Press, 1984), 130. Quoted in Humphrey, 31.

[45] O'Donnell, 37.

[46] Lenehan, 17.

[47] Goffman, *Frame Analysis*, 24.

[48] Rowena d'Anjou, "Medieval Verisimilitude" seminar at West Kingdom Arts and Sciences Tourney, Petaluma, California, 22 July 1985.

[49] Erisman, 166.

[50] See his work at http://www.billdawsonmetalsmith.com.

[51] Evreinov, 85.

[52] Hollander, interview.

[53] Ibid.

[54] Ibid.

[55] Ibid.

[56] Ibid.

[57] Greg Rose, *An Explanation of the SCA* (accessed 1 April 2000); available from http://www.theroutiers.org. (this link now appears to be broken)

[58] Ibid.

[59] Morril.

[60] Ibid.

[61] Ibid.

[62] David D. Friedman, *A Miscellany*, 9th Edition (2000, accessed 4 May 2003); available from http://www.daviddfriedman.com/Medieval/miscellany_pdf/Articles_about_Persona.pdf.

[63] David Wiles, *The Early Plays of Robin Hood* (Cambridge: D. S. Brewer, 1981), 20.

[64] Friedman.

[65] Georges Duby, *William Marshal the Flower of Chivalry*, trans. Richard Howard (New York: Pantheon Books, 1985), 43-44.

[66] P. Meyer, ed., *Historie De Guillaume Le Maréchal*, 3 vols. (Paris: Société de l'Historie, 1891-1901). Quoted in Duby, 44.

[67] Duby, 46.

[68] At a recent Estrella War they set up a "Period Camping Demonstration Area" in an area of high foot traffic. This alleviates Gavin's first complaint, but marking the activity as unusual by putting it on a stage makes it no less liminal.

[69] Rodwell, 24.

[70] Evreinov, 94.

[71] Ambrosius, 57.

[72] Ibid., 25.

[73] Anonymous, *Origins of the Middle Kingdom* (Middle Kingdom, accessed 1 May 2004); available from www.midrealm.org/midrealm_origins.html.

[74] Mikhail Bakhtin, *Rabelais and His World*, trans. Helene Iswolsky (Bloomington, IN: Indiana University Press, 1984), 7.

[75] Tony Horowitz, *Confederates in the Attic* (New York: Pantheon Books, 1998), 7.

[76] Ibid., 12.

[77] Eco, 65.

[78] Morril.

[79] Kramer-Rolls.

[80] Lenehan, 23.

[81] Taylor, 170.

[82] Lenehan, 24.

4

ON THE FIELD OF THE SUMMER KING

While the SCA is not a reenactment of the Middle Ages, the game they play is a re-creation of a medieval game. The king game was a peasant festival that was popular during the Middle Ages and Renaissance in several variations both in England and on the continent.[1] Lawrence Clopper notes a link between seasonal rites and the king game, and adds that in some places "king games or *ludi* of the king and queen of May seem to have been occasions on which the locals chose their royal couple to preside over feasts and entertainments[.]"[2] The central element of the king game is the setting up of a mock king or other authoritative figure to reign over a festive period of misrule. In towns it was sometimes a mock mayor, and on occasion it was a mock bishop. Folk heroes and quasi-mythical figures were also variations of the game, as peasants would sometimes set up courts under Jack Straw or John Barleycorn. The most popular version of the game in England during the Middle Ages, and the version that is still with us today is, of course, Robin Hood.[3]

When the nobility played a type of king game it was usually the subject of either a masque or tournament that reinscribed the social order. There is nothing very transgressive when the Crown Prince of England dances the part of Oberon the Fairy Prince. Instead, as Stephen Orgel notes, "Masques were essential to the life of the Renaissance court; their allegories gave higher meaning to the realities of politics and power, their fictions created heroic roles for the leaders of society."[4] Even on that rare occasion when the king participated in a version of the game more closely related to the peasant version, the royal order was maintained. When Henry VIII and his court were "kidnapped" and entertained by Robin Hood and his merry men in 1515, Henry's kingly status was never truly inverted, and the performance played out more like a masque than like the rougher and more dangerous peasant Robin Hood game.[5]

E.K. Chambers insists that the king game grew out of Celtic practices of human sacrifice:

> [O]ne ceremony which, as has been seen, grew out of human sacrifice, has been the election of a temporary king. Originally chosen out of the lowest of the people for death, and feted as the equivalent or double of the real king-priest of the community, he has survived the tragic event which gave him birth, and plays a great part as the master of ceremonies in many a village revel. The English "May-king," or "summer-king," or "harvest lord," or "mock-mayor," is a familiar personage, and can be more abundantly paralleled from continental festivals.[6]

Chambers was highly influenced by James George Frazer's *The Golden Bough: A Study in Magic and Religion,* which was published at about the same time Chambers was publishing *The Medieval Stage.* It is from Frazer that Chambers gets the concept of the "year king." Following Frazer, Chambers saw all forms of play, game, and drama as traceable to religious ceremony of one form or another. However, O.B. Hardison and John Cox have both noted that Chambers had to take this position because, like Frazer, Chambers' overall thesis was that "an enlightened secularity was bound to flourish in the long run in its opposition to benighted superstition."[7] According to Hardison, Charles Darwin had a profound impact on nineteenth-century literary criticism, and his theory prompted Chambers and others to posit an evolutionary theory of the drama, which in turn led to the belief that all forms of play, including the drama, had to start as a religious ceremony.[8]

Richard Axton identifies another type of game that intersects the king game; the "hero-combat" (which survives in English mummings, in which champions fight and at least one of them dies, is lamented, and then, usually, returns to life):

> If the pagan people of northern Europe ever thought of their own traditional drama in any generic sense, it may well have been as a kind of contest of physical combat. This sense is within the Roman meaning of *ludus,* which include sports and physical exercise as well as spectacles and "shows."[9]

Following Chambers, Axton suggests that these types of games are descended from ritual sacrifice and associates them with fertility rituals.[10] Axton makes no inquiry into whether the combats represented in medieval hero-combat plays were staged or in earnest. David Wiles suggests that it was most likely the latter, and that combat plays may have been merely a dramatic device to frame games, including fighting with staves or with swords and bucklers.[11]

Clopper notes that, among other things, king games are often associated with king of the mountain games,[12] an instance where, as in the SCA, the mock king is chosen in a physical contest. This, according to Sandra Billington, is an important element in many summer king games. In *Mock Kings in Medieval Society and Renaissance Drama,* Billington argues that the king game in summer had as its central metaphor Fortune's Mountain, which, like the better known Fortune's Wheel, represented man's rise to the pinnacle of achievement before tumbling, or being thrown, down again (Billington divides her discussion into summer and winter king games, which proves very useful for a discussion of the SCA). The king of the mountain is an obvious manifestation of this idea, and the king who achieves the top of the mountain must eventually be replaced by another. As Billington noted in her discussion of the Elizabethan tragedy *The Misfortunes of Arthur,* this cyclical rotation of mock kings can even be related to the Arthurian legend that inspired so many of the festivals and tournaments of the Middle Ages: Arthur is chosen king either by pulling a sword from a stone or having it handed to him by the Lady of the Lake, and then is eventually overthrown by another would-be king.[13] Carrying this idea further, the sword in the stone version of the story can be seen as a type of contest and, in fact, young Arthur's pulling out the sword often takes place while a tournament is being held, the winner of which is to become the actual king.

Among the many summer games Billington discusses, the most interesting are the Cotswold Summer Games staged by Robert Dover, probably around 1618 after King James issued the *Book of Sports,* which declared many traditional country games to be legal. The Cotswold games were not medieval but a very early re-creation of the type performed by the SCA. However, they clearly involved several medieval traditions that had survived in rural festivals.[14] They are referenced in several sources, including a set of poems written about the heroic deeds performed there. Staged around a castle made of boards standing on a hill, these games included men playing at cudgels and wrestling, women dancing, feasts, riding, coursing greyhounds, and various other contests.

On the continent fighting games also took the form of mock battles. Richard Barker and Juliet Barber describe a game played in the cities of northern Italy among the foot soldiers and townsmen (though it was not played in summer: soldiers were busy fighting real wars in summer), which resembles SCA combat almost exactly. In Pisa, where the game was called *mazzascudo,* a section of the town square was chained off as a kind of open combat area from Christmas to Shrove Tuesday. In this space townsmen on foot and armed with cudgels and shields would stage a kind of tournament:

> [I]ndividuals could challenge each other as and when they liked. On holidays, a general battle took place, which attracted a large audience. This opened with single combats; lovers would paint their lady's face on their shields and fight in their honour, until the general combat was announced by a trumpet-blast. In the later version of the game, played on the Ponte Vecchio in Pisa, the players wore the equivalent of footsoldiers' armour, except that a great deal more padding was worn.[15]

Looking at all of these examples we find many medieval and Renaissance precedents for the SCA king game. Although there was, in fact, only a queen of May at the first SCA tournament (and that was not even the title she used), the central core of all SCA activities is the same as that described by Clopper: a rotating system of monarchs who preside over various entertainments. The cycle of elevation and descent described by Chambers and Billington is also the cycle of the SCA king game, as one person rises above the rest by winning a ceremonial contest, in this case a tournament, revealing himself to be the "true king," is crowned, reigns in splendor, and then is replaced by another who has gone through the same process.

The SCA combat game shares a great deal with the *mazzascudo,* in the manner in which a specific place of combat is marked off (ropes in the SCA, chain in the *mazzascudo*), in the progression from single combat to melee, in the romantic subtext of the combats, even in the equipment used. Barker and Barber show an illustration of *mazzascudo* armor that includes a helmet with a bar-cage face grill, a type rarely worn in the Middle Ages but ubiquitous in the SCA. What we know about the Cotswold Summer Games closely resembles the SCA's large interkingdom wars, particularly Gulf Wars, the SCA's third largest event, which includes all of the elements listed as part of the Cotswold Games, including riding, coursing greyhounds, and a castle made of boards that the armies take turns storming. In a description that could easily be made of the SCA Billington says of the castle:

> The Poems further suggest that the castle was painted silver and that Dover conducted the games from inside. Some events involved storming it, but it was the victor of the sports who was crowned and made king of the castle. In the evening, and during the night, it was used for feasting, music, and other entertainments, with Dover host to the whole gathering.[16]

Most interesting of all, "the honour of kingship . . . passed from the host king to the winner,"[17] just as it does in the SCA. These games, particularly the *mazzascudo* and the Cotswold Games, offer medieval and Renaissance examples of exactly the types of combat games that the SCA reinvented in 1966.

The King Game in the SCA

The SCA is built around two complementary versions of the king game: the summer king game, based on fighting, and the winter king game, based on court ceremony (the subject of Chapter 5). The SCA's reinvention of the king game is remarkable in that it was more or less accidental. SCA members did not set out to reinvent the king game but to live a romantic fantasy, and they built their fantasy around a king game of their own invention. Even today, most members seem to have little knowledge of the king game as played in the Middle Ages. However, the similarities between the medieval king game and the SCA version are striking. Both are entertainments in which nonnobles pretend to be noble, temporarily elevating one or two people to the status of "royalty" and giving them a symbolic power over the other participants, who are organized into a hierarchical mock "court." In this way, both games are transgressive, upending the social order and putting a new one in its place. Significantly, in both games, members of the group can become "king." And, ultimately, both games are relatively unthreatening to the social order, as the old order is always reinscribed when the game is over and everyone returns to his or her day job. Meg Twycross in *Festive Drama* notes that Michael J. Bristol finds festive misrule fundamentally conservative, and states: "What we know of these folk entertainments— Robin Hood plays, King Games, Lords of Misrule and the like—suggests that they would have offered images of resistance to authority before culminating in gestures of concord and obeisance."[18] Likewise, Victor Turner notes: "[S]ome seasonal rites (whose residues are carnivals and festivals) elevate those of low status before returning them to their permanent humbleness."[19]

According to O'Donnell, the SCA's invention of the position of "king" arose out of a practical need. Citing an interview he conducted with Paxson, O'Donnell contends that the SCA created kings so that they could have somebody to preside over the tournaments. Since everybody wanted to fight, the solution was to make the winner of the last tournament sit the next one out and put him in charge. This was the first king. As O'Donnell puts it, "one bureaucratic decision had led to hundreds of fighters striving for a position created just to get them to do work."[20] Seeking to confirm this I contacted both Hollander and Forgue. They recalled a much different rationale for having a king in the SCA, one that was much more rooted in the romantic. According to Forgue, there are kings in the SCA because there were queens. As Hollander put it, the queen was sitting up there all by herself and they decided they needed someone to sit in the chair next to her. This became the king. Reading accounts of how the first SCA king came to be crowned suggest that it was from a more romantic impulse rather than a practical one.

Conflicting remembrances such as the ones above are an important part of the way SCA members wax nostalgic not only about medieval history but also about their own history. Just like the SCA itself, SCA history is organic and always changing. Erisman notes a desire among SCA members to record their own history and make it official, and that the resulting written histories often conflict with the SCA's oral tradition.[21] Even official SCA histories are full of inconsistencies. As mentioned in the introduction, The West Kingdom History Project is made up of an official history with annotations by people who were there, and these often conflict. Friedman reportedly refuses to write down an "official" version of how the Pennsic war started (see below) because he prefers the inconsistent and ever changing oral version.[22] In this way SCA histories come to be more mythic, larger and grander than actual events, satisfying a need among the participants to be heroes and not merely history.

The ceremony scroll from the first official SCA court seems to outline what the purpose of the SCA was in 1968 (different from its official purpose now). It states: "[I]t be the prime business of our society to present such Revels and Tourneys as are pleasing to the populace, and . . . the prime pleasure of that populace is to see the great sport of the tourney."[23] There is no mention of scholarly research or of living history, but only of the spectacle of the tourney. Clearly, the SCA was viewed at this time as a social organization and not, necessarily, a scholarly one. Officially, it existed in this instance so people could play the king game.

The SCA's king game is a re-creation of a peasant game pretending to be a re-creation of an aristocratic game. Crucial to the SCA myth is that members are re-creating knights in shining armor doing battle for the pleasure of beautiful ladies. Most members of the SCA see themselves as engaged in the chivalric pursuits of the medieval aristocracy. SCA members are Arthur and Guinevere and William Marshal. They are trying to recreate a medieval tournament culture and their inspiration for this, originally Tolkien and the Victorians, is now more likely to be Malory and Froissart and Duke René of Anjou. The tournaments

SCA single combat. *Photo by Ron Lutz II*

A battle at the Estrella War. *Photo by Kelli Thompson*

A Tuchux Warrior in fantasy armor.
Photo by Ron Lutz II

The Army of the East at Pennsic. *Photo by Ron Lutz II*

A latter-day Achilles at Pennsic War. *Photo by Ron Lutz II*

A knight wearing twelfth-century armor. *Photo by Ron Lutz II*

A Knight in Maximilian Plate Armor. *Photo by Ron Lutz II*

SCA Musicians. *Photo by Bill Toscano*

SCA Craftsmen. *Photo by Bill Toscano*

The Kingdom of Æthelmarc processes to opening ceremonies at Pennsic. *Photo by Ron Lutz II*

Fighters lined up for invocation. *Photo by Kelli Thompson*

Royalty at the opening ceremonies of Pennsic. *Photo by Bill Toscano*

they wish to emulate are those of the upper classes, and they are encouraged by the fact that medieval nobility did, indeed, do the same sort of thing—hold tournaments in which they would portray romantic or legendary figures such as Arthur and his knights.

The tournament in the Middle Ages has been closely analyzed in books such at Barker and Barber's *Tournaments* and Keene's *Chivalry*. However, it is important to note a few elements of the aristocratic tournament because, even though the SCA more closely resembles the peasant king game, SCA members take romantic images from the aristocratic tournament as their primary inspiration, and how SCA members see themselves and their courts is important to understanding how their game is played out. Roy Strong lists the royal entry, the tournament, and the masquerade as the three main types of aristocratic festival forms in the Middle Ages and Renaissance, and all of these exist in the SCA.[24]

The medieval tournament began as practice for war. Groups of mounted knights and squires would meet at a particular time and place and fight one another. Usually there was a safe area within which a person could not be attacked, but otherwise the fight ranged over hill and dale and even into the towns. Wealth could be obtained by capturing a knight and ransoming him back, usually for his horse and armor. This form of tournament, with slight modifications, continued through the fifteenth century and was an important part of chivalric life, representing a source of income and prestige for the knights who participated. Steven Muhlberger/Duke Finvar de Tahe, a professor of history at Nipissing University in Canada who is also one of the founders of the Middle Kingdom, has published a translation of Geoffroi de Charny's questions on the joust, and notes that most of the questions can boiled down to "in such and such a situation, who gets the horse?"[25] Tourneying was the spectacular professional sport of its day, much like football or boxing today, but with a romantic underpinning.

The joust, or single combat, developed as an ancillary activity but soon overtook the tournament in popularity, as jousting was done in a more confined space and could be better enjoyed by spectators. Winners of these contests were often declared by affirmation, and at other times the winner was the person who broke the most lances. By the fifteenth century, an elaborate scoring system had been developed.[26] Although the practical purpose behind the tournament and joust was preparation for war, as a means of securing wealth and as a social gathering for an elite social class its excitement, spectacle, and drama spurred development in other areas. Tournaments throughout the Middle Ages became increasingly theatrical.[27] Knights began to dress as Arthur and his knights, or as the Nine Worthies, or even as pagan mythological figures such as Apollo or Venus. Elaborate machines, pyrotechnics, fire-breathing dragons, and the like formed a framework around the physical sport of getting on a horse and running into one another, a framework that placed the sport in the context of romance, and constructed as its purpose the pleasing of ladies. "The tournament was by itself dramatic to a high degree and possessed at the same time of a highly erotic ambiance."[28]

In the fifteenth century, the most elaborate form of tournament was the *pas d'armes*, in which individuals or teams publicly announced that they would defend a specific place for a certain amount of time against all comers. Single or group combats would be staged, with all challenges recorded by a herald or "king at arms" for the tourney. Because it was in a controlled space, spectators could get very close to the action. Often, knights would form tournament companies for the purpose of staging *pas d'armes,* a practice that continues in the SCA. The victors would be determined either by the combatants themselves or else by "the gallery," meaning the ladies watching the fighting, or occasionally based on the number of lances broken. Strong describes it as "a festival form which united the arts of war and peace by overlaying onto an exercise designed to train knights for battle the trappings of allegory, plot, poetry, ceremonial and music."[29]

As the courtly romance became the preferred literary expression of the nobility, and the tournament became more and more an expression of that romantic ideal, masculine violence came to be defined by its relationship to the feminine, and the presence of women as spectators became essential. As with the *mazzascudo* in Pisa, combat in tournaments was performed for the glorification of one's lover. In this way, as the Crusades attempted to control the violent tendencies of knights by co-opting them in the service of a religious ideal, romance, through both literature and the tournament, channeled that same violence in the service of a feminine ideal. This romantic underpinning to chivalry, filtered through Victorian literature and filmic images, forms a core value of the SCA and the relationship between the SCA combatant and his or her consort. This sense of the Middle Ages, of the aristocratic tournament of chivalry, is how the SCA views itself.

From the outside, looking at the activity as a twentieth-century phenomenon and then comparing it to the Middle Ages, it is clear that, however refined or romantic it may attempt to be, the SCA bears a much stronger resemblance to the king games played by the peasantry than it does to the games played by the royalty. SCA members are not members of a titled aristocracy. They are pretending to be. Their kings are not actual kings taking on mythological roles to draw allegorical comparisons between themselves and legend, thereby increasing their prestige and their power (although many SCA kings make this kind of allegory part of their SCA performance). SCA kings are mock kings who, at the end of the weekend, have to go back to work. Because there is no king in the area where the SCA primarily operates—the United States—and because the rigid hierarchy of medieval society no longer exists, it cannot be said to be a social inversion in the way the king games of the Middle Ages were. Instead the SCA can be seen as a inversion of society as a whole, acted out through a game similar to one played in the Middle Ages. SCA kings are chosen by contest like summer kings. They reign for a short period of time and then hand the kingship off to another winner. Most of all, the SCA is made up of everyday people escaping their everyday lives in a carnivalesque game where they can create their own roles regardless of where society has pigeonholed them. So the SCA's king game is a reinvention of a peasant game, but it contains elements taken from or inspired by aristocratic games, such as chivalric tournaments and masques.

SCA Combat

The SCA enacts its version of the summer king game through combat. Fighting is the SCA's central activity and, to many, the activity that defines the organization. It is certainly the SCA's greatest contribution to medievalism. Thousands of people in the SCA have had the experience of donning armor, marching out onto the field, and fighting, sometimes in heavy rains, sometimes in blistering heat. Even though the combat is stylized, it is nonetheless full contact, unchoreographed, and often painful. SCA fighting provides people with some sense of what a physical competition in armor actually feels like.

Fighting in the SCA is not only how SCA kings are chosen, it is also the way in which their kingly status is best performed. Although the role of the sovereign involves being the ceremonial center for SCA activity, recognizing achievement by handing out awards and rank, and even making some governing decisions, an SCA monarch's most important jobs involve combat: overseeing the tournament to choose an heir (in the SCA it is often plural: crown tournament chooses the "heirs" both to the king's throne and to the queen's), leading knights in SCA wars, and, of course, winning the crown in the first place. Above all, as Hollander points out, SCA kings are supposed to appear heroic. This is how kingship is performed in the SCA, and how the king game is reinterpreted.

As discussed in above, the SCA's king game arose out of an attempt to re-create the Last Tournament at Eglinton and, like Eglinton, was heavily influenced by Sir Walter Scott's *Ivanhoe*. In *Ivanhoe* a tournament is held at which a "Queen of Love and Beauty" is to reign. Prince John is supposed to choose a girl to play the role, but instead decides to defer to the victor of the day's jousting, giving him the honor of choosing the festival queen. When the disguised Ivanhoe is victorious, he chooses his long-separated love Lady Rowena and gives her the chaplet. At the backyard party in 1966 the victor was allowed to crown his lady "fairest" and give her either a pearl necklace or a crown (those who were there still disagree over this point), making her their queen of love and beauty for the day. It was only later that they decided that they had to have a king.[30]

By having a mock queen, who for all intents and purposes functioned as a queen of the May, the SCA had already entered into a type of summer game, a "queen game" if not a king game. In *Mock Kings* Billington writes of a summer game in 1469 in which one Margaret Moore was installed as queen and reigned over a summer court in a barn referred to as "Sommerhouse." Although there was a king, a man named Thomas Barker, there is little mention of him in the account, and the queen appears to have been the focal point of the performance as in the early SCA. According to Billington, N.M. Davis has suggested that it was "a game designed to bring into the open romantic feelings which in normal life would have remained hidden."[31] This is also true in the SCA. Flirting and romantic trysts are a common part of SCA activity. Kissing and flirting games are ubiquitous, and people are constantly engaging in "courtly" flirting whether it is centered on the dance floor or on the combat field. Romantic displays which in contemporary society would seem foolish are integrated into the SCA lifestyle, making Davis's description of the Sommerhouse game applicable to the SCA as well.

By the first Twelfth Night in 1967 the SCA had started talking about having a king, and at the tournament on March 25, AS I (1967), de Maiffe, who had won the Summer Solstice tourney, called up Henrik Olsgaard/Henrik of Havn, who had won the Fall Equinox tourney. Thewlis, who had knighted David Breen at the first tournament, knighted Olsgaard, and then de Maiffe crowned him king. Olsgaard then presided over the tournament to determine the new crown prince and crown princess.[32]

The creation of the position of king in 1967 combined with the ceremonies established at the second Twelfth Night in 1968 institutionalized the SCA framework in a process Goffman discusses in *Frame Analysis*:

> There seems to be a continuum between playfulness, whereby some utilitarian act is caught up and employed in a transformed way for fun, and both sports and games. In any case, whereas in playfulness the playful reconstitution of some object or individual into a "plaything" is quite temporary, never fully established, in organized games and sports this reconstitution is institutionalized (stabilized, as it were) just as the arena of action is fixed by the formal rules of the activity. (That presumably is what we mean by "organized.") And as this formalization progresses, the content of play seems to become further and further removed from any particular replication of day-to-day activity and more and more a primary framework unto itself.[33]

The SCA suddenly had "traditions." The summer king game was now firmly established (and the winter king game, as we shall see, was in the process of being formed). From now on the SCA's unique brand of combat would determine the SCA's mock king.

SCA Fighting as a Game

First and foremost, SCA fighting is a game. The style of fighting the SCA developed, which has since been copied by some other groups, is full-force fighting with swords made of cane while wearing armor. Under current rules the head, groin, larynx, cervical vertebrae, knees, elbows, and hands must be protected by rigid armor, usually steel (always, in the case of helmets).

Weapons are made of rattan covered with either cloth-backed tape (such as duct tape) or leather. Occasionally they will be padded with some type of foam to represent the head of an ax or a mace, or to make them a little less painful when used for thrusting. The most popular weapons form in the SCA is sword and shield, although two-handed weapons are also used, and occasionally combatants fight with a weapon in each hand. Fights are scored on an honor system. If a fighter is hit on a limb with sufficient force (what constitutes sufficient and excessive force is always a matter of debate and changes from region to region), he loses the use of that limb. If he is struck in the torso or the head he is defeated and is required to fall down and pretend to be dead, a bit of theatre which is disparaged by serious reenactors but is considered essential to the romantic milieu in which the SCA operates. If the SCA is recreating a medieval tournament in which combatants were not intended to be killed, then pretending to fall down dead is an anachronism. However, if the SCA is creating a performance based on romantic or epic poetry, then the vanquished falling dead is somewhat appropriate. Other elements of SCA fighting that engender similar debate are the number of blows it takes to defeat someone, the use of two-weapon forms, and the practice of losing a leg when struck, which leads to fighters either having to yield the fight or continue on their knees. None of these conventions existed in the Middle Ages (except possibly two-weapon fighting, but that is a matter of debate as well).

In Goffman's hierarchy discussed in Chapter 1, even fighting activities are considered unserious if they are controlled in any way. Martial sports are confined by rules and therefore fall into the realm of play:

> Consider sports such as boxing, horse racing, jousting, fox hunting, and the like. The literal model seems to be fighting (or hunting or fleeing from) of some kind, and the rules of the sport supply restrictions of degree and mode of aggression.[34]

In Goffman's formulation, a boxing match would be less serious than a street fight, because the boxing match is a sporting contest where the aggression is controlled, the stakes are not as high, and the animosity is not as real as in a street fight where people are intent on doing real bodily harm and where the combatants are fighting to protect themselves and (possibly) for their lives. Huizinga agrees, writing, "all fighting bound by rules bears the formal characteristics of play by that very limitation."[35]

In fact this is often not the case—men die in boxing matches, the stakes can be very high in terms of money and prestige, and the animosity can be quite real. Goffman admits that sport does not always stay in the realm of unserious activity. If it is a professional sporting contest then the fighters' livelihoods are involved, and earning a living is clearly a serious activity to Goffman. But he maintains that play, as it is not necessary for survival or social advancement, is frivolous.

> [T]he framework of these actions does not make meaningless events meaningful, there being a contrast here to primary understandings, which do. Rather, this play activity is closely patterned after something that already has meaning in its own terms—in this case fighting, a well known type of guided activity. Real fighting here serves as a model, a detailed pattern to follow, a foundation for form.[36]

As Huizinga writes, "The Medieval tournament was always regarded as a sham fight, hence as play."[37]

At the first SCA tournament in 1966 SCA participants decided that they wanted to fight like knights in shining armor, and then went out and did it to the best of their ability. The combat was based primarily on the re-creations done by de Maiffe and Thewlis. They approached this from what little knowledge they had, relying mostly on images of medieval knights from books, Hollywood, and some fencing or martial arts experience. Since they were not wearing armor other than helmets, they made the weapons they used out of wood or aluminum. Very quickly they abandoned the use of modern fencing weapons and settled on rattan, a solid grass, like bamboo, used to make furniture and some martial arts weapons, because they found it had a good mass but did not break easily. Later they realized that rattan flexed enough to take some of the impact out of a blow, making it safer than other materials.

The combat system the SCA invented does not accurately replicate medieval combat. Early members of the SCA did not decide to re-create medieval sword play, then search out available sources, translate them, and carefully reconstruct them through interpretation and experiment. Most of the resources necessary for this experiment—the fifteenth-century German and Italian *fechtbücher* or fighting manuals—were not widely available in 1966. That project is going on right now among several historical fencing societies throughout Europe and North America, and has only become widespread over the last ten years as more of the medieval sword manuals have been published and the internet has facilitated communication among groups interested in this project. Early SCA members were just playing knights the same way kids do with bamboo sticks and garbage can lids. Their experiments in medieval combat were just that, experiments. Theatricality and fun were more important than historical accuracy. They had no sure reference point other than modern fencing and the games children play with wooden swords as guidelines as to how to do this. Pictures of early SCA tournaments show fighters wearing almost no armor, sometimes fighting in just a fencing mask and a tunic, with some basketball elbow and knee pads. Fighting in this instance was basically just a game, adults playing make-believe like children do, and much of this ludic quality has been maintained in the SCA.

SCA Fighting as Martial Art

The influence that took SCA fighting from a re-creation of a child's game to a martial art came not from medieval sources but from Asian martial arts. Several of the early SCA members looked to kendo, the Japanese sword art, and to escrima, a South Pacific form of stick fighting, as places to find techniques that would work for SCA fighting. The person most responsible for this transition was Paul Porter/Duke Paul of Bellatrix (whose name comes from a star in the constellation of Orion and whose arms included three red compass stars in a line). In 1972 Porter entered the SCA as an accomplished martial artist, with a black belt in judo and some experience in international competition. He applied the techniques of body mechanics, distance, timing, and psychology he had learned in judo to SCA sword work, and developed a style wherein the legs were used to generate power, creating an extremely hard blow. This fit in much better with the SCA dictum that a blow should be hard enough to break mail. Porter's techniques of distance, timing, and footwork, although based on judo, are very similar to many found in medieval fighting manuals. Porter was also a great spur to the SCA armor industry, as people began to get injured on a much more regular basis with deep bruises and some broken bones, and armor standards were raised as a result.

Mr. Porter's success earned him a large following. When he and several other Western dukes, now trained in his style, traveled to the Pennsic War in 1976, they brought an entirely different method of fighting to the most populous areas of the SCA. They hit much harder than people there were used to, and were extremely effective. Afterwards Porter was highly sought after as a trainer, and groups all over the SCA, including branches in Europe and Asia, would take up a collection from fighters and fly Porter to their area so he could teach a workshop. Porter's success led others to study different martial arts, and apply them to SCA fighting, so that other styles, based on boxing, tae kwon do, or eventually German sword manuals, were developed. From this point on the SCA's king game would revolve around a martial art that could be studied and practiced for its own sake.

Gender and SCA Combat

In the 1999 David Fincher movie *Fight Club*, a group of young men form a secret organization whose sole purpose is to provide an arena for them to fight one another. The fighting serves a dual purpose for the men involved. It allows them to express their masculinity in what they perceive to be an increasingly feminized world through violent interaction, and it gives the men a single-gender group within which to bond. SCA combat provides a similar release and bonding. SCA fighters are part of an exclusive, mostly male club that dominates the group, a made-up warrior class from whom all the SCA's leaders are taken. To many SCA fighters, everything in the SCA not directly related to fighting is feminized. This gendering of activities is inscribed in the traditional division of responsibilities between the masculine monarch (martial, judicial) and his feminine consort (arts and sciences). However, like aristocratic women of the Middle Ages, the SCA uses the traditions of courtly love to channel this masculine violence into the service of women, as fighters (supposedly) relinquish their place of precedence to the feminine by declaring that all honor they win is by the inspiration and for the glory of their consorts.

The SCA fighter performs a particular type of heterosexual masculinity, both violent and erotic, what Maurice Keen describes in *Chivalry* as a scene "in which colour and violence fuse together in the display of the male before the female."[38] The SCA reinterprets the Victorian concepts of the knight and his lady in the relationship between SCA fighters and their consorts. In the Middle Ages fighters in mail would perform feats of bravery at tournaments for a gallery of ladies. SCA fighters, clad in armor covered in brightly colored surcotes, parade in front of mostly female spectators and risk pain and injury for the avowed purpose of pleasing and honoring them.

But this tradition of placing the female on a pedestal to be worshiped symbolically keeps the woman passive and framed within a masculine ideal. Combat is the arena in which the highest prestige in the SCA is won, and for the most part women receive only the prestige and power granted to them by men. As Erisman says: "[b]ecause heavy fighting is so central to the SCA and because female participants tend not to be involved in it, SCA women often find themselves known primarily as an appendage of the men in their lives."[39]

However, the Victorian image of the passive and demure princess is often far from SCA reality. Sometimes the queen or princess will accept the traditional submissive role, but at other times she will come to dominate a reign and the kingdom. Quite often it is the queens who run things. A common axiom is that the king reigns while the queen rules, and members of the Order of the Rose, particularly duchesses, are often seen as being the most powerful group within the SCA.

Most often a fighter champions his or her romantic partner, but this is not always the case. Young male fighters are notorious for changing consorts on a regular basis, and often they fight for the girlfriend *du jour* or even someone they merely want to sleep with. Other fighters choose consorts with whom they are not romantically involved but who have been in the group long enough to understand how the politics and bureaucracy of the group work (often better than the fighter himself). The stereotype associated with this couple is that of a fighter who goes out to wars, leads the troops, and plays with the boys, while his queen actually runs the kingdom. Whereas there is one qualification for being king—being a good enough fighter to win crown tourney—there is no qualification for being queen (other than being a paid member of the society, which all combatants and consorts in Crown tourney must be). Although some women in the SCA base their performance on the romantic ideal of the submissive princess, patterning their persona after a Guinevere or Iseult, others emulate the more powerful women of the Middle Ages, attempting to portray themselves as another Eleanor of Aquitaine or Elizabeth I. Furthermore, women occupy most of the administrative positions in the SCA, which gives them a great deal of actual power.

The medieval king game was not so different. The summer king is often a braggart and a lampoon of a king while his queen is more virtuous. Drawing on evidence from the Wistow game involving Margaret Moore and Thomas Barker in 1469, Billington suggests that "the character of the king could have been a boastful figure and that his queen was a model of virtue."[40] Although many in the SCA would be loath to admit it, this is often how the royal couple in an SCA court is viewed. SCA kings take their romantic and heroic role seriously and usually try to perform it to the best of their ability, but some perform as despots or drunken revelers. When a prince or king behaves in this way he risks ridicule and shame, as well as being ostracized when he is no longer king.

In royal lists the relationship between fighter and consort is highlighted, and the roles they play, taken from both medieval and Victorian romance, are very gender-specific. The consort is expected, if she is present, to accompany the fighter to the invocation of the list and stand by the side of the field when he is fighting. She is also expected to offer support and encouragement, to make sure the fighter is drinking enough water, etc.

Before each fight the fighters bow not only to the king and to their opponents but also to their consorts. Often this salute is more elaborate than the others. While one fighter may merely raise his sword in the direction of his consort, another will go down on bended knee. The consort often has a ritual of her own, which she performs as part of the salute, blowing a kiss or curtsying in return. One lady I have seen carries a rose, and as her fighter salutes her with his sword she curtsies and salutes back with the rose. The most elaborate such ritual I have witnessed is performed by Sir Ragnar Beowulf and his lady Skye O'Brea. When the salute is called for Ragnar marches to the side of the field and kneels before his lady so that she may tie her favor to his arm, and then returns to the field to salute his opponent.

The favor is the most important prop in the performance of the relationship between fighter and consort. It derives from the medieval tradition of a lady giving a token to a knight, and fighters are expected to wear the favor of their consorts prominently displayed at all times. The favor is therefore a mark of association, linking fighter to consort publicly, even when the consort is not present. Although some ladies give as favors the same types of items used for this purpose in the Middle Ages—sleeves, gloves, scarves, etc.—most favors in the SCA are not re-creations of historical artifacts but are yet another SCA invention: a piece of cloth with a loop sewn in one end so that it may be hung securely on a belt, and embroidered with the lady's arms or badge or initial.

As Huizinga notes, the giving and receiving of favors can be highly sexual:

> The erotic element of the knightly tournament is most directly revealed in such customs as the wearing of the beloved's veil or other garment that carries the fragrance of her hair or that of her body. Caught up in the excitement of combat, women offer one piece of jewelry after another; when the game is over, they sit bare headed with their arms stripped of their sleeves.[41]

This eroticism is an important element of both SCA and medieval tournaments, and the practice of giving favors may function as part of an elaborate courting ritual rooted in SCA combat. However, favors can symbolize many things other than a romantic relationship. Sometimes a favor is given as a token of recognition for a heroic or chivalric deed, and groups of ladies will occasionally organize together to give out favors in order to promote overt displays of romantic or heroic behavior. The queen, princess, and baroness also have a tradition of favors, quite hierarchical, which they give out as part of the performance of their duties. The queen or princess usually has a personal guard, composed of up-and-coming fighters who are being considered for knighthood. While they may act as a ceremonial guard for the queen and even guard her on the battlefield if she fights, the actual duty of the Queen's Guard is to act as set-up crew for the royalty. They will set up the thrones for court, erect the royal pavilion, and strike all the regalia at the end of an event. In the ceremony inducting fighters into the Queen's Guard fighters are given a favor from the queen. Unlike the other badges of their office, usually a baldric and/or a livery tabard, which must be returned at the end of each reign, these favors are personal tokens from the queen. They are produced for each individual queen, and fighters keep them once the reign is over. These are often more elaborate than normal favors, and sometimes will be a piece of garb or even armor. The captain of the guard will get a more elaborate favor marking his position, and sometimes the queen or princess will ask the king to appoint a knight to counsel her guard, who will receive a unique favor as well. The queen and princess also have champions. Sometimes they chose their champions, and sometimes the champion is the winner of a tournament (the tradition varies from kingdom to kingdom). This champion will receive the most elaborate favor of all. On the other end of the favor hierarchy are war favors. At the large interkingdom wars such as Pennsic and Estrella, the queens of each kingdom will often present favors to every fighter in their armies. This necessitates the construction of several hundred favors for this single event. These favors are extremely simple and are made by volunteers who produce a certain number (usually between five and twenty). One person, always a woman, is assigned to direct this project.

The romantic ideal of masculinity—that of the chivalrous knight defending all ladies—which is present in both medieval and Victorian literature, is challenged in the SCA by the presence of female fighters, especially when one of these women wins a royal tournament and makes her male consort the "prince-consort of love and beauty." In the romantic medieval paradigm, women are simply not supposed to display martial traits:

> Ladies, after all, do not hold swords; or rather (since they can, of course, help to arm the knight) they do not hold naked swords. Note, for instance, King Anguin's words in the Prose Tristan, when he sees his wife clutching a "naked" sword: "Hearing these cries King Anguin arrives all amazed because he sees that the queen holds the totally naked sword. . . . 'Now hand the sword to me,' he says, 'because it is not right that a lady should hold a sword in this way.'" The naked sword is (or should be) the exclusive property of men.[42]

Billington also notes a prejudice against women participating in martial activities in Shakespeare's *Henry VI*, where Joan of Arc and Princess Margaret are both considered unnatural women because of their martial traits.[43] Medieval (and Victorian) prejudice places women apart from men as objects to be worshiped and prizes to be won, and not as participants in the actions of society.

In the SCA contemporary values of fair play and antidiscrimination trump such prejudice. Women in the SCA fight and they fight against men. The first female fighter in the SCA was Sir Trude Lacklandia. According to Thewlis, who was on the SCA Board of Directors at the time, Trude petitioned the Board for permission to fight and they told her she would have to prove that women fought in the Middle Ages. Trude presented several examples of women combatants to the board and she was allowed to become an authorized fighter. Later she was made the SCA's first lady knight. This was one of the few times that the SCA Board based a decision specifically on historical practice, which indicates the strong resistance that existed at the time against women fighting. That resistance still exists: one (anonymous) knight says simply, "it messes with my game." He feels he is unable to perform his role as a knight if he has to fight women, since a knight's oath often included a vow to "do no harm to ladies."

When a lady fighter enters the lists, her consort is often expected to perform the traditional consort's duties. When a man stands by the side of the field to watch his lady fight, brings her water and food, accompanies her to the invocation, etc., the reversal of the traditional fighter/consort roles is plain for all to see. One way this tension with his traditional role is relieved is when the male fighter, instead of relinquishing the role of heroic champion, performs it alongside his lady. Most lady fighters are the consorts of men who also fight, and it is not uncommon to see a man and woman, both in armor, march together in the parade preceding the invocation of the lists. This creates an obvious double standard—while the woman has abandoned her role as a traditional consort and taken on the masculine role of fighter, the man in this case has kept his traditional role, and does not risk being feminized.

The SCA constructs a very traditional set of gender roles and has trouble reconciling them with contemporary sensibilities. The biggest example of this problem is that, although SCA governing policy holds that the king and queen are equal and reign together, custom in most kingdoms holds that the king is the source of law and, as "sovereign" rather than "consort," he has the final say on kingdom policy. Although it is rare, there have been a few occasions when a woman has won a coronet list and (to date) one occasion when a woman won a crown tournament. In this case the gender role reversal cannot be avoided. The sovereign and consort have very distinct duties and traditions that are part of the performance of these roles, and they are highly gendered. By SCA tradition the king is the source of law and martial strength for the kingdom while the queen is patroness of the arts, most of which are considered feminine activities. Lisa Snook/Countess Svava Thorgiersdottir, a fighter with a Viking persona and a recent Queen of the East, says the duties of an SCA queen are "to show support for the arts and sciences and encourage the nonmartial activities—hence why it is a pain in the ass to be fighting female royalty. They schedule all the teas and exhibits during the battles."[44] This is a common complaint but it underlines the gender differences built into SCA performance. Fighters are not supposed to be interested in arts competitions and teas. They are there to do manly things like "swing stick." Ladies are supposed to be delicate and demure and to confine their activities to gentler pastimes. Snook's aggravation over the conflict between her duties as queen and her desire to go out and fight ("have fun with the boys"), reveals that her pleasure in the SCA derives from her position in a masculine field of endeavor, but once she became queen her duty was to feminized activities.

There are many artists and artisans in the SCA who are men. Men in the SCA are encouraged to participate in the arts, and a knight is supposed to be able to compose poetry and dance, at the very least. Many knights take this duty seriously. However, not all of them do, and this requirement is often passed by with a wink and a nod. Although men, including many knights, sew, paint, dance, and sing and are rewarded for doing so, the only arts that are truly considered masculine are those that provide the materials necessary for the performance of masculine roles: specifically, making armor and brewing beer. For this reason having a man, especially a male fighter, be a "patroness" of the arts is often snickered at—even though there is no requirement that a female consort actually have any artistic inclinations herself.

What to call a male royal consort is also a problem. The first woman to win a coronet list was Dana Kramer-Rolls/Viscountess Maythen Gervaise, who won the coronet of the Principality of the Mists, part of the West Kingdom. The Principality is roughly contiguous with the San Francisco Bay Area and includes the area where the SCA originated. Just a year before her victory, Kramer-Rolls had reigned as Princess with her husband, Bill Rolls/Duke William of Houghton, after he won the coronet fighting for her. When she won coronet they wanted to clearly establish that she had the sovereign's role. Kramer-Rolls took the masculine title Prince, citing the period example of Elizabeth I, while William took the out-of-period title of Prince Consort, which was first used by Prince Albert in the nineteenth century.

During their reign Prince William used camp to foreground the reversal of gender roles. In addition to taking on the feminine role of patroness of the arts, he called the members of his court his "laddies in waiting," and they spent a great deal of time combing his beard, braiding his hair, and at one point mockingly fighting with one another, portraying stereotypes of gay men. Susan Sontag famously wrote of camp, "the essence of Camp is its love of the unnatural: of artifice and exaggeration."[45] To Sontag, writing in 1964, camp was the celebration of bad taste, and she claimed to be both attracted to and repulsed by it; however, looking at her list of camp artifacts, which includes the Brown Derby restaurant, *The Maltese Falcon,* Tiffany lamps, and *Flash Gordon* comics, all things which she considers to be in incredibly bad taste, Sontag seems to be prefiguring postmodernism and its destruction of hierarchies—in this case taste. Notably, to Sontag, camp is apolitical. Kim Michasiw writes of a much more political version of camp, breaking it down into camp-performative and camp-recognition (the latter term she takes from Eve Sedgwick). Michasiw sees in camp-performative a complex layer of coding that, when peeled back, reveals a truth to those who understand all the codes, while in camp-recognition she sees a self-identification that is necessarily political.[46] It is also worth noting that, to Sontag, the SCA itself would likely be camp, since, as she put it, "To perceive Camp in objects and persons is to understand Being-as-Playing-a-Role. It is the farthest extension, in sensibility, of the metaphor of life as theater."[47]

The political element of camp was not important to the straight Prince William. He was most concerned with camp as performance, of which Michasiw (following Leo Bersani) says, "camp is entirely parodic, a self-conscious approximation of what one is not (female, feminine, tasteless, trailer-trash, whatever)."[48] In other words, Rolls was, through camp, displaying what he was not: he was not a woman even though he had taken on a feminine role.

This actually has some historical precedent if we understand Rolls's performance as drag, which Sontag would agree is nearly always camp. There is a great deal of transvestitism in chivalric literature, and on occasion knights would use drag as a theatrical device. The most famous example of this was Sir Ulrich von Liechtenstein, who during his famous "Venus Quest" in 1226 fought a series of tournaments disguised as "Lady Venus."[49] A.D. Putter in "Transvestite Knights" notes that, as in the case of William and his laddies-in-waiting, transvestitism in chivalric literature is often treated as a joke.[50] The cross-dressing Putter discusses is often very campy, so the cross-dressing knight's sexuality is never in question.[51] He further notes:

> The extra advantage that cross-dressing offers over other types of disguise is that it makes masculinity an inseparable part of that incontestable identity. . . . But the knight's desire to prove the "incontestability" of his gender, his desire to re-encode his body's masculinity in rituals of dressing and undressing, also exposes just how fragile and incomplete his sense of masculinity actually is.[52]

Turning his reign as consort into camp allowed Rolls to assume the traditionally feminized role of princess while protecting his own masculine identity.

Women who have reigned as princess are normally given the title Viscountess, but in the Mists they were also admitted to the Order of the *Dames de la Mer*. Kramer-Rolls was already a member but William Rolls accepted membership after this reign, and they normally walk up together when the order is called forward. Recently Duchess Bryn McClellan won Mists coronet for her brother, Viscount Brand McClellan, and they performed their roles in much the same way.

As Putter points out, by donning the trappings of knighthood a knight both reinscribes and questions his masculinity.[53] Donning masculine signs (armor, sword, belt, and chain) says, "I am a knight," but it also says, "I am masculine," since the knight is a figure of masculinity. The existence of this statement points up that the question must also exist: "Am I masculine?" The presence of female fighters and knights in the SCA complicates this. Are they saying they are masculine by donning armor, or are they saying, "I am feminine but I can compete with the boys"? Kramer-Rolls's position was always that when she was in armor and fighting she was becoming masculine. She insisted on always being treated as "one of the guys" and refused to take part in women-only tournaments. Tobi Beck/Duchess Elina of Beckenham seems to be saying the opposite. Tobi Beck is author of *The Iron Rose*, a training manual written specifically for lady fighters. Whereas Kramer-Rolls, a product of seventies feminism, insisted on stressing sameness and a leveling of gender differences, Tobi Beck, a product of nineties feminism, stresses gender difference. Based on her experience as an officer in the United States Army and methods used by her drill instructor during her basic training, Tobi Beck grounds her training methods in both physical difference between men and women and what she considers to be the psychological conditioning women experience in contemporary society.[54]

Some women fighters don signs of their femininity along with their armor, further calling into question the masculine nature of combat. Eichling von Arum, a lady fighter from CAID who has been offered knighthood several times but turned it down (she has given a variety of reasons for this), wears a skirt when she fights and a breastplate that accentuates her breasts. Other lady fighters go so far as to wear Roman-style breastplates with breasts molded into them.

The title used by lady knights is also an issue. Patty Winter/Viscountess Gwenllian Rhiannon of Dragon Keep, the first female Master of Arms, uses the title "Mistress of the Pelican" and even "Viscountess," though she too is one of the few women who has won a coronet tourney, but she uses the title "Master of Arms" to refer to herself as a member of the Chivalry. Mary of Uffington and Kramer-Rolls, the second and third female knights, used the title "Sir." However, during her knighting ceremony, Bolverk of Momchilivik objected to being dubbed "Sir Bolverk," shouting at the king "That's *Lady* Bolverk! I got tits, see?" and pointing to her chest.

The issues raised by this form of participation are many. Women fighting against men on the field of honor shatters the chivalric paradigm under which the SCA operates. The tournament culture as it developed in the Middle Ages was constructed, as early as the thirteenth century, around the ideal of honor, protection, and service to women. A knight usually vowed never to harm ladies. When a lady is standing in front of him swinging a sword, this becomes difficult.

Furthermore, as shown by Kramer-Rolls's portrayal of a sovereign princess and her husband's performance as her prince consort, this type of participation is also a form of drag. Just as fighting is a masculine activity and the signs associated with fighting are signs of masculinity, armor is, by association, a masculine uniform. When a woman dons armor she is dressing in drag and giving a drag performance by participating in a masculine activity. Even those women whose armor emphasizes their femininity through skirts or molded breastplates are participating in a drag performance, one which involves several layers of coding—feminine signs on a masculine uniform on a female body performing a masculine activity—much like a woman pretending to be a gay male drag performer.

In addition to being a fighter Snook is also an actress and director familiar with drag and with queer performance, and she rejects the idea that women fighting is a form of drag, or that by accentuating the feminine in their armor women are engaged in a double coding. She sees it as purely a practical matter. Her own armor, at first glance, appears to be a faux-Roman leather breastplate and skirt, but on closer examination is actually based on a corset and leather miniskirt. Snook insists that this is so her armor will fit better: "Look, I've got curves," she says. "Armor that accentuates my curves fits and moves better than armor made for a guy."[55] To her, armor that accentuates the female is the opposite of drag: it is an expression of the feminine on a female body.

In this postmodern, post-Xena world, that doesn't sound too far-fetched. We are used to representations of women in popular culture who can be feminine and still fight and, in Xena's case, fight in armor with a sword. In fact, the influence of Xena on female SCA fighting is profound. Since Xena became popular, the number of women fighters has grown exponentially, and women now make up ten percent of the authorized fighters in the SCA (though less than one percent of the knights). However, the great appeal of warrior women in pop culture, from the Amazons of Greek mythology, to the Calamity Jane of nineteenth-century dime novels, to Xena, is the shock and surprise that they can compete against men and succeed. The traditional image of the knight in shining armor and the highly gendered roles of knight and consort, not only in the SCA but in medieval and Victorian romance, continue to mark fighting as a masculine activity, and female fighters as gender-bending.

Men who do not participate in fighting are considered by many of the male fighters (and some of the female fighters) to be unmanly. Men who participate in combat activities not associated with heavy fighting, those who act solely as missile troops or fencers, are often seen as effeminate, not willing to risk the bruises and possible broken bones that come with SCA fighting. The truth of the matter is that fighters see themselves as particularly masculine. Those who make the study of the Middle Ages an important part of their performance see themselves as maintaining the cult of chivalry, and therefore are trying to re-create a particularly medieval form of masculinity. Those with more modern views see SCA fighting as something akin to a game of football, a sport (mostly) for men in which they risk injury and endure pain for the purposes of proving their masculinity.

As is to be expected in a society deeply rooted in a heterosexual machismo, the SCA is extremely heteronormative. Putter argues that the chivalric audience was "fiercely homophobic."[56] This is also true of much of the chivalry of the SCA (though again with regional variation: it is less true in the California kingdoms than elsewhere, and less true in urban branches than in suburban and rural branches). SCA rules state plainly that a fighter may only champion someone of the opposite gender.[57] Same-sex couples are thus prevented from taking part in the romantic ritual at the center of SCA culture. Nonetheless, Erisman correctly points out that gay and other alternative lifestyles are more welcome and prominent in the SCA than in society as a whole.[58] While mundane society is in flux over this issue, and it creates a great deal of conflict, nonetheless, even among conservative members of the SCA, gay and other alternative lifestyles are more or less accepted. There is a thriving gay community in the SCA. Many belong to a group called Clan Blue Feather. According to their website:

> The primary reason for the establishment of Blue Feather, and for its continued existence is education: to encourage and facilitate research on homosexuality in the Middle Ages and the Renaissance, and to teach other members of the Society about homosexuality in the Current Middle Ages. We also exist as a social organization, to facilitate interaction among the members of the Society, especially those who are gay, lesbian, or bisexual.[59]

Although Blue Feather's activities are threatening to the romantic hegemony that dominates the SCA, and they are occasionally met with derision and scorn, particularly among some members of the heavy fighting community, nonetheless to the society as a whole they are not seen as a threat. It should also be noted that many of those same heavy fighters that heap scorn upon Clan Bluefeather direct the same sort of derision toward archers, fencers, many artisans, and just about any other nonfighter types. From my observations, openly gay men who fight are not targets of such scorn. They are welcomed as part of the masculine fighting community.

Fighting for the Crown

Royal rank in the SCA is gained through single combat in a crown tournament. This is an often violent combat that is highly ritualized and contained within a frame of civility and romance established by the ceremonies that surround the tournament and each fight.

Traditions as to how Crown is fought and what kind of event it is to be— indoor or outdoor, with a feast, with camping—vary from kingdom to kingdom and change mostly due to weather conditions and where the event will be held. The SCA owns no land. Whether holding an indoor revel or an outdoor tournament, organizers need to rent space from somebody else, which means they have little control over the appearance of their venues. Although an authentic Twelfth Night celebration would call for a medieval or Tudor hall, more often than not they take place in VFW or Shriners' halls. Occasionally the SCA will be able to rent a church for an indoor event, in which case the ambience will be better. A coronation in a neogothic church feels more authentic than a coronation in a modern convention center with concrete floors and exposed duct work, which no number of banners hung from the ceiling can disguise.

Crown Tourney is usually held out of doors. For outdoor events the SCA is able to create a more complete setting for its activities, one that transforms field and meadow into a liminal place where past and present are supposed to mix. SCA members co-opt existing space and through a carefully chosen set of traditions write a temporary architectural text on the space they've occupied, complete with a type of symbolic "civic architecture" in the form of official pavilions and spaces marked with signs of authority—flags, banners, heraldic devices. Starting with a cow pasture or a meadow or a county park, members write their imprint onto the landscape through careful coding.

If it is a weekend-long event, sometime midday on Friday the SCA begins its process of taking over whatever space it will use for the weekend. By erecting medieval-style pavilions and other structures, members create a suitable faux-medieval frame for their activities. The center of this activity for Crown Tourney is the tourney field, which is usually called the "lists" or in some places "the Eric." The layout of the Eric is symbolic and delineates the power structure of the kingdom. At camping events modern tents spring up around the site, mixed in with medieval-style pavilions, but only pavilions are allowed to be set up on the Eric, making the frame more attractive and more medieval in appearance for the rituals that will take place there. Because space next to the Eric, other than for official pavilions, is usually granted on a first-come, first-served basis, groups that have a lot of fighters will show up early to claim a spot. At night the martial activities give way to parties and revels. At those kingdoms where feasting is a common part of the SCA, arrangements will have been made for a kitchen and a feast hall (if there is not one at the tourney site a separate site will be rented). Socialization in the form of feasting, song, and usually court dancing will go on into the night as the king sits in state. In kingdoms where Crown Tourney is a camping event without a central feast, people will gather together for parties of various sorts, sometimes with campfire singing, sometimes with a dramatic performance, sometimes with belly dancing, and sometimes just to drink and talk. Often the largest party will be hosted by the king on the Eric.

Owning a medieval pavilion, like owning any luxury item, is a sign of status. They are expensive to purchase and both difficult and time consuming to build. Whether owned by an individual or purchased by a household or local branch, a pavilion demonstrates that someone has not only disposable income but also a dedication to the group as a whole and a desire to contribute to the ambiance of the event. In the early years of the SCA, most pavilions were home-made, but as with many of the items necessary for SCA performance, they are now available for purchase from several companies in the United States and England. In yet another SCA compromise, the most common pavilions used in the SCA are large marquis-style pavilions with side poles, which are based on a design from the eighteenth century. But they look old and are obviously not Coleman tents, so they'll do. Other pavilions are used as well, such as the more accurate marquis without side poles, round pavilions, Viking A-frames, and Bedouin-style tents, all styles that fit into the SCA's time frame.

Camping on the Eric is also a sign of being part of the SCA hegemony. Because the official activities happen on the Eric, the farther away from the Eric one camps the less likely a person is to be involved in those activities. As with the Bog at Pennsic War (see below), many people on the outskirts of the camp at a crown tourney show up simply to party and dress weirdly. These people refer to those who are involved in the SCA's rituals (often derisively) as "Eric people." Sometimes, off to one side, there is a much smaller rapier Eric. The rapier Eric's size and location illustrates the position rapier combat occupies in the SCA in relationship to heavy combat in many kingdoms. Rapier combat, representing sixteenth-century dueling and using flexible steel rapier blades, is the poor stepchild to heavy combat. In some kingdoms rapier is well integrated with the social fabric of the SCA. In others it is not accepted by the mainstream. In a few kingdoms it is not permitted at all. Camping on the rapier Eric is a little like sitting at the kids' table at Thanksgiving. Those who are on the rapier Eric have less power and significance in the group as a whole, and placing them in a special spot removed from the town square isolates them from other official activities and hides them from view. Rapier fighters are thus excluded from "serious" (grownup) activities.

Like the area in front of the camp store at Pennsic, the Eric functions as town square for Crown Tourney. Three offices are necessary for running the tournament: the heralds who announce the fighters into the lists, the marshals who are there as safety officers, and the lists office, which organizes the pairings and keeps track of the progression of the fighters. Usually, each of these offices has a pavilion set up on the Eric. Others who may camp on the Eric are the Constable, in charge of security, and the Arts and Sciences pavilion, where competitions will be held and where there will be a display of members' recently completed projects. These are placed on the Eric so they will be centrally located and easy to find. In the center of one side of the Eric (usually placed so that the sun won't be in the occupants' eyes) is the royal pavilion. This is where the king and queen will sit in state, watch the tourney, and hold court. During most of the tourney the king will be sitting in state, occupying the throne and wearing the crown. If he leaves the pavilion (other than for a bathroom break) it will be to walk out onto the field to confer with his marshals or with the herald. As the ultimate authority over how his heirs are chosen, it is the king's duty to watch all of the fighting. During the day people may come to the royal pavilion to confer with the king or present him with gifts, but, for the most part, the king pays attention to the fighting. Sometimes the queen, who is also sitting in state, will speak to visitors so that the king can keep his attention on the combat. This sets up the type of relationship Orgel discusses between Renaissance monarchs and their populace watching any form of entertainment. The spectacle is not just the fighting but also watching the king watch the fighting.[60]

In *From Ritual to Performance* Turner cites Arnold Van Gennep's three phases in a rite of passage: separation, transition, and incorporation.[61] All SCA ceremonies, whether based on historical or contemporary models, follow this pattern. This is also true in SCA tourneys, especially Crown. Turner elaborates on Van Gennep:

> The first phase of separation clearly demarcates sacred space and time from profane or secular space and time. . . . It includes symbolic behavior—especially symbols or reversal or inversion of things, relationships, and processes secular—which represents detachment of the ritual subjects (novices, candidates, neophytes or initiands) from their previous social statuses.[62]

The SCA does this through the invocation ceremony in which the fighters are welcomed into the sacred space in which the competition to determine the heir will take place—the tourney field or "Eric." At about noon, fighters competing in the lists are asked to gather in front of the thrones. This separates the fighters from the rest of the society. Fighters enter a liminal space that they will occupy until they are eliminated from the tournament. One by one, the names of the fighters are announced, sometimes as part of a "grand march" as they and their consorts process into place. Once all the fighters have been introduced, the earl marshal of the kingdom steps forward to explain the conventions of combat. These almost never change from tourney to tourney (though they vary from kingdom to kingdom) and everybody is familiar with them already. This being done the herald administers an oath of invocation, in which the fighters swear to obey the rules of the list and rule justly if they are victorious. They are then paired up for the first round, often by having fighters of lesser rank challenge one of the fighters above them.

Continuing his discussion of Van Gennep, Turner goes on to say:

> During the intervening phase of transition . . . the ritual subjects pass through a period of ambiguity, a sort of social limbo which has few (though sometimes these are the most crucial) of the attributes of either the preceding or subsequent profane social statuses or cultural states.[63]

In Crown Tournament, this phase consists of the fighting itself, as with each round the field shrinks and one by one the fighters are eliminated, until only the victor remains to be named crown prince.

A series of smaller rituals surrounds each fight in Crown Tournament. Each field has a herald to announce the fights, plus at least two marshals, who are in charge of the field. The pairings are sent from the list table to the herald in the form of index cards, and the herald calls the fighters to the field and calls the next pair to "arm and stand ready." By entering the lists, like boxers entering a ring, fighters are symbolically cut off from the crowd until the outcome of their bout is decided. The herald, reciting a prescribed litany, introduces the fighters and asks them to salute, in order, the crown, their consorts, and each other and, in some kingdoms, the crowd. The marshal asks them if they are ready and then, with the marshals knocking their staffs together, he cries "Lay on!"

Rituals serve to ground us, to steep us in tradition, and to build community. All rituals serve either an individual purpose, a community purpose, or both. One might feel they are oppressive (and in one sense they are, since they expect people to conform to a ritual tradition), but to most people they build bonds of togetherness through shared experience and a type of shared reverence for certain aspects of life. The rituals surrounding a tournament fight offer a good example. The first phase of this ritual prepares the fighters for the combat to come—asking if they have all their armor on, etc. The second phase is designed to honor and acknowledge those elements that go into a combat, and to acknowledge the three (or four) different audience/participants in the combat (crown, consort, crowd, and opponent).

A ritual affirms the importance of an act. A group ritual, by affirming the importance of an act to a group, serves to strengthen the bond of community within that group, whatever else its purpose might be. As Turner notes:

> Ritual is, in its most typical cross-cultural expressions, a synchronization of many performance genres, and is often ordered by dramatic structure, a plot, frequently involving an act of sacrifice or self-sacrifice, which energizes and gives emotional clarity to the interdependent communicative codes which express in manifold ways the dramatic leitmotiv.[64]

The ritual of a crown tournament fight is clearly dramatic: two people compete against one another for a prize and one of them is victorious. The rituals that frame the fight acknowledge the seriousness of the act about to take place and isolate the combatants within a sacred space. SCA fighters are symbolically separated from the rest of society when they walk past the Eric rope and onto the field during crown lists. Ideally they should be like the warriors who travel out to an island to do combat alone, only one of them to return. Once the "lay on" is called they and they alone are supposed to determine the outcome of the fight and whether or not any blow landed with sufficient force.

The reality is often much different. The opportunity to cheat is great in an activity governed strictly by an honor system, and every kingdom has had one or more controversies surrounding blow-calling in a crown tournament. The cheating is rarely intentional, most often being brought on by adrenalin and emotion. In some kingdoms, especially those that have had several disputed crowns, the marshals take an active role in determining the outcome of a fight up to and including calling a fighter "dead." This practice often causes conflict at interkingdom wars that involve kingdoms with differing marshalate policies. In a column in the first issue of "Thinkwell" (a pre-internet discussion group of SCA issues) Sandra Dodd/Mistress Aelfled of Duckford points out that opinions on these policies, no matter the side, are always expressed in terms of what is and is not honorable. In kingdoms where the marshalate adheres to the principle that only the fighters can determine a blow, the policy is based on the idea that it is dishonorable to interfere because it takes away from the fighters the honor of making the right choice. In kingdoms where the marshalate is active in a bout, it is based on the idea that it is dishonorable *not* to get involved, since to have a disputed crown makes the king himself look dishonorable and reflects poorly upon the kingdom. Dodd writes:

> [T]he way a person was "raised" in the SCA would determine what he believed when he was "grown" (an officer, marshal, knight, etc.), and that people would understand, accept, and repeat what was taught to them by people they respected when they were new in the group.[65]

Those who believe that only the fighters should be able to call their blows are concerned with the individual fighter's honor. To them, there is no opportunity to behave honorably if conduct is dictated by a higher authority. The ease of cheating and the temptation of victory make resisting that temptation and behaving honorably an accomplishment. Those who think marshals should be able to call blows are concerned with the collective honor of the kingdom and the crown. They wish there to be no taint on the outcome of the lists lest it reflect badly upon the group. They see themselves as protecting the honor of the kingdom. Predictably, these regional differences often correlate with other differences, particularly in force and calibration. Those kingdoms that hit harder tend to favor the individual fighter's right to call a blow. Those kingdoms where fighters hit and take lighter blows tend to favor determinate marshaling.

All this conflict exists because of the performative nature of SCA combat and the presence of an audience for the fighting. If it truly were two fighters alone on an island then there could never be any question about who was victorious. It would always be the one who came back. But people are watching and making note of what each fighter does. The crowd controls a fighter's reputation, and will be quick to label someone a "rhino hide" if they think he's ignoring blows.

In all kingdoms the person most responsible for policing the conduct of a fighter is his or her consort. Since the fighter is supposedly fighting for his consort's honor, any transgression he commits, within the society's romantic paradigm, would reflect poorly upon her. A consort will often tell her fighter if there appeared to be any transgressions on his part. In some cases, consorts have been known to publicly chastise their champions if they have engaged in behavior that embarrassed them, on or off the field. The most visible display of this disapproval is when a consort, believing her champion to have behaved dishonorably during a list, will demand her favor back, sometimes immediately after or even during a fight. A fighter to whom this has happened is publicly disgraced and must withdraw from the lists, as he no longer has anyone to fight for. This is the most effective way in which the feminine exercises control over masculine behavior in the SCA. So even though ideally and symbolically fighters are isolated when they enter the lists, in reality there is a great deal of pressure, official and societal, prompting a fighter to conform to the group standards of conduct.

Most SCA fighters approach combat as a serious business, but some place as high a value on theatricality as they do on efficiency. They will show off their skills and banter with their opponents. I once saw a fighter struck after his opponent told him that his cuisse was unbuckled and he looked (his opponent laughed, refused to accept the victory, and told him to get back up and continue the fight). Quotes from popular movies such as "There can be only one" (from *Highlander,* 1986) and "Come to the dark side" (*The Empire Strikes Back* 1980), etc., are sometimes heard, especially during final round. All this is done for the enjoyment of the audience. Much more common are overt displays of courtesy or ferocity. If a fight is long, one fighter will offer his opponent a chance to rest and take refreshment. Sometimes a "point of honor" is given when, for instance, a fighter strikes his opponent in the leg, forcing him to fight from his knees, and kneels himself so as not to take too great an advantage. More common is giving up an arm after having taken one. SCA fights usually last less than three minutes, though they can go on much longer.

When a fighter falls down "dead" it provides another opportunity for theatricality. Some people cry out something like, "I am slain!" Others go through comical death throes. Some do somersaults and then lie down as if having expired. Still others stiffen and fall forward onto the victor. There are often awards to acknowledge these types of performance and theatricality. The oldest award in the SCA is "The Muckin' Great Clubbe," a huge wooden club with a spike driven through it, which is awarded for ferocity (and specifically *not* for skill). Another award, almost as old, is "The Old Battered Helm," given for the "best death." Every fighter receiving this award is supposed to leave his or her mark upon it "with live steel." The helm has been hit with swords, axes, and maces and even shot a couple of times with a Colt .45. Every kingdom has some form of award to recognize overt displays of valor or courtesy during crown lists. All of these awards expressly acknowledge the theatricality of SCA fighting.

The third phase of initiation plays out slowly in the course of the day, culminating in the crowning of the crown prince. Turner writes, "The third phase. . . . includes symbolic phenomena and actions which represent the return of the subjects to their new, relatively stable, well-defined position in the total society."[66] The culmination of this reintegration, and of the tournament, is the final round, which is more elaborate than the earlier rounds in the tourney. The consorts of the two finalists are invited either to sit with the queen or stand with her at the edge of the field. Traditionally, the chivalry is invited to sit within the lists to watch the combat.[67]

Each combatant is given his or her own herald who announces not only the combatant's name but his or her arms and the name of his or her consort. Usually the finals are best two out of three. In some kingdoms the finals are even more elaborate than this, requiring three of five or even five of seven victories, often with the fights being fought with a variety of matched weapons, both to demonstrate that the victor is well rounded and to give the spectators a better show. Once the fights are over the victor will be proclaimed crown prince and crown his consort crown princess. The symbolic purpose of these rituals, taken together, is the same as the ritual of the sword in the stone from Arthurian legend or of the Cotswold Summer Games, but also echoes any war of succession: the participants are fighting it out to become king.

The pomp and circumstance of the crown tourney masks a game that would be easily recognizable to townsmen of the Middle Ages as a variation on the summer king game. It is a game in which people, usually men, strive in a physical contest to best all others and be crowned as the group's mock king. This postmodern communal fantasy is the basis of all SCA activity.

War Fighting

The other part of the summer king's duty is to lead his troops in mock battle. The first SCA war was held on an island in a reservoir in Marin County, California, in 1967 (AS II). As there were no other kingdoms at that time, the combatants divided up into teams and invented a scenario. They decided to kidnap a young maiden, Dorothy Heydt/Mistress Dorothea of Caer Myrddin. One side would be the kidnappers and the other the rescuers. This scenario was popular in the SCA for many years but fell out of favor when people started complaining that it would be unchivalrous to have knights kidnap defenseless maidens.

The kidnappers took their captive to the top of a nearby hill, and one fighter guarded her while the rest fought the rescuers down below. Eventually the other kidnappers were all killed and the rescuers charged the lone fighter on the hill. The finale of the war as described on the West Kingdom History Project website by Sir Stephen de Loraine was obviously inspired by romantic literature and filmic imagery, so I quote it here in full:

> The final confrontation was rather spectacular, I am told (by Siegfried shortly after the event, as a matter of fact—I didn't go). He and Dorothea had decided that they were doomed lovers being pursued by the evil Richard. Richard, on the other hand, was of the opinion he was the valiant rescuer of the fair maiden. The rock had two methods of access. One was a tricky path going up one sloping side. The other was a series of handholds going up the sheer back of the rock. Siegfried stood at the top of the path, downing attackers as they tried to assail him single file. Then Dorothea screamed. Richard had climbed up the backside of the rock. Seeing his doom before him, Siegfried scrambled to interpose himself between Richard and Dorothea, and gently swung his sword back to touch the fair maiden (thus "killing" Dorothea) while Richard cut him down. I am told that Richard was really upset that they weren't following his idea of the situation. But then, I'm sure there have been any number of real life similar situations where the participants had similar two [sic] different ideas of what was going on.[68]

The image of the doomed lovers standing atop a windswept crag while a villain creeps up behind them is something out of a movie or a Gothic melodrama. These three SCA members had cast themselves in roles adapted from a theatrical genre; however, a conflict arose because both fighters saw themselves in the role of hero.

Chivalry and War

One of the most difficult issues facing SCA re-creators surrounds the subject of just how to re-create war. Wars in the SCA can most closely be associated with medieval tournaments. Like medieval tournaments, they occur at a specific time and within a controlled space. Like tournaments they are not fought over territory but for sport. There is no death nor mayhem, and tactics are often quite gentlemanly. Most importantly, they are imbued with a sense of chivalry and fair play.

But this puts their status as reenactments or even re-creations on questionable footing. As the first SCA war demonstrates, SCA wars like SCA tourneys are imbued with a high degree of romanticism. Knights and other warriors take the field in service of their mock kings and to honor their ladies. According to the SCA's official documents, they are all considered to be nobles and they are all required to treat one another with chivalry and courtesy. But what exactly does that mean? Over the course of the SCA's history rules have been established, which vary from kingdom to kingdom and also for each of the major wars, as to what constitutes acceptable chivalric behavior. You cannot strike someone on the ground, but if someone falls must you let him regain his feet or is he automatically considered dead or captured? A flanking maneuver may place you behind enemy lines, but is it chivalrous to kill them from behind? And what of the status of missile troops, who would rarely (but would on occasion) be of noble blood?

In some kingdom traditions wars are simply seen as large chivalric tourneys and fighters are expected to display the exact same behavior as they would were they fighting in the lists. Often there is to be no killing from behind. Sometimes, opponents who lose their footing must be allowed to regain it. In other kingdoms, war is a distinctly different form of combat from tourneys, and allows for greater latitude of behavior. For some knights, their main pleasure in the SCA comes from re-creating in some way medieval warfare, with tactical maneuvers and strategies, including flanking, running charges, and the combination of missile and melee troops. The arguments over these issues are among the most contentious in the SCA. Fighters from those kingdoms who see some or all of these as unchivalrous often cite Geoffroi de Charny and other fourteenth century warrior philosophers, who railed against archers and other tactics as unknightly (but who, it must be admitted, were otherwise as warlike as Sherman marching through Georgia). Knights from kingdoms where SCA war is meant to re-create medieval war are labeled as unchivalrous, even as villains.

Nowhere is this argument more heated than in discussions of the place of combat archery. Archery existed at the first SCA war mentioned above, and from then on was a part of warfare in the West Coast kingdoms where it was extremely popular in the 1970s and 1980s. The only other place where archery developed as a war tactic was in the Kingdom of Meridies and its spawn, the Kingdom of Trimaris. But the two styles of archery differed greatly. In the Western kingdoms archery was done primarily with light (35 pound draw weight or less) bows shooting arrows with ¼ inch bird blunts on them. This necessitated the use of woven or perforated steel to cover the face openings of helmets, which were allowed to have openings up to one inch wide. Use of such steel mesh annoyed some fighters. Thee West Coast kingdoms also had "light archers," which were meant to represent peasant levies. Archers had only to take the field wearing tunic, pants, fencing mask, a cup, and elbow and knee pads.

They could not be struck but had to be declared dead by proximity: a fighter approached to within a set distance—ten or fifteen feet, and declared "archer, you are dead." In Meridies on the other hand they shot arrows with heads the same diameter as a sword, so that extra eye protection was deemed unnecessary. There were also no light archers in this area. All archers could be struck with a sword. Eventually, this second form of archery was declared the SCA standard, greatly angering people on the West Coast (The Kingdom of Lochac threatened to leave the SCA over the change, and was granted special permission to keep using the old rules).

Like the French in the Hundred Years War, many SCA knights are fully contemptuous of archery in SCA combat. As did Charny, they consider it unchivalrous to shoot at a knight from a distance, not putting oneself directly at risk. Knights, they say, should fight hand to hand where they can strike and be struck. The masculinity, courage, and ethical character of archers and those who support archery are attacked by knights and fighters who hold this opinion, and the fights that ensue are the most vitriolic the SCA knows.

The basic philosophies of each side of the argument are completely incompatible. They show no sign of ever reconciling.

Pennsic War

The SCA's largest event is the Pennsic War. In the kingdoms east of the Mississippi River, all roads lead to Pennsic. It dominates the SCA calendar and SCA activity. For many people, Pennsic is the only SCA event they attend. As were the Cotswold Summer Games, Pennsic is a huge summer-king festival. It provides the largest stage for the SCA's mock kings to perform upon. All the kings of the SCA try to attend Pennsic if it falls during their reign. They will stage many royal performances, some public and some private, throughout the two weeks. They will all hold some kind of court, march in the Grand March, stroll through camp and the merchant areas with their retinues, and attend various dinners and parties.

Within the overall performance that is Pennsic there are hundreds of smaller ones: parties, ceremonies, courts, rituals, battles, plays, dances, masks, singing, and storytelling.

The conflict of the war itself runs very much along the lines of the rupture/conflict/resolution pattern identified by Turner. The principal kingdoms declare their intention to go to war in the opening ceremony, which is held the Sunday of "war week," the second week of the event. The ceremony begins, as is appropriate, with a royal entry. Each of the kings and queens marches about the camp accompanied by his or her retinue and followed, in long parades, by all the local branches and great households of the kingdom, each marching behind its banner with drums, horns, and bagpipes making a great cacophony. The full parade is more than a mile long. They meet at the battlefield (or the barn if it is raining). The whole thing will ideally look like the meeting of the kings on the Field of the Cloth of Gold. Once the parade reaches the site, the marchers become the audience for the annual ritual of the opening ceremony, a ritual that is both highly symbolic and slightly ironic.

The ritual begins when the King of the East presents an arrow to the King of the Middle. Together they break the arrow, symbolizing the rupture between the two kingdoms. This ritual goes back to the origins of the Pennsic War. The legend goes that when Friedman was the first King of the Middle he issued a challenge to the King of the East that went unanswered until he himself moved to the East, won Eastern crown and answered it (thereby declaring war on himself). He appeared at a Middle Kingdom event with an arrow which the Middle king broke, and the two kingdoms went to war. This, although not the oldest war in the SCA, was the first between two mock kings.

The next phase of the ritual is the gathering of allies. A Midrealm household, House Darkyard, is summoned to bring forth "The Pennsic Horn," which they are traditionally charged with keeping, and which is supposed to be blown only once a year. The two kings take turns blowing the horn, symbolically summoning their allies. This, of course, references several mythic tropes: the Horn of Gondor from *Return of the King,* which Boromir blows before he dies; The Horn of Roland from *The Song of Roland,* which was Tolkien's main source; and the Gjallerhorn, which Heimdall blows to summon the Gods for Ragnarok. In answer to the call the assembled kings declare their allegiance. Each in turn steps forward and announces which side his army will fight on. This is, in a way, a gathering of the tribes, symbolically framing the mundane act of picking teams.

At smaller events there may be a coronation procession or parade of fighters, but Pennsic is one of the few places in the SCA where large processional performances take place. In addition to the Grand March there are several other parades at Pennsic. Late in the war Clan Caminari, a Japanese household (which also provides taiko drummers to accompany the battles), stages one of the most unusual processions, a reconstruction of a Japanese fertility festival. The entire household dresses in fundoshi (loin cloths), drinks a lot of beer, and parades around the campground carrying a twenty-foot-long pink paper maché phallus. They stop in front of each camp and scream, "May everyone in this camp be fertile!"—a blessing many people are not thankful for. They end the day with "oiled squire wrestling" which is exactly what it sounds like. An even more popular version of procession that takes place at Pennsic is the Fool's Parade, in which a group of people clad in motley and wearing jester's caps marches about the campground, banging drums and screaming, basically causing as much mischief as they can.

One of the better period-style performances I have witnessed in the SCA took place at the royal dinner hosted by the King of the East for all the crowned heads at the war. During dinner a herald entered the room announcing the arrival of the "Lord of the Forest" who had come to bless the gathering. Two men then entered carrying a model of a white hart with an arrow in its side on a green palanquin. When the arrow was pulled out red wine flowed from the wound. This was an innovative bit of medieval-style pageantry. It also nearly caused an international incident. Among the guests was the King of the Outlands, and the symbol of the Outlands is a white stag on a green field. The king, named Artan, wasn't paying attention when the hart was carried in and I said to him, "Artan, are you watching this?" He looked up and screamed, "Hey! That is a white stag there, isn't it?" The assembled royals laughed as the herald fell over himself to apologize, saying they hadn't considered the Outlands arms when planning the ceremony, and meant no offense. It was all in fun, and everybody took it that way, but it could have truly offended some people. Mock kings or not, SCA royalty take their roles seriously.

The battles at Pennsic include several traditional SCA scenarios. There is usually an open field battle, a "mountain pass" (rows of hay bales with a big gap between them), a "Bridge Battle" (several rows of hay bales with narrow gaps between them) and a woods battle in real woods. This last is a "resurrection battle," an armored game of "capture the flag," during which dead fighters may go back to their resurrection point and then return to the fighting until the time limit for the battle is up. There are also numerous champions' battles, wherein small handpicked teams compete against each other. The so-called "heroic champions" is one of the highlights of the event for spectators, a series of single combats fought between the best fighters at the war. Each of these battle scenarios is worth a war point. There are also points for rapier combat and archery. The king is central to each of the war point performances. The kings of the two principal kingdoms are expected to lead their armies in the battle, and if they don't show up, it is likely that many of their knights will skip it as well.

At the end of the week a closing ceremony is held, representing the reconciliation of the two kingdoms, and completing the resolution phase of the ceremonial conflict. At this ceremony the kings emphasize their mutual friendship and common bonds. The results of all the war point competitions are announced and the winner officially proclaimed.

The Geography of Misrule

Pennsic is not a typical SCA event, and many of the people who go to the war are not SCA members. They include other re-creationist groups such as Medieval Scenarios and Recreations (a group that split off from the SCA), fantasy groups such as the Tuchux (a group based on the barbarians from John Norman's S&M fantasy series, *The Chronicles of Gor*), and various elves, fairies, and live action role players, who come mainly for the parties. This all turns Pennsic into a combination market fair, science fiction convention, medieval tournament, and Burning Man-style postmodern fertility festival, all depending on whose camp you visit.

As at Crown Tourney, people arrive at Pennsic on the first day of the event to occupy and begin to transform the space, though the land grab at Pennsic is much more elaborate and much more controlled. Plots of land have already been allotted to groups based on the number of people they have registered for the event (250 square feet per person), and the first day mostly involves negotiation over where exactly to place a boundary line. Many groups spend the first week building their camp to provide an appropriate stage set for their performance. Some groups have large gates and towers made of plywood, foam, and steel to mark their territory. One group erects an elaborate Italian villa out of scaffolding and plywood. Another builds the gates of a Roman fort out of logs. Still another group erects a foam-brick castle. There is even a plywood pirate ship. A group of merchants erects a scaled-down representation of a medieval Wealdon house, with sleeping lofts at either end and a central peaked hall. A household led by a professional stonemason camps in a grotto which, over time, they have paved with cut stone, creating a series of steps, pathways, and multi-level patios that are quite elaborate. Theirs is the only camp at Pennsic that is not dismantled at the end of the event.

Pennsic is one of the few events in the SCA that can develop a geographical history, and the SCA has been able to write its text into the landscape in a more lasting fashion here than anywhere else. The place of Pennsic has become part of the story of Pennsic. The land is associated with stories and memories of events, and provides a literal grounding for SCA activities and for SCA myths. It is likely for this reason that some SCA members consider Pennsic to be the "home" of their persona, and greet each other with the phrase "welcome home" when they arrive, as though they have spent the other fifty weeks of the year out wandering in the wilderness and have just now returned for a brief respite before going out again.

Large groups at Pennsic camp on the same ground year after year, and they are very protective of their allotments. Traditional camping areas become associated with the groups who camp there, or once camped there, as the event has grown in size and new areas have opened up for camping. There is a certain amount of status associated with site location. The choicest camping areas are those near the permanent camp store because they are an easy walk from the battlefield, merchants' row, and the barn, where most of the official activities of the week take place. This is where the royal encampments of the two principal kingdoms can be found. The area known as the Serengeti, so called because it is flat, dusty, and there is no shade to be found, lies directly to the east of the battlefield and to the north of the merchants, and close to the parking lot. This was once the battlefield, and later the parking lot, and at one time contained a small dirt race track. It has been taken over for camping as the event has grown.

The area known as "Rune Stone Hill" is a long slope heading away from the barn on which several camps are set, including the Enchanted Ground. There is indeed a rune stone there. It was placed there several years ago on a leveled spot. No one is allowed to camp next to the rune stone, and it is used for gatherings and special events, as when SCA members will occasionally get married at the war.

In a wooded area down the hill near the lake, which was also once part of the battlefield, people now camp in the shade of the forest. In a nearby brook there are two swimming holes, one of which is clothing optional. This is where the SCA is at its most carnivalesque. It is far removed from the main activities of the event, and most of the non-SCA groups attending the war, the elves, fairies, and vampires, not welcome among many SCA members, usually camp down here. As a result this is the location of the event's biggest and wildest parties. These include an annual slave auction, an S&M party hosted by someone elaborately dressed as Satan, a "men without pants" party, a Mardi Gras party, and lots of topless belly dancing. Known as "the bog," this is a liminal space in its own right, similar to those areas of a town where respectable people don't spend much time. It is the Southwark of Pennsic (O'Donnell, who uses *Henry V* to frame his book, makes a similar observation referring to the "party camps" in the Bog at Pennsic as "the society equivalent of Falstaff and the rest of the tavern crowd"[69]).

The problems associated with carnival also exist in the SCA and, although not restricted to the Bog, are certainly concentrated there. As Goffman notes, king game gatherings, winter or summer, "fall into the category of the carnivalesque; they have in common overindulgence and (temporary and non-threatening) inversions of the social and patriarchal orders."[70] This overindulgence also exists at SCA events and can cause a great deal of tension among participants. Many people who are in the SCA for scholarly or reenactment pursuits resent the fact that the SCA functions on one level as a large party. There is a great deal of alcohol consumption at SCA events and a great deal of sexual license. One of the complaints against this type of behavior is that it conflicts with the romantic ideals that many see as the basis of the SCA, that the Middle Ages was (or should have been?) more courteous than this. Another complaint is that alcohol consumption can lead to incidents of violence at SCA events, including sexual harassment and rape. The same dangers of misrule identified by Billington, which existed in king games and ales, and exist today at Mardi Gras, rock concerts, and many fraternity parties, can be found in the SCA as well. According to the autocrat (organizer) of the 2004 Pennsic War, reportable crimes in which the local police are called to the site occur, on average, four times a year. Although this is not many in a gathering of 12,000 people, it is still significant, and there is no way of knowing the number of unreported crimes.

At Yahoogroups.com, an email support group called SCA-skeletons provides a forum for discussion of such issues. One recurring theme is that people who have been involved in such incidents feel let down because the SCA was supposed to be a more chivalrous society and that people had felt safer in the SCA than in the contemporary world. This echoes through inversion the idea that the courtly love tradition was created to control masculine violence by subjugating it to feminine desire. When a crime of any nature occurs at an SCA event, the common complaint is that the SCA has not lived up to its romantic paradigm. Many people feel safe when they enter the SCA because the SCA bills itself as an organization built on the values of courtesy and honor. On SCA-skeletons, the overwhelming opinion is that this is a lie.

Snook, when I asked her about this, countered this argument, saying it is unrealistic to expect the SCA to be safer than the real world or to assume that acts of violence will never occur. She further noted that the SCA is full of men with a "knights in shining armor" complex, who itch for the chance to ride to someone's rescue.[71] Indeed, whenever there is a call for help of any kind at an SCA event a group of men in white belts will come running to see what they can do and whom they can protect, and are disappointed if it turns out to be something harmless. I once asked a king of Meridies how his kingdom handled incidents of sexual harassment and he told me (in a deep southern twang), "Oh, we don't have any problems like that. Whenever somebody gets outa line a couple of the good old boys with the white belts take him out behind the royal pavilion for a talking to and the problem is solved."

The problem in these instances is the carnival nature of misrule, the inversion and suspension of societal rules, which allows bad behavior to occur. The consumption of alcohol, sexual license, and violence were prominent elements of medieval king games (some of which were called "king ales," indicating what the main activity involved was to be). Wiles notes that fist fights were an accepted, even welcome, part of meetings between mummers even into the nineteenth century.[72] Like other carnivals—including Mardi Gras, another seasonal form of the king game that has survived from the Middle Ages—this suspension of society's rules is an integral part of the festivities and, like Carnival, it occasionally leads to behavior that even those involved in the game cannot tolerate. This element of misrule is also a part of the king game in the SCA, just as it was in the Middle Ages.

The Quest for Renown

There is one way in which SCA fighting strongly resembles the aristocratic chivalric model as opposed to the peasant king game. One thing that SCA fighters share with medieval knights is the quest for renown. Two performances from Estrella War in 2004/AS XXXVIII demonstrate this well. Someone had made a war banner for the West Kingdom out of gold silk. It had not been intended to be carried on the field, as there was no regular banner bearer, but Hollander, who was at the time the Queen's champion as well as a former banner herald, offered to bear the banner on his pike so long as he could still fight with it (which would undoubtedly damage the banner). The West was on the losing side in most of the battles, and a couple of times they were kept as the last reserve. Toward the end of the battle the banner and the king would wade in, fight, and then end up making a "last stand," in which Hollander would fight beside the king and die defending the royal standard, just as Geoffroi de Charny did at Poitiers (only Hollander got to do it over and over again). In every battle the banner became more and more shredded, until it was in tatters, barely hanging onto the pole. After Saturday's battles the king called a court and tore the banner into strips, which he handed out to the units who had fought with the West so they could hang them from their own standards.

There was a Queen's equestrian tourney at this same Estrella and the Queen of the West was asked for someone to represent her. Not having an equestrian champion, she went to Olsgaard, who is one of the most accomplished equestrians in the SCA, and asked him to be her equestrian champion for the weekend. Unfortunately, Olsgaard was using a rental horse that spooked at the quintain and absolutely refused to run the course. In order to keep competing, and to maintain his queen's honor, Olsgaard picked up his lance and his shield and ran through the course three times on foot, actually scoring a point against a mounted opponent. Unlike most SCA equestrians, when Henrik rides he does so dressed as a Norman knight in a knee-length mail hauberk and uses a heavy lance. Bearing all this weight he ran, full out, three times through the tilt. This so impressed one lady that she retired from the competition and gave him her horse, at which point Olsgaard's scores improved markedly

These were not young men in either case, but two of the SCA's founders, both of whom had fought at the first tourney in 1966. Hollander at the time was in his late fifties and Olsgaard in his early sixties. That both of these men were champions for the mock queen highlights how even the performances of people other than the royalty are part of the king game. These performances displayed the type of physical prowess and courage typical of medieval romances, and both, appropriately, will be celebrated in song and story—and in staging them they brought renown not only to themselves but also to their queen.

Battle Re-creations

SCA combat resembles the medieval aristocratic model of combat because it takes the form of group battles framed by history or literature, as opposed to reenactments of history. The differences between reenactment groups and the SCA become apparent when we examine the ways the SCA and other groups approach medieval battles. In October 2000, amongst a frenzy of millennial activity, an organizing group put on the Hastings 2000 reenactment. This was one of the largest medieval reenactments ever staged, with thousands of participants on both sides. There were even some SCA members present. Olsgaard attended and rode as a Norman knight. In an article for *Tournaments Illuminated,* the SCA's quarterly journal, SCA members who attended noted that strictures put on participants in terms of their garb were far more stringent than those found in the SCA. Some elements resembled SCA events, such as the tent where everyone had to sign in once they arrived, an armor inspection, and even an authorization fight to make sure the participants were safe. But unlike the SCA the primary emphasis was on authenticity. The armor inspection was actually an authenticity inspection, and there was no plastic or aluminum allowed. They fought with real swords and worked *not* to hit each other.[73] The purpose of this reenactment, as with most reenactments, was to both commemorate a historical event and to provide an entertaining show for a crowd of spectators.

In the SCA historical battles are rarely ever reenacted. Unlike Civil War reenactment in the United States or medieval reenactment in Europe, the US offers no space that is appropriate for staging a medieval reenactment. Reenactment in its purest form takes place, like Hastings, on the location of the original event. It is possible still to march across the field at Gettysburg (though probably not without tripping over a monument) in a reenactment of Pickett's charge, but it is not possible to recreate the battle of Hastings on this side of the Atlantic, or anywhere else other than Hastings, with any kind of accuracy. Place is a character in such reenactments. If you can't look up from the old oak tree and see Little Round Top, you are not getting the full Gettysburg experience (never mind that the topography of Gettysburg has changed in the last 140 years). Reenactors try, as closely as possible, to stage their battle reenactments on the same battlefields on which the original battles were fought. In Europe medieval reenactors have the ground and the physical artifacts around which to stage their performances. The SCA, at least in North and South America, Australia, New Zealand, and Asia, does not. Members stage their events in campgrounds, in schools and county parks, sometimes even in Civil War forts or battlefields. At best an event may be held in an undeveloped cow pasture or on the grounds of one of the large renaissance faires (Members of SCA groups in Europe occupy a middle ground in this case. They can stage an event in a castle, and often participate in other medieval reenactments, but the majority of their activities still center around the SCA's make-believe social structure rather than a particular historical event).

On occasion, however, the SCA will mark an anniversary of a particular event in medieval history with a re-creation of the event. This type of framing device resembles medieval tournaments wherein the combat would take place framed by either romantic fantasy or historical event. In 1992 I took part in an SCA performance which provides a good example, a war between the Principality of the Mists (the San Francisco Bay Area) and the Principality of Cynagua (the Sacramento Valley plus northern Nevada). The Saturday of the war fell upon the 577th anniversary of the Battle of Agincourt, and so the two princes decided that their war should be a re-creation of the Agincourt campaign, including a beach landing, the siege of Harfleur and, of course, the battle of Agincourt itself. As opposed to the thousands of reenactors who took part at the Hastings event, in the SCA re-creation there were a little more than one hundred fighters competing on both sides.

Prior to the battles a joint court was held in which the king inducted Patty Winter/Mistress Gwenllian Rhiannon of Dragon Keep into the order of chivalry. In keeping with the custom of those who initially trained her in the East Kingdom (specifically Vermont), she chose not to swear fealty and became a Master of Arms. This was a grafting of modern attitudes onto her SCA performance. According to Winter, there is an abundance of Masters of Arms in the New England states because "it is part of our cultural heritage to be able to tell the king to go screw himself." Her elevation was certainly in keeping with the fact that the French created several knights the morning before the battle of Agincourt.

At the end of the court a knight entered and recited the prologue from Act IV of *Henry V*:

> Now entertain conjecture of a time
> When creeping murmur and the poring dark
> Fills the wide vessel of the universe.

From camp to camp through the foul womb of night
The hum of either army stilly sounds,
That the fixed sentinels almost receive
The secret whispers of each other's watch[74]

. . . etc., effectively setting the stage for the battles. This performance placed this re-creation within a literary and not a historical frame. The war was not to be the historic battle of Agincourt but Shakespeare's version of it. This framing continued when, before the castle siege battle, a different knight delivered Hal's challenge to Harfleur, and before the Agincourt scenario a third knight (me) delivered the Crispin's Day speech.

The way each of these scenarios worked was typical of the SCA. They simply adapted common SCA scenarios: a boat landing, a castle siege, and an open-field battle. Each scenario was fought twice and each principality got to take turns portraying the French and the English; it was possible for the side playing the French to win any one of them and, in fact, Cynagua won the battle of Agincourt while portraying the French.

This was obviously not a reenactment. It was a tournament that had been framed in reference to a historical event and through a literary filter. Such tournaments were common in the Middle Ages. Keen, Huizinga, Barker and Barber, and others give numerous examples. Consider also that what the SCA fighters at this event were doing was what Shakespeare's version of King Henry promised they would be doing when he said, "and Crispin Crispian shall ne're go by from this day to the ending of the world, but in it we shall be remembered."[75] They were "remembering," not just the historical Agincourt but also Shakespeare's propaganda rendering of Agincourt. They were placing themselves among the mythic versions of historical figures that Shakespeare created. After all, it was not the kings of England and France who were staging this tournament/war, it was Alfred and Cathan, mock princes of imaginary principalities. As I was reciting the list of heroic names in the Crispin's Day speech, "Harry the king, Bedford and Exeter, Warwick and Talbot, Salisbury and Gloucester,"[76] someone added "and Cathan and Alfred," placing these two mock princes in the nostalgic setting of Shakespeare's play. When, after the speech, the fighters all cheered, they were not cheering the performance or Shakespeare's text or the real Henry V, they were cheering themselves, exhorting themselves into the fray. Instead of a reenactment they had created a postmodern participatory performance of *Henry V* in which they were both audience and actor. Thus the war was about not only the battle of Agincourt, but it was also about Shakespeare's play and the popular filmed versions of it with Lawrence Olivier and Kenneth Branagh, and also the audience/actor SCA combatants themselves.[77]

Historic Tourney Models

SCA members do occasionally re-create medieval aristocratic tournament forms within the confines of their stylized version of medieval combat. Attempts

to more accurately represent medieval fighting styles have not been very successful with the overall population of SCA fighters, who tend to prefer their
stylized, modern way of fighting. The one exception to this has been the rising
popularity of *pas d'armes* of the type discussed by Barker and Barber. Based on
Duke René of Anjou's *Livre de Tournoi*, these events take elements of medieval
tournaments and graft them onto SCA combat. There is no pyramid-style list to
advance through. Great efforts are made to construct a wooden list enclosure
and, usually, a barrier. Counted blows are sometimes used instead of the normal
SCA system, so that no one has to fight kneeling. The form is always more or
less the same. A group of knights, called the *tenans*, issue a challenge to all
comers, referred to as *venans*, to meet them at a specific place on a specific day
(often over several days). Many SCA knights have formed tourneying companies after the style of the fourteenth- and fifteenth-century companies and orders
for the purpose of promoting this style of tourney, and they have taken names
like "The Company of St. George" or "The Company of the Swan." Several
shields are hung either from the lists or a nearby tree indicating different types
of combat—weapon choices, group combat, etc. The *tenans* stand in the list as
the *venans* present themselves and strike one of the shields indicating what type
of combat they wish to engage in. Performance elements such as courtesy, lar-
gesse, and poetic challenges are expected from all participants. Sometimes this
is taken to extremes: at Pennsic War XXXIII, a *pas d'armes* was held that was a
re-creation of the Combat of the Thirty (a famous mêlée from 1350). Everyone
who entered was required to have an accurate and fairly elaborate fourteenth-
century harness. One fighter made a brand-new suit of armor for the event and
then paid it as ransom to the fighter who defeated him. Another fighter fought
with a representation of an "iron bar."

The most elaborate of these *pas d'armes* to date in the SCA was held at the
SCA's thirty-year celebration, a ten-day event held in St. Helena, Washington,
in 1996.[78] The *pas d'armes* had been announced by several means, both contemporary and medieval, months beforehand: fliers went out, announcements
were placed in newsletters and on the internet, and heralds cried *banns* throughout the camp. Fighters were asked to appear a few days before, with a herald to
announce them, to register for the lists. On the day of the *pas* the *tenans* waited
in the lists as the *venans* and their entourages were called into the lists in order
of precedence, kings first (there were three kings competing), to issue their challenges.

As the fighters were being paraded into the lists an entourage arrived late,
appearing over a hill. They were more elaborate than any who had yet arrived
because, in addition to heralds, banner bearers, and retainers they also had period musicians playing a processional. The knight at the center of the procession
had taken tufts of tall grass and stuck them about his armor, and had placed a
garland of the grass upon his helmet. In each hand he held a massive club, like
one would see in an Ally Oop comic, about four feet long with knobs all over
them. Around his neck the knight wore a rope woven out of the same grass,
which was used as a lead, the other end of which was held by a barefoot five-

year-old girl, who led him into the lists as his herald cried, "Make way for *le Chevalier Sauvage!*" The knight's herald challenged the *tenans* to send one of their knights out to meet him at the barrier with "the gnarly clubs" and a knight, Tim Bray/Sir Colin deBray, accepted. After Bray won he demanded that the knight reveal himself, and the knight threw off his helmet and proclaimed "I am Vissevald Selkirkson, a duke of the East," to great applause.

This type of scenario is discussed in "Transvestite Knights," wherein Putter writes:

> A knight in disguise creates that fascination around himself by means of a strip-tease that turns his potential rivals for attention into voyeurs. "Who am I?" he asks, and the momentary withholding of the answer serves to fix public attention on the dramatic moment when his identity is unveiled: "It is me!" Behind the disguise stands the principle of deferred gratification, the principle that the sum total of received recognition will be greater the longer recognition is refused. The tournament thrives on disguise. . . . Louise Fradenburg has written suggestively about the function of the incognito in the tournament, relating it to the cult of honor that asks that knights must be seen in order to be, must capture attention and fascination. . . . In Fradenburg's words, "the desire of knight and king, in romance and in tournament, to efface identity, is produced by the desire to prove the incontestability of identity."[79]

In literature the disguise of an incognito knight is never pierced until he himself reveals his identity. Ulrich von Liechtenstein was clear on this point. He insists that even his gender was never discovered during his Venus Quest (which scholars dismiss). I think it likely that knights disguised in tournaments were often recognized. Some people recognized Duke Vissevald in his disguise, but that was not the point. To many of the rest he was unknown. They accepted him as *Le Chevalier Sauvage* until he was defeated and revealed himself. It was a conceit much appreciated by the participants and the spectators, who were happy to go along. Thus his disguise probably worked as well as it would have in an actual medieval tournament. Both the bout and his eventual discovery were highly theatrical, moving the *pas d'armes* even closer toward the type of mimetic event that the later medieval tournament represented. Of course Putter's point is made very clearly by the nature of an SCA tournament. Vissevald's identity is contestable because Vissevald himself is a disguise put on by a twenty-first-century person named Thomas Courtney who only plays a duke on the weekends. His donning of the *Chevalier Sauvage* disguise and his eventual unmasking may have indeed served to reaffirm his fame as a duke and a knight, but that fame and that identity are themselves part of a fantasy. Although the self-making of identity is a very postmodern concept, that concept is rooted in the idea that all identity is fragmented to begin with. Each person has multiple identities and multiple roles he or she plays in life. Duke Vissevald is only one role. He could, after having exposed himself as Duke Vissevald, have exposed himself once again as his mundane self which, though it would not have fit into the game, would have been equally spectacular and even more shocking. In reaffirming his identity by casting off his disguise, Vissevald clearly displayed how fragmentary SCA identity is.

The King's Game

In these and many other ways the SCA plays out its postmodern king game. Vissevald's disguise was unique not only because he was playing a medieval game with a fairly high degree of accuracy, but also because he was a duke, a member of the highest station within the SCA's king game. The fighters at the Pennsic war might still go out and fight anyway because fighting is fun, but their activity is framed by kings who lead them into battle in a romantic tourney setting. And, of course, those fighting for the crown are playing the king game in its purest form. As Goffman points out, "Taken all together, the primary frameworks of a particular social group constitute a central element of its culture."[80] The king game, the SCA's primary activity, the framework within which all SCA activity operates, is the central element of SCA culture. As Forgue once put it,

> We're all here for the Crown. The fighters exist to fight for the Crown and to follow the Crown into battle. The laurels exist to dress the king and queen and to decorate the SCA and provide the stage set on which the crown performs, to feed the king and queen and sing their praises. The pelicans exist to keep the game going so the Crown can do its thing. And all of us together exist so the Crown will have someone to rule."[81]

Not everyone shares this paradigm, but is nonetheless an accurate description of how the SCA's postmodern king game works.

NOTES

[1] Chambers, 143.

[2] Lawrence Clopper, *Drama, Play and Game: English Festive Culture in the Medieval and Early Modern Period* (Chicago: University of Chicago Press, 2001), 122.

[3] Wiles, 8.

[4] Stephen Orgel, *The Illusion of Power* (Berkeley: University of California Press, 1975), 38.

[5] This incident, perhaps because it is so filmic and resonates with modern versions of Robin Hood, particularly the Errol Flynn film, is discussed in many different sources on both the king game and Robin Hood. See Sponsler, 47.

[6] Chambers, 143-144.

[7] John Cox, *The Devil and the Sacred in English Drama, 1350-1642* (Cambridge: Cambridge University Press, 2000), 1.

[8] O. B. Hardison, *Christian Rite and Christian Drama in the Middle Ages* (Baltimore: Johns Hopkins Press, 1965), viii.

[9] Richard Axton, *European Drama of the Early Middle Ages* (Pittsburgh: University of Pittsburgh Press, 1975), 33.

[10] Ibid., 37.

[11] Wiles, 39.

[12] Clopper, 281.

[13] Sandra Billington, *Mock Kings in Medieval Society and Renaissance Drama* (Oxford: Clarendon Press, 1991), 134-35.

[14] Ibid., 80-83.

[15] Barber and Barker, 84.

[16] Billington, 83.

[17] Ibid.

[18] Meg Twycross, ed., *Festive Drama: Papers from the Sixth Colloquium of the International Society for the Study of Medieval Theatre, Lancaster, 13-19 July, 1989* (Cambridge: D. S. Brewer, 1996), 36.

[19] Turner, 25.

[20] O'Donnell, 169.

[21] Erisman, 268.

[22] O'Donnell, 208.

[23] Kingdom of the West, *West Kingdom Coronation Ceremony Scroll—2nd Twelfth Night* in Keyes.

[24] Roy Strong, *Art and Power* (Woodbridge, UK: The Boydell Press, 1984), 6.

[25] Steven Muhlberger, "Practical Chivalry, 1350: Geoffroi De Charny's Questions on War," seminar at *39th International Congress on Medieval Studies* 6 May 2004 Kalamazoo, MI.

[26] Barber and Barker, 192-193.

[27] Maurice Keen, *Chivalry* (New Haven: Yale University Press, 1984), 92-93.

[28] Johan Huizinga, *The Autumn of the Middle Ages*, trans. Rodney J. and Ulrich Mammitzsch Payton (Chicago: University of Chicago Press, 1996), 85.

[29] Strong, 12.

[30] Keyes.

[31] Billington, 59.

[32] "The First Coronation Tournament" in Keyes.

[33] Goffman, *Frame Analysis*, 57-58.

[34] Ibid., 56.

[35] Huizinga, *Homo Ludens*, 89.

[36] Goffman, *Frame Analysis*, 40-41.

[37] Huizinga, *Homo Ludens*, 89.

[38] Keen, 92.

[39] Erisman, 319.

[40] Billington, 59.

[41] Huizinga, *The Autumn of the Middle Ages*, 88.

[42] Putter, 290.

[43] See Billington, 139-141.

[44] Lisa Snook, to author, 13 October 2004.

[45] Susan Sontag, *Notes on Camp* (Partisan Review, 1964, accessed 11 February 2005); available from http://interglacial.com/~sburke/pub/prose/Susan_Sontag_-_Notes_on_Camp.html.

[46] Kim Michasiw, "Camp, Masculinity, Masquerade," *Differences: A Journal of Feminist Cultural Studies* 6, no. 2/3 combined (1994): 151.

[47] Sontag.

[48] Michasiw: 161.

[49] Barber and Barker, 49.

[50] Putter, 280.

[51] Ibid., 295.

[52] Ibid., 286.

[53] Ibid., 288.

[54] See Tobi Beck, *The Armored Rose* (San Jose: Beckenhall Publishers, 1999).

[55] Snook.

[56] Putter, 288.

[57] The Society for Creative Anachronism, *The Society for Creative Anachronism, Inc., Organizational Handbook*, 10.

[58] Erisman, 57.

[59] Clan Bluefeather FAQ (accessed 15 October 2003); available from http://www.bluefeather.org/about.htm .

[60] See Orgel, 9. See also James Saslow, *The Medici Wedding of 1589* (New Haven: Yale University Press, 1996), 148.

[61] Turner, 24.

[62] Ibid.

[63] Ibid.

[64] Ibid., 81.

[65] Sandra Dodd, "Ethnocentricity," *Thinkwell* 1, no. 1. (accessed 13 September, 2003); available from www.sandradodd.com.

[66] Turner, 24.

[67] In some kingdoms this has been expanded to all the peers as an answer to a common complaint that the knights have too many privileges.

[68] Stephen de Loraine, quoted in Keyes.

[69] O'Donnell, 290.

[70] Wiles, 41.

[71] Snook.

[72] Ibid.

[73] Michael Cady and Henrik Olsgaard, *Hastings 2000: Our Experiences at the Battle of Hastings, October 4, 2000.* (Stefan's Florilegium, 2002, accessed 11 February 2005); available from http://www.florilegium.org/files/CELEBRATIONS/Hastings-2000-art.html.

[74] *Henry V*, 4.Chorus.1-7.

[75] Ibid., 4.3.59.

[76] Ibid., 4.3.53-4.

[77] Interestingly, O'Donnell uses *Henry V* to frame his whole book, labeling each chapter with act and scene numbers, and using quotes from the play in several introductions. Apparently, the questions of honor and valor so important to Hal resonate strongly with SCA members.

[78] I took part in this event, and this account is based on my observations.

[79] Putter, 286.

[80] Goffman, *Frame Analysis*, 27.

[81] Forgue, "S.C.A. History."

5

IN THE HALL OF THE WINTER KING

The young man was nineteen and he was beautiful: tall and slender with thick black hair and a handsome face. His one flaw, a slightly crooked smile with one chipped tooth, gave him a playful and rather mischievous appearance. He looked as though he had stepped out of one of Edmund Blair Leighton's Pre-Raphaelite paintings of idealized knights. His armor was a tricolored coat of plates—that is, a leather jacket of three colors with steel plates riveted to the inside. It was the nicest coat of plates anyone could remember seeing. The day was sunny and warm for March. The evening before, the young fighter had attained the final round of the crown tournament, along with two knights just slightly older than he. The three of them had battled in single combat, one striking down the other only to be struck down himself, so that there was no victor and the tournament was stopped on account of the hour. Now, the morning had dawned clear and bright, and before the tournament could be finished the young fighter was called before the king (a funny little man with mutton-chop sideburns who looked like Mr. Pickwick in royal robes and a crown), and knelt before him to receive the accolade of knighthood, the very image of the "parfait gentil knight." He was given the signs of the order—a white belt, a gold chain, and spurs—marking him as a knight, and sent out onto the field to complete the tourney, which he promptly lost (though, as it turned out, Dan Hunter/Duke Radnor of Guildemar would win every tourney he entered subsequently for the next twenty years).

This simple ceremony, though it took place on the field beneath a warm sun and involved a fighter, does not belong to the summer king image from which SCA fighting is descended, but to the realm of the winter king. Billington divides her examination of medieval mock kings into "summer kings" and "winter kings" and this division suits the SCA mock kings as well. Billington indicates that the difference between the two types of game was that the first tradition was based on "competitive king games [summer]" while the second employed "the stately excesses of the winter court."[1] Although SCA fighting is a re-creation of summer king games, SCA court and ceremony are variants of the winter king festivals. These two tropes were sometimes combined in the Middle Ages, and the SCA combines them as well, holding royal courts at fighting events, including crown, but the traditions are nonetheless distinct.

In most kingdoms there is a clear division between the winter and summer reigns, to the point where the kings are often referred to as "winter king" or "summer king" respectively. Nowhere is this division more pronounced than in the East and Middle Kingdoms. Because of their status as the principal combatants at Pennsic, activities in these two kingdoms tend to revolve around the war. A summer king in the East and the Middle is expected to be a warlike king and to lead his troops in battle. A winter king's reign centers on the kingdom's main ceremonial event, Twelfth Night. In addition to Twelfth Night, there will be many more indoor-only events on the calendar during the winter reign, so this reign is more dedicated to the arts and sciences, primarily indoor activities.

Unlike the SCA's unintentional re-creation of the summer king game, there was a conscious attempt among SCA members to re-create a winter king game in the first year of the SCA. Prior to the first SCA Twelfth Night in January AS I/1967 people had begun to discuss having a king, and at that event they informally referred to Olsgaard, who had won the tournament in September, as "King Henrik," but it wasn't until the following March that there was a coronation. They did have a king game, however:

> No one was too sure what to do with a King at the time, but someone (Fulk?) came up with the idea of a Lord of Misrule. They decided to choose the Lord of Misrule by having a little wooden figure put in a square of a cake baked (I believe) by Ellen Hodghead. He (or she) who bit upon the cake became the self-same Lord. I got one of the early pieces. Nothing. I was told later that David Hodghead was the one to bite down on the figure and promptly complained that he didn't want to spend the evening thinking up entertainment for everyone else. Steve Henderson, who was passing the cake around, said "No problem." They put the figure into the biggest piece left and brought it to me. I said I had already tried. They said that everyone had tried and there was still no Lord. I, as Steve knew I would, grabbed the biggest piece and bit down. Unfortunately, the piece was so big that I missed the wooden figure with my first bite. David and Steve were somewhat surprised, but assumed that maybe they had forgotten which piece they put the figure in. I kept chewing and said "Wait a minute," as they were walking away, looking for another sucker.[2]

The Lord of Misrule installed his girlfriend as Lady of Misrule and she presided over various contests such as "moustache measuring." This game has become a tradition that is still played at West Kingdom Twelfth Night.

Chambers identifies this "king of the bean" game (usually a bean, not a wooden figure, is baked into the cake) as a yuletide activity.[3] More to the point, Billington notes, "at Twelfth Night in kings' courts, a *rex fabarum* was selected through the chance portion of cake containing the bean."[4] Scholars agree that mock kings, and the Lord of Misrule in particular, functioned as a symbol of resistance to kingly rule, whether or not the practice of inversion was sanctioned. At this time the SCA was still unsure what to do with the king, and yet they created a game that inverted his authority by setting up an anti-king. One possible reason is that, as seems clear, more was known at the time of the king of the bean/lord of misrule tradition than was known of the revolving summer king tradition, so this was an obvious way to frame the SCA's first winter revel. However, I suspect that the real reason this game was employed, and the reason it was a success, is because inversion and a carnival sense of fun are what the SCA has been about from the very beginning. Selecting a set of mock rulers to lead them through a series of liminal flirting games was an obvious choice for a group of young people who had banded together out of a combined desire for a medieval fantasy world and dissatisfaction with contemporary society. Turner notes, "In a sense, every type of cultural performance, including ritual, ceremony, carnival, theatre, and poetry, is explanation and explication of life itself."[5] The SCA provides a wealth of such material.

SCA Ceremony

Most official SCA ceremonies take place at a formal court, called by the king or the prince to hand out awards and elevate people in status. As with ceremonies of elevation in all cultures, SCA ceremonies affirm the value of the rank attained as well as the value of the person receiving it, and assigns him or her a new place in society. The public nature of the act impresses upon witnesses the importance of the rank, and upon the recipient the solemnity of the occasion. Goffman writes:

> Ceremonials: Social ritual such as marriage ceremonies, funerals, and investitures are examples. Something unlike ordinary activity goes on in them, but what goes on in them is difficult to be sure of. Like scripted productions, a whole mesh of acts are plotted in advance, rehearsal of what is to unfold can occur, and an easy distinction can be drawn between rehearsal and "real" performance. But whereas in stage plays this preformulation allows for a broad simulation of ordinary life, in ceremonials it functions to constrict, allowing one deed, one doing, to be stripped from the usual texture of events and choreographed to fill out a whole occasion. In brief, a play keys life, a ceremony keys an event.[6]

This is the nature of all SCA ceremony. It keys certain events within the SCA cycle (because the SCA is cyclical: they cycle through royalty as they cycle through a year).

SCA ceremonial forms were established at the second Twelfth Night in AS II (January, 1968). At this event the king presided over the SCA's first formal court and created the SCA peerage, originally called the Order of the Laurel. All those made peers because of their fighting were called "Knights of the Laurel," while those made peers for their artistic abilities or service were referred to as "Master" or "Mistress of the Laurel." Originally, not anticipating that there would one day be thousands of members, the king gave specific titles based on the reason each person was elevated, such as "Master Musician to the King." This is also the source of the SCA invention the "Master of Arms," a member of the chivalry who is not required to swear fealty. Another peerage created at the same event was "Duke," for those who had reigned as king twice.

In her article "There Are No Scrolls," Catherine Helm-Clark points out that many of the elements of SCA ceremony that trace their roots to this event are blatantly anachronistic. They were instituted because they "felt right" and because they were highly theatrical. This includes the most ubiquitous prop in SCA ceremony, the scroll (which, she points out, would more accurately be called a writ).[7] The first SCA court was very carefully scripted, with the herald reading everything from a single scroll (which is how the word "scroll" acquired its meaning in the SCA vocabulary). This is also when the standard oath of fealty, written by Heydt and based on Pippin's oath to Denethor, the Steward of Gondor in *The Lord of the Rings*, came into use.[8] From this point on we can analyze the coronation ceremony and the knighting ceremony in several variations, as well as the use of scrolls, heraldry, and pageantry.

SCA ceremonies follow Van Gennep's separation/change/reintegration pattern of a rite of passage, as discussed in Chapter 2. A person called into court for an award enters a sacred space, removed from the rest of society, and will not emerge from that space unchanged. If the award is a small one, such as an award for winning a contest, the person will simply be presented with a token and congratulated. The more prestigious the award the more complex the ceremony.

When a person receives an award in the SCA it is usually accompanied by a decorated writ, in the SCA referred to as a scroll. For instance, in the Award of Arms ceremony, the scroll contains a proclamation saying, in one way or another, "We, King so and so, grant unto this person arms." The scroll is decorated with the arms of the recipient. Usually, these do not resemble historic legal documents but instead take their stylistic cues from books of hours and other illuminated works. Once the scroll has been read the herald will call for three cheers and the new armiger will be given leave to depart, signaling his or her reintegration into society in a changed state. All SCA award ceremonies follow this basic pattern.

Knighthood

The ceremony for knighthood in the SCA is an extremely elaborate rite of passage. The ceremony, with its complex symbols and regalia, was adapted from medieval example, but also from literature. In most kingdoms a candidate for knighthood is told of his or her impending elevation ahead of time so that he or she can make preparations. Often new suits of clothes are sewn for the occasion and new accessories, such as a new banner, might be prepared, all so the new knight can look the part. Like many things in the SCA, knighthood is about appearance, and dressing in fine clothes and armor is considered in the SCA to represent the knightly virtue of franchise.

Huizinga writes, "The ceremony conferring knighthood is an ethically and socially elaborated puberty ritual."[9] This is not quite true in the SCA. People in the SCA are almost never knighted as teenagers. Most SCA knights are made when they are in their twenties and thirties, so SCA knighthood cannot be accurately called a "puberty ritual." However, this ceremony, like those for Orders of the Laurel and the Pelican, does elevate a person to the upper stratum of society by making him or her a peer, and this is demonstrated symbolically in the way that the ceremony is framed as a plea. In the knighting ceremony the knights are called forward and inform the king, "Our numbers are not complete." By structuring it in this way, the act of knighting a person is represented as a plea from the chivalry to the king to recognize the candidate. This places the ultimate authority with the crown but the initiation of the act with the group.

The SCA knighting ceremony takes one of two forms. In the older form, the candidate is either called forward or else a group of knights and/or masters is sent to fetch him or her. The candidate is brought before the king and kneels, and the king says, "We are minded to admit you to the order of chivalry. Will you accept?" Assuming the candidate says yes, he or she will be asked a series of other questions, centering on the ability to conduct oneself as a knight. The Chivalry of the SCA is separated into two branches, knights and masters of arms. During the ceremony the candidate will be asked if he/she is willing to swear fealty. If the answer is yes then the candidate swears an oath of fealty on a sword held by the king, and he/she will become a knight. This basic ceremony, including the fealty oath, was adapted from Tolkien's *The Lord of the Rings*, in which Pippin offers his service to the steward of Gondor and then swears an oath of fealty on a sword held by the steward.[10]

If the candidate chooses not to swear fealty then he/she will become a master of arms, a title that was created at the second Twelfth Night out of tension created by the SCA's secularity and the religious nature of medieval knighthood. As Keen points out, the link between knighthood and religion, as discussed by late medieval writers such as Raymond Lull and Geoffroi de Charny, can be very problematic, and it often obscures the secular origins of medieval knighthood.[11] Lull wrote in *The Book of Knighthood and Chivalry*, "The office of a knight is to maintain and defend the holy Catholic faith."[12] Knighthood in late medieval practice and in Victorian perception was often seen as a religious station. When offered knighthood before the second Twelfth Night, Richard Barnhart/Duke Richard the Short said he would not be able to swear fealty, and so could not become a knight. Barnhart was in seminary and thought it would be improper for him to swear fealty to an earthly power. Furthermore, by officially eschewing religion, the SCA had stripped knighthood of an element Barnhart thought was essential. SCA knights were not Christian enough for him. The king and his advisors decided to create a special rank for Barnhart called "Master of Arms." For all intents and purposes, this is an SCA knight who is not required to swear fealty at his or her elevation. Masters wear slightly different regalia, using a white baldric instead of a white belt. Officially they are a separate order from knighthood, but the two function as one order, and are referred to collectively simply as "the Chivalry." At the same time, Zimmer/Master Edwin Bersark took the opposite position from Barnhart. To Zimmer, who was active in the neo-pagan movement in San Francisco, knighthood was too Christian an institution. When the title Master of Arms was created for Barnhart, Zimmer, who was elevated at the same ceremony, decided that he would take it as well. Therefore, of the first two masters of arms, one took the title because knighthood was too Christian, while the other took the title because knighthood was not Christian enough.

The newer form of the knighting ceremony, primarily used in kingdoms east of the Rockies, breaks the ceremony into two phases separated by a vigil. When a candidate is called forward, he/she is asked not whether or not he/she will become a knight but instead is sent off to vigil so he/she can take counsel from other peers on what his/her answer should be to the questions: Will he/she join the chivalry, and will he/she become a knight or a master of arms. As Turner and Van Gennep point out in their discussion of rites of passage, the candidate is sometimes removed from society for a long period of time for contemplation, purification, etc. The SCA vigil is a clear example of this. Candidates are taken to a specially prepared space. The signs of their new station are laid out before them and the symbolism of each is explained. Knights and sometimes other peers come to the candidate to offer guidance and wisdom. Often, the candidate will take a ritual bath. I have even known candidates to arrange to have their armor blessed and to hear mass as part of the vigil. Once the ceremony is over the candidate is ready to assume a new station, which will be consecrated when he/she receives the accolade and the signs of the order in public. This part of the ceremony is the same as in the older form.

As Katherine Helm-Clark says, "back in our early beginnings, we did a whole bunch of things that were off the mark [historically inaccurate]. We did them because they were good theater."[13] Good examples of this are the gold chain, white belt, and spurs used as regalia for an SCA knight and presented to him or her as part of the knighting ceremony. They were taken primarily from Victorian sources, not medieval ones. There is a medieval source for a white belt being used in the knighting ceremony in the thirteenth-century poem, the *Ordene de chevalerie*. This poem, in which Saladin is knighted by his prisoner Count Hugh of Tiberius, is the most detailed medieval source for a thirteenth-century knighting ceremony. It explains the use of a ritual bath, the vigil, several symbolic items of clothing, and the knight's regalia, including a white belt, signifying a knight's purity and reminding him not to be lustful.[14] However, according to both Hollander and Muhlberger, this poem was not known to early SCA members. The source they cite for the SCA knight's regalia is the Sir Arthur Conan Doyle story *Sir Nigel,* in which the first knight Nigel meets is wearing a white belt and a gold chain (and, presumably, gold spurs). Using this as source material, the SCA knighting ceremony includes the decorating of the new knight with the signs of the order: a white belt to symbolize prowess, a chain to symbolize the bond of fealty, and spurs to symbolize the knight's rank (originally this was not the case. The chain and belt were simply tokens of rank: the belt was to be a knight's mark of station when fighting, the chain was his mark of station when not in armor. It was only later that they came to symbolize prowess and fealty).

Conspicuously marked with the signs of their status, knights are the most visible segment of the SCA society. This performance of status through regalia is appropriate from a medieval standpoint to the extent that knighthood, at least according to Huizinga, was a work of art: "[A]s the ideal of the beautiful life the idea of knighthood has a particular form. In its essence, it is an aesthetic ideal, built out of colorful fantasies and uplifting sentiments."[15] It is worth noting that in a group where the carrying of swords, axes, and other weapons is common and encouraged, knights are rarely seen carrying any edged weapons. They are required to do so in certain ceremonies, but otherwise they rarely go armed.

Their chains and belts are signs not only of their rank but also of their martial abilities, and they have no need to stress their masculinity by wearing a lot of pointy objects. Morril likes to say that the more knives a person carries the less likely he/she is to actually fight.

As Helm-Clark points out, "Historically, knights were not peers. . . . We cannot document nor justify the unification of peerage and knighthood: such a beast did not exist."[16] Knights in the Middle Ages were among the lowest ranks of nobility. They were, at best, aristocratic soldiers. True power rested with the upper levels of nobility. However, as Keen points out, in the early Middle Ages the nobility began to assume the titles of knighthood due to the increasing symbolism associated with the rank.[17] As the arm of military might in the Middle Ages, in their newly constituted role as defenders of the faith, and as the administrators of justice, knights symbolically occupied a station much higher than they actually had. Lull writes that the first knights were made by choosing the best man out of each thousand.[18] In story, song, and legend, up to and including contemporary images from film and television, whether in *Star Wars* or *Excalibur*, knights are at the top of the medieval hierarchy. This is an image most people bring with them to the SCA.

SCA knighthood is clearly based on Victorian popular culture. While SCA members now consult primary sources such as Lull and Charny as inspiration for their performance, the structure of SCA knighthood, the regalia, and the ceremonial forms were all taken from nineteenth- and twentieth-century sources: Tolkien, Kipling, and Conan Doyle. Just as the SCA is a loose collection of ideas about the Middle Ages, SCA knighthood is a loose collection of ideas about knighthood, which can only be demonstrated by performative means. The symbology of the knightly regalia only exists because of the way it is employed in performance of the knighting ceremony. SCA knights dress in highly theatrical garb and code their bodies with the signs of their order, granting them instant recognition and status within the group while at the same time binding them to one another. Knighthood in the SCA is a performance enacted through ritual and careful coding of the body.

The Great Western Purification Ritual

As mentioned above, one element that the vigil might include is a ritual bath. During Ayers's first reign as King of the West this became an important performance element that demonstrates the hybrid nature of the SCA—serious re-creation of medieval modes of thought combined with tongue-in-cheek parody of those same ideas. A squire named John Schmidt/John Theophilus was to be knighted and held a vigil (in the western kingdoms a candidate is not called into court and then sent out to vigil: candidates are usually told of their elevation ahead of time and choose to hold vigil or not on their own). As a queen's guardsman, Schmidt had been given a favor from the queen that would be used in the ceremony. The queen must release a guardsman from her guard before he can be knighted, but always asks the guardsman to keep her favor. But Schmidt had lost the favor. Losing a favor is usually a major social *faux pas,* and losing the queen's favor is worse, but to lose your queen's favor right before your knighting is a major embarrassment.

The site for this event was a campground in the coastal mountains of California, north of the Napa Valley, which had a swimming hole. At dawn (when it was very cold) Schmidt, dressed only in a white shirt and without telling anyone what he was going to do, waded out into icy waters of the swimming hole and scourged himself with his queen's guard baldric. A practicing Catholic, Schmidt viewed this as an act of penance that was coded as medieval. What he did not know was that his act had been witnessed. At court, after knighting Schmidt, Ayers told of how he had gotten up to go to the toilet that morning, had witnessed Schmidt's act of penance, and "was amazed." Ayers, the serious reenactor who is always looking for ways to incorporate medieval attitudes and behavior into the SCA, charged all his knights to join him the next morning for "a mass purification of the chivalry." One of the knights asked if he could bring his squires along and was told "absolutely." So the next day the entire kingdom got up to watch the knights and squires make fools of themselves. The knights and squires gathered in front of the royal pavilion and marched out to the swimming hole with the rest of the kingdom following behind. When they got there, they found three ladies, all peers of the realm, clad in white chemises and drenching wet, standing on the diving platform in the middle of the water. One of them held aloft a rattan fighting sword and proclaimed that their presence proved that not only his majesty's knights but all of his peers could be silly and stupid. Stan Haley/Sir Gerstan Heah Leah marched up with three of his squires, all chanting "We will, we will purify! Purify!" (à la Queen's "We Are the Champions"). They performed a bit of shtick in which Haley tested the water with his toe and proclaimed it too cold. One squire poured a bowl of hot water into the swimming hole and Haley tested it again. This was repeated with a tea cup and a sake cup until Haley proclaimed the water "just right." Then, on the king's count of three, all the knights and squires charged into the water screaming and whipping themselves with their belts. The spectacle was an impressive bit of postmodern theatricality. It combined images from several different sources, from Malory to *Goldilocks and the Three Bears,* and ended up as a parody of a ritual bath. Schmidt's original act of purification had been a serious form of penance for what he considered a grave transgression. By parodying Schmidt's ritual, the other knights ended up mocking Schmidt's original act of penance, turning it into a joke. In this way the master narrative of Christian knighthood and the symbolism of the ritual bath were undermined.

Twelfth Night as Social Occasion

Twelfth Night is the only event that is universal in the SCA. Every kingdom holds crowns and coronations, but they are spread throughout the calendar. Only two kingdoms hold a coronation at Twelfth Night, but in all the SCA kingdoms Twelfth Night is still a crown event—that is, one sponsored by the kingdom rather than a local branch, and one the king is always expected to attend. This is due to the importance the second Twelfth Night has in SCA history as the source of SCA ceremony. Twelfth Night is each kingdom's big annual indoor party. It is the time when people put on their best garb (or make new garb), sit at an extremely long court (often five or six hours long), and feast and revel with the whole kingdom. It is as integral to the SCA as is Crown Tourney. That it is indoors is another link to the winter king. Obviously, winter festive rites were mostly held indoors, but Chambers thinks it important to note the "domestic quality" of the winter festival.[19] Winter festivals take place in the hall, and Twelfth Night, symbolically, is when the people gather in the king's hall in grand style and display their devotion to the game through elaborate ceremony and ostentatious display of consumption, celebrating two of what James Saslow identifies as "the three broad concerns of the wealthy elite in which depth and surface interlock: social rank, titles and protocol; [and] magnificence of display, especially fabrics and fine jewelry."[20] (The third concern, "the physical prowess and competition of the military-chivalric tradition" is, as I've already discussed, on display elsewhere.)

"Arts and sciences" is a nebulous term in the SCA. Originally, it referred to everything in the SCA that didn't involve fighting, those activities that came under the purview of the Order of the Laurel.[21] However, the terms are poorly defined at best. For a long time there has been a tendency among members of the Order of the Laurel to only consider accomplishments in the arts when evaluating prospective new members, and no one was quite sure how to define a "science."[22] Someone who uses medieval instruments to study astronomy, for instance, might get a laurel if he makes his own instruments, but is unlikely to be elevated simply for practicing astronomy. Archery, horseback riding, fencing, and other martial pursuits are even more challenging, since the Chivalry is limited to heavy fighters only. The same division between art and science existed in the Renaissance, and both were represented in winter festivities. Billington notes that George Ferrer's procession as a winter Lord of Misrule in 1552 included "representatives of the sciences and arts."[23]

Twelfth Night in the Middle Ages and Renaissance was also the masquing season. It was the time for wearing extremely elaborate and expensive garb, and this is also the most important activity associated with Twelfth Night in the SCA. Twelfth Night is a fancy dress ball. As early as the previous spring SCA costumers begin planning next year's Twelfth Night outfits. Billington discusses an equally elaborate sartorial display in association with winter king festivals. In the George Ferrer procession mentioned above, Billington says, "His costume was a purple velvet robe, coat and cape, lined with simulated ermine, and also had an elaborate velvet hat or headpiece, and pages carried a shield, sword and ax."[24] The conspicuous costumes of SCA Twelfth Night also recall festival days in Renaissance Venice when, in order to make the city appear more magnificent, the authorities suspended sumptuary laws.[25] It is a time when many people, seeking the most elaborate garb possible, will move out of their personas (assuming they have them), and several Vikings can be seen in Italian or Elizabethan garb. Examples of such extravagance can also be seen in the costumes of Robert Dudley as Winter King at the Inns of Court in the late sixteenth century.

"The Constable Marshal [Dudley] entered in full carnival dress . . . white and gilt harness, many coloured feathers 'upon his crest or Helm, and a gilt Pole-axe in his hand.'"[26] An eyewitness account by Gerard Legh in *The Accedens of Armoire* describing Dudley's Christmas Prince court marvels at the "Arthurian Splendor" of the hall and the dignity of Dudley. "His narrative transforms the Master of the Horse into a second Perseus,"[27] according to Billington. Dudley, a suitor to Elizabeth I, was quite serious about his position as a mock king and used it to stress his worthiness to assume the real crown. For this reason his misrule courts were as spectacular as those of any king.

The splendor and extravagance of this type of winter king imagery is what SCA members strive for at Twelfth Night, especially in their garb. By doing so, they are carrying on a well-documented tradition of splendor, often of gaudiness, that is out of place in contemporary society. In the twenty-first century, this type of extravagance is limited to Las Vegas, Superbowl halftime shows, rock concerts, and traditional Lenten carnivals like those in New Orleans and Rio de Janeiro (all, of course, carnivalesque spaces in their own right).

Awards, Titles and Regalia

Turner sees performances of ritual as "distinct phases in the social process whereby groups become adjusted to internal changes."[28] Official SCA rituals usually mark a passage of some kind: coronation of a king, elevation in rank, etc. However, following Goffman's discussions of serious and unserious activity, they fall under the category of what Turner calls "liminoid" as opposed to liminal activity:

> Liminoid phenomena tend to be more idiosyncratic, quirky, to be generated by specific names, individuals and in particular groups—"schools," circles and coteries. . . . [T]he liminal found in the activities of churches, sects and movements, in the initiation rites of clubs, fraternities, Masonic orders and other secret societies, etc.—is no longer world wide. Nor are the liminoid phenomena which tend to be the leisure genres of art, sport, pastimes, games, etc.[29]

The SCA has created a complex system of signification for its members to employ. Station in the SCA is clearly defined, not necessarily by the consumption of valuable goods but by coding of the body through the wearing of regalia. A new member of the SCA may be able to afford an expensive suit of Tudor garb, and this will bring him or her some recognition and status, but a duke wearing a broadcloth tunic and a very plain coronet marked with strawberry leaves will rank far above the person in the extravagant outfit and will receive deference from other members of the group not afforded to the newcomer. SCA regalia signifies instantly to what stratum of the society that person belongs.

At the Twelfth Night in January 1968 the awards structure of SCA was formally established. Dukes were men who had won Crown twice. Knights and masters of arms were made specifically because they were good fighters. The Order of the Laurel was essentially for everyone else. Each order was given its own regalia. Knights were given a gold chain (usually in those days a lamp chain from a local hardware store) and a white belt. Masters of arms got a white baldric. Members of Order of the Laurel were given a medallion with a laurel wreath upon it.

There were no duchesses at the time. The Order of the Rose, a patent order equal to that of knight, was created about this time because there was no royal peerage title available to ex-queens and women were not allowed to fight.[30] It has long been redundant, because during Early's second reign in the West Kingdom he created the titles "count" and "countess" for men and women who had reigned as king and queen once, making the Order of the Rose superfluous. The third peerage, the Order of the Pelican, was created by the SCA Board of Directors in 1972 to reward those who had served the SCA corporation as opposed to a particular kingdom. This created a conflict with the existing kingdoms and, after awarding three pelicans, the board gave the peerage over to the crowns. A separate title, "Court Baron," was created because a king of the West wanted to give something special to his father who was not actually an SCA member. The other title universal to the SCA is the Grant of Arms. This ranks between the Award of Arms and a peerage, and was created for a specific purpose: to reward a kingdom officer who was stepping down from her office but who was not deemed to be ready for membership in the Order of the Pelican. Initially, the grant was only given to retiring kingdom officers. However, it soon became a kind of "junior-peerage," and was attached to all sorts of awards for activities as diverse as horseback riding and fencing.

This plethora of titles has led to the SCA's merit-badge-style award system. Kingdoms quickly began creating awards for specific activities, such as cooking or archery, and attaching the SCA-wide awards to them. In some kingdoms an archer (for example) can progress from a simple archery award to one that carries an award of arms to one that carries a grant of arms, and finally to a laurel for achievements in archery. It is a completely modern hierarchy of achievement and has no medieval precedent. A person can collect all the awards, and people who have the three awarded peerages—knight, laurel, and pelican—are referred to as "triple peers."

The SCA continued its tradition of giving each order of peerage its own regalia, most of which was not based on medieval precedent. Duchesses as well as dukes are allowed to wear coronets of strawberry leaves. Counts and countesses wear embattled coronets. Viscounts and viscountesses, created to honor those who have reigned as prince and princess of a principality, are allowed simply a "little crown." These design elements are taken not from a medieval source but from Sir Arthur Charles Fox-Davies' *Complete Guide to Heraldry.* Fox-Davies did not mean these coronets to represent those actually worn by peers in the Middle Ages. Rather, they are used in crests by the English College of Arms when painting achievements of arms. Nonetheless they are used in the SCA as though they were medieval symbols of authority.

Marks of association are extremely important in a society based on feudal relationships, and so the regalia for the peerage orders was adapted for personal use. Squires, as vassals of knights, are usually given belts of red, and in some kingdoms wear silver chains and spurs. Not to be outdone, pelicans and laurels began to take on vassals of their own, called "protégés" and "apprentices," who are given yellow and green belts respectively. Often, the device of the peer to whom one is in fealty will be painted on the tip of the belt. More traditional forms of livery taken from the Middle Ages, such as tabards and badges, are used but with far less frequency.

While the signifiers used in the SCA are modern, they perform a medieval function. SCA members are usually very conscious of rank, and the SCA is very hierarchical. If a person's rank is unknown he or she is addressed as "my lord" or "my lady," but other ranks have specific forms of address: "Master," "Mistress," or "Sir" for the peerage orders, "Your Grace" for dukes and duchesses, "Your Excellency" for barons, counts, and viscounts, "Your Highness" for princes and princesses, "Your Majesty" for the king and queen, "Your Lordship" for holders of a grant of arms, and "my lord" for everyone else. Some people take rank seriously. However, some SCA members often approach rank from a modern mindset and refuse to use titles and rank unless in a formal situation such as being called into court. They look on rank as a conceit that some people take too seriously and they make it a point to resist it. Helm-Clark often complained about what she called "The Western pretentious unpretentiousness," referring to some subjects of the Kingdom of the West and their habit of eschewing persona and rank. Having come from an SCA kingdom that celebrated rank and reveled in pomp and circumstance, she was often bothered that some peers chose to underplay rank. Peers in this group often introduce themselves by nicknames and insist that their titles not be used. They frequently do not wear the signs of their rank or else do so subtly. One Western peer wears a pendant earring as his pelican medallion. One woman wears her laurel as a leather hair tie. That doesn't make it any less of a performance—underplaying is merely a performance choice. But it is a direct challenge to the concept of the SCA as living history. By foregrounding their modern selves as part of their SCA performance, these peers are making the political statement that the SCA is not about the Middle Ages but instead is specifically rooted in the now. This, as Eco would point out, is using the Middle Ages in his first variation, as pretext. In the Middle Ages as pretext, "There is no real interest in the historical background; the Middle Ages are taken as a sort of mythological stage on which to place contemporary characters."[31]

The forms of address occasionally cause some problems among SCA members, particularly among the three peerages. Many members of the Orders of the Laurel and Pelican feel that the Chivalry have a title and regalia that place them above the other two orders, even though they are supposed to be equal (as Early used to say, "Nobody ever told stories about King Arthur and his Pelicans of the Round Table."). Furthermore, some female members of those orders object to the use of the title "Mistress."[32] To alleviate this, Mistresses of the Laurel and the Pelican are now allowed to use the title "dame" (although some people would consider that title to be equally demeaning).

This echoes a late medieval reality. Huizinga notes that conflicts over rank between nobles and nonnobles was an important point of debate in the late Middle Ages, revolving around how to reconcile the rising powers of the bourgeoisie with the medieval tradition of the three estates. According to Huizinga, one way in which this conflict was negotiated was in the elevation of scholarship, a realm dominated by the burghers, to the same level as martial prowess. Scholarship was equated with knighthood in the late Middle Ages, and the doctoral degree was often accorded the same privileges as knighthood.[33] This was especially true, and especially important, with the awarding of the Juris Doctor, or law degree, up to the point where lawyers began to take on the appellation "Esquire," (a title occasionally used by squires in the SCA). In the SCA this is not often discussed, but a similar situation occurs nonetheless. The Order of the Laurel was established as the peerage for nonfighters, those who had no means of attaining royal rank or knighthood. Although it is often looked on as an order for artists, the Laurel always involves an element of scholarship, and some members of the Laurel don doctor's robes as part of their laurelling ceremony. In Ranaissance Engand most of the activites that are considered "service" in the SCA would be performed by members of the Inns of Court—that is, lawyers. In this context it is not too far off to consider the elevation of artists and servants of the crown to the peerage as born out of that same tension discussed by Huizinga. They are, essentially, bourgeois activities, which nonethess in the SCA demand status as edqual to that of knighthood. This is another way in which the SCA echoes medieval and Renaissance practice.

The Performance of Mock Kingship

The Society Seneschal, who is the chief administrative officer of the SCA, sends a letter to all victors of crown tourneys advising them to do basically nothing and reminding them that they have no real authority. For many years she admonished royalty to "Think of yourselves as the lead characters in a play." (many incoming royalty find this particularly offensive). The Board has a clear understanding of the idea of kingship as a performance within the SCA context. However, the seneschal's metaphor can be turned on its head when one recalls Elizabeth I's statement that princes must be players always. She understood that as a Renaissance monarch she was putting on a show for her populace, just as SCA monarchs do. Her performance was part of her power.

The role of a monarch is highly theatrical, and this was true of monarchs from Charlemagne to Elizabeth I and beyond. A monarch is the lead actor in a drama, one in which his or her performance can strike fear into enemies and inspire subjects. If a Renaissance monarch failed to meet expectations, or went too far in the performance, it could cost a monarch a crown and even the head it sat upon. Medieval and Renaissance monarchs used performance as an instrument of policy. Kingly performance is always political. The Society Seneschal's letter was meant as a warning to SCA monarchs that they have no real power, they are merely "actors in a play," but in fact they *do* have power and that power stems from the very fact that they are actors in a play. They have power to inspire the populace (even to the point of defying the Society Seneschal and the Board of Directors) stemming from the performative nature of mock kingship. Part of the SCA is, as I have argued throughout, based on a carnivalesque game in which a mock king is set up as a kind of antiauthoritarian figure, and in the SCA, attempts by a higher authority like the Board of Directors to impress its will upon the group are often met with open defiance. SCA monarchs do not have the power of life or death over anyone, so they strike only minimal fear in their subjects or rivals, but they do have a bully pulpit. A popular SCA king will field more troops at a war, throw bigger and better parties, and even have some leverage with the Board of Directors. If the populace as a whole refuses to follow the Board there isn't much the Board can do about it. The same is true of the crown, but the crown has the advantage of familiarity and also the desire of the populace to live out a romantic fantasy, which often includes an Arthur-like true and just king, and not a Twenty-first century corporate entity.

The effect of the SCA's institutionalized ceremony and ritual, although not nearly so elaborate as its medieval predecessors, is still much the same. It does more than simply build community. SCA ceremony, within the game of the SCA, exalts certain people and creates an almost cult-like atmosphere around the monarchs, which may be serious or tongue-in-cheek depending on who is playing the role. In *The Medici Wedding of 1589* James Saslow writes of the Medici:

> [T]he rigid and formal court etiquette adopted by Cosimo I under the influence of his Spanish wife, Eleonara of Toledo, with its niceties of hierarchical ranking and respectful rituals, was continued by Ferdinando as a way to sacralize the monarchy and the persons of the ruling family by surrounding them with an aura of mystery and pomp. Elaborate public and courtly spectacles, from the wedding to similar festivities for baptisms, deaths and military victories, were an integral part of this social integration.[34]

As mentioned earlier, the SCA social structure, when looked on as a "court," most closely resembles a late medieval or Renaissance court such as the Florentine aristocracy under the Medici. Although no one in the SCA has the resources to create the types of spectacle used in the 1589 wedding and coronation, that type of grandiose display of pomp and circumstance is what most SCA members imagine going on around them as the crown prince marches up the aisle to be crowned king.

As Saslow points out, "since Machiavelli, Italian political theorists had held that the prince's essential art is 'looking the part'—that is, playing the public role of statecraft with conviction and splendor."[35] The SCA, a game of mock kings wherein there is no real political power, no life-or-death wars to fight, and where what governing there is takes place only in the context of a game, is therefore a space where monarchy is all about show. Most SCA kings echo Elizabeth's opinion that acting the part is what's important, and some of them recognize monarchy as a type of performance piece. Duchess Natayla de Foix could be echoing Machiavelli when she writes, "More then (sic) the duties the monarchs must fulfill, they are the stars of the play, actors from whom all others must take their cues throughout the reign. . . . It is improvisational theatre at its most challenging[.]"[36]

The SCA court structure is made up of a small group of people, all of them supposedly representing the nobility, who interact with one another through their interaction with the crown. Forgue's dictum that the fighters exist to protect the crown, the laurels to dress the crown and the pelicans to keep things running, is very revealing when examined in the context of a Burgundian or Florentine court. These late-medieval and early-modern courts were very similarly organized. Medici Florence had an elaborate civil service that planned, organized, and recorded every detail of court life (pelicans). They also had to deal with a warrior-based aristocracy that not only fought the Medicis' wars for them but also carried out diplomacy and were integral to Florentine ritual and ceremony (knights). And, of course, Florence had an artistic community, the main function of which was to glorify and entertain the nobility (laurels). The same conditions existed in Tudor England, Maximilian Germany, and, in the fifteenth century, ducal Burgundy. In other words, as confirmed in Castiglione's *The Courtier,* end purpose of every activity is to serve, support and glorify the Prince and his court. Forgue's dictum, which is not appreciated by many members of the Laurel of the Pelican, turns out to be true in period.

Saslow notes that a fundamental quality of theatre is as a space of controlled artifice,[37] and that the world was seen in the Middle Ages as a *theatrum mundi* in which the prince was the lead actor. The SCA creates its own, small world (or knowne world) in which SCA princes play this same role. As Saslow points out: "[T]he audience for all these events were also performing a large-scale social ritual costumed and staged throughout the capital city over several weeks: they were cast as actors themselves, as well as viewers."[38] This condition, central to Florentine society, is also central to the SCA. As in Renaissance Florence, everyone at an SCA event is both performer and audience member and, as with a Renaissance court, their performance revolves around the king or prince who is the lead actor in the show. SCA monarchs occupy a space that every SCA member has created, a space in which they are able to perform a ceremonial role that provides SCA members with a desired figurehead, a "true and just king" who can protect them from the evils and inconsistencies of the mundane world, at least within the context of this game. As did Renaissance monarchs, SCA monarchs provide a focal point for SCA members' pride and group identity. When an SCA king appears at an event, be it a crown event or one sponsored by a local SCA chapter, he immediately becomes the center of attention and reframes the event with his presence.

According to Roy Strong, the Elizabethan progress was developed as "an elaborate ritual and ceremonial with which to frame and present the Queen to her subjects as the sacred virgin whose reign was ushering in a new golden age of peace and plenty."[39] Progresses were designed to focus loyalty and enthusiasm on the monarch while allowing the monarch to perform a ritual taking-over of the land by occupying it for a time, reaffirming her authority. In many SCA kingdoms, when the king attends an event it is referred to as a "royal progress event." Such events are considered to be part of the king's imaginary procession through his kingdom by which he takes possession of his lands, impresses his rule upon the people, and inspires them by his presence, mockingly echoing the agenda of Elizabeth I. In practical terms a progress allows the king to hold court in many parts of his kingdom and give out awards and recognition, his main ceremonial function, to members of his populace who would not otherwise be in his presence to receive them, because they couldn't make the drive to crown or coronation or the war.

Performance is the central element of SCA monarchy. Elaborate clothing and complex ritual, elements of the winter king game, are used in the SCA as the basis for a monarchy that fulfills the desires and fantasies of the SCA's members. Nowhere is this more clear than in the coronation ceremony.

Coronation

The most elaborate SCA performances are those surrounding the coronation. Since royalty changes regularly in the SCA, an SCA coronation involves not only the installation of a new monarch but also the culmination of the previous reign. It is necessary for the departing royalty to bring their reign to a close, giving thanks and recognition to those who have helped them, releasing their queen's guard, and saying goodbye as king and queen. All outgoing royalty perform these rituals. Household members and retainers are released and the queen usually gives out tokens to those who have served her. Once these rituals are complete the actual coronation can begin.

SCA coronations are a microcosm of the grand pageants that accompanied state occasions in the fifteenth and sixteenth centuries. Coronation always begins with a procession in which the crown prince enters the king's hall accompanied by his guard and retainers. A herald or spokesman usually announces the arrival of the prince. Either the herald or the prince will announce the prince's intentions to claim the thrones. Usually, the outgoing king invites the new king to approach and the crown prince and princess, sometimes together and sometimes separately, kneel before the thrones, where they swear fealty to the kingdom, and are crowned (in some kingdoms the outgoing king is not always part of the coronation ceremony itself). After this the ceremony differs greatly from kingdom to kingdom. Sometimes the herald, marshal, and seneschal each come forward to affirm the crown's succession. In some kingdoms the retainers simply change places and the ceremony is over. In others an elaborate progression of peers takes place as the various orders of peerage come forward to swear fealty.

The original SCA coronation ceremony was very simple. The scroll of the coronation ceremony at the second Twelfth Night states simply that the herald cried, "Let the Grand March begin." The stage directions follow:

> The musicians shall play, and all shall present themselves to the king and queen. The last to present themselves shall be the New King, William the Si-

lent, and his Queen, who will stand before the throne. There will be silence. King Henrik will step down and place the Crown on William's head. The queen will stand and give her crown to King William, who will place it on his Queen's head. Henrik and his lady will bow and back away, King William and his queen will mount their thrones, and there will be a fanfares, shouts, etc.[40]

No oaths of fealty were involved, no announcements, no speaking at all.

Women were conspicuously silent. Although the king and the knights have lines later in the ceremony, exchanging oaths of fealty, the queen says nothing. Both of the kings are mentioned in the scroll by name but their queens are not. Although just a few months earlier the Queen of Love and Beauty had been the reason behind the SCA's king game, at this, the original coronation ceremony, the queens existed only as ornaments. They had no franchise. Duchesses came much later, and the only mention of their possible presence is that the consorts of the first three dukes were invited to stand with them behind the throne. The ceremony scroll also assumes that all members of the Order of the Laurel will be men, as the only titles listed for the order are Master or My Lord. There is no Mistress of the Laurel yet. Even the queen is silent (However, some sources say that the Order of the Rose was created at this event by Queen Sheryl of Thespis.[41] It is possible that the existing scroll for the ceremony from that event it incomplete).

This lack of franchise for the queen is much like the situation in the ceremonies surrounding Ferdinando de Medici's wedding to Christine of Loraine, in which, as Saslow notes, women are part of the spectacle, merely ornaments to be admired and possessed by the men.[42] Saslow says of Christine's coronation, which accompanied the 1589 state entry:

> Fifteen bishops blessed her richly worked crown; the Archbishop of Pisa, Carlo Antonio Puteo, handed it to Ferdinando, who placed it on the head of his kneeling bride. As a consort, Christine received her crown from her husband, not, as he had, from higher clerical and secular authority; her status and prerogatives were henceforth dependent on him.[43]

This (minus the blessing by the bishops) is the same way queens are crowned in the SCA. In the SCA it is considered important for a queen to be crowned by the hand of her king since his entire purpose (supposedly) for winning the tournament was to elevate and glorify her. The crowning (literally) symbol of his achievement is his placing the crown on her head. However, the nature of the ceremony creates the same sort of relationship between consort and monarch that Saslow notes existed in sixteenth-century Florence: the queen only has status through her association with a powerful man, the king. Her crown is not her right; it is his right to bestow it upon her.

Although the span of time that the SCA covers makes verisimilitude a difficult goal, the royal court is one place wherein a specific culture and time period can be performed. Court rituals, especially coronations, gives a large group of people the opportunity to take "center stage" and portray a single time period and culture. In the early SCA a king and queen's court—that is, their retainers and servants—was made up of their friends and members of their household, and was a rather amorphous group. It operated simply as a loose collection of supporters who stood behind the thrones, fed the royalty, and passed things back and forth between them. It was separate from the heralds, who were part of an official body within the SCA, and from the Queen's Guard. As time went by the performative nature of the court began to be realized, and courts became, like some households, one of the few places in the SCA where a group of people could present a cohesive performance of a particular time period or culture. Usually this is based on the time period the royalty normally portrays.

It is in the coronation ceremony that this quest for verisimilitude is taken to its greatest lengths. Most of the time, and in most kingdoms, the coronation takes place as a part of the game and without any attempt to disguise its ludic nature. Only rarely is an effort is made to find a plausible explanation as to why one king is handing over his crown to another. But in some kingdoms there is a tradition that the outgoing monarchs do not attend their successors' coronation ceremony. In this case a bit of theatre is usually devised to mark the division between reigns. The king has been poisoned, assassinated, killed in battle, entered a monastery, and just plain "died."

This need to explain why the king and queen are giving up their thrones is a problem that can occasionally link the ideologies of the romantic and the reenactment versions of the SCA. Among the most theatrical solutions to this problem, enacted not only in the coronation but throughout the whole reign, was the one adopted by Scott Farrell/Sir Guillaume de la Belgique. Farrell reigned twice over the Kingdom of CAID, the same kingdom the members of the Red Company came from, and like them he had a keen sense of the theatrical. He and his queen, whose name was Felinah Tifarah Arvella Memo Hazara Khan-ad-Din, wanted their two reigns to be seen as "six months of 'interactive theatre.'"[44] To accomplish this Farrell used small dramatic vignettes to add a narrative to their coronations and their abdications (often called in the SCA "decoronation" or, more commonly, "stepping down"). Since Farrell's persona is that of a Norman knight during the Conquest, and since his name was indeed Guillaume, he framed his first coronation as a Shakespearean-style history play written about the Norman Conquest, complete with some court intrigue, a chorus, and the former king, Edric, appearing as a ghost to crown his successor. The whole of his six-month reign was framed by the Norman Conquest, to the point that he carried a "Domesday Book" around to events with him so his subjects could record their "assets." His second reign was even more complex. The theme was inspired by Felinah's persona, a fourteenth-century Spanish Moor. The reign was conceived as a historical novel, full of family and court intrigue, in which Felinah was to play a Moorish warrior princess and Guillaume a Christian prince who wed one another in order to end an imagined conflict between the Moors and Christians of CAID. (Interestingly, in an email exchange I had with him, Farrell said that he had no intention of referencing the *Chanson de Guillaume,* or the rest of the cycle dedicated to Guillaume d'Orange, which contains a number of similar elements, including battles against the Saracens and Guillaume's marriage to a Saracen princess, with which Farrell had only a passing familiarity at the time).

Once again Farrell wrote a play to frame their coronation, but this time he created a villainous anti-king, a *Richard III*-like hunchback named Syrivald, who was twin brother to the king. Of course, Farrell played both roles. Syrivald was actually introduced at an event weeks before the coronation as a plotting usurper, and his story line was carried throughout the reign, as various intrigues were launched by Syrivald and then put down while his twin brother was "away" somewhere fighting various wars. For their stepping down this time Farrell created a Corneille-like neoclassical tragedy that played out in several scenes between the business of their final court. Syrivald, finally given a chance to lead an army, redeems himself by rescuing the crown prince in a battle against marauding Atenveldters (thus setting the stage for that year's Estrella War), but while seeking to hunt down the Atenveldters the king is slain. Appropriately, all this action happens off stage and is related by various messengers.

This was a complex example of using theatricality to help frame SCA performance. In these two reigns Farrell went beyond the normal SCA-as-counterculture paradigm and created pieces of mimetic theatre. However, they were clearly not reenactments. Framed by Shakespearean and neoclassical tragedy, with invented casts of characters and carefully constructed plot lines, these two reigns were fictionalized in a way that SCA reigns are not supposed to be. If we analyze these reigns from a performance studies perspective, we see the dichotomy between theatricality and performance come up again. As I argued earlier, this dichotomy need not be employed when analyzing the SCA. However, these were not typical SCA performances. These performances represented the type of falseness that comes from a script in which people play characters as opposed to a ritual in which they represent idealized versions of themselves. While the same thing was done at the Mists/Cynagua war discussed earlier, that could be seen as an elaborate tourney with historical references, as was common in the fifteenth and sixteenth centuries. In the cases of Farrell's two coronations, framing ceremonies with a fictional dramatic text made their reigns, in a sense, less real.

The addition of a villain is also subversive. Because of Syrivald's intrigues, Farrell's second reign was much more like the mocking renaissance faire model. Someone is always trying to overthrow the monarch at renaissance faires, whether it is scheming Spanish spies or a scheming Mary, Queen of Scots. Acting in this way, Syrivald represented a different type of historical reference from that commonly seen in the SCA, especially at court. In the introduction I discussed Rodwell's argument that in pursuit of a romantic ideal the SCA eschews irony because irony would undermine the so-called dream. This example demonstrates that Rodwell is both right and wrong. Syrivald was ironic and was embraced by the kingdom as a creative and entertaining innovation, but he clearly undermined any sort of romantic paradigm. In attempting to achieve verisimilitude by turning their reign into a play, Farrell and his wife ended up subverting the SCA.

The Coronation of Thorvald and Svava

Coronations are a bit like weddings. A couple plans for months to walk up an aisle and take part in a ceremony that will link them to one another and to a larger group. Both parties will have their supporters, usually of the same gender, who will march in with them. Preparations for a coronation are similarly elaborate. The ceremony must be adapted to suit the people involved while retaining its basic function. Sumptuous clothes will be constructed, and the retainers, like bridesmaids and groomsmen, will have some form of matching garb. Rarely is it as uniform as in a wedding, with bridesmaids all in the same dress and groomsmen in matching tuxedos, but their clothing will often be color-coordinated, or perhaps they will all be dressed heraldically, wearing tunics in their personal colors or displaying their arms.

The coronation of Chris Butler and Lisa Snook/Thorvald (Thorson) Halvorsen and Svava Thorgiersdottir, which took place on October 2, 2004, is typical. Preparations for this event began five months in advance, when Butler won the crown tournament. Two sets of garb were created for both Snook and Butler, one set for their coronation and another for their first court and the royal feast. Snook's coronation overdress alone took eighty hours of work. Butler's was trimmed with an elaborately hand-couched interlace trim. The fabric for the garb they wore that evening had been dyed by hand. According to Snook, as many as twenty people were involved in the construction of these outfits.[45] As noted above, Snook is an actress and director, so when she became queen she took full advantage of the dramatic opportunities provided by the coronation ceremony. Like Farrell, she approached the ceremony as a play and wrote a script that covered all the day's activities, and she included an explanation as to why the king and queen were abdicating. However, she did not create the type of dramatic framing device Farrell had created for his coronation, and so Butler and Snook's coronation was more in keeping with SCA traditions of ludic ceremony.

Snook presented herself and Butler as Viking rulers come to take over the kingdom (a common theme for royalty with Viking persona). The site lent itself to this well. It was an outdoor coronation (unusual for the East Kingdom), which took place at a lakeside Boy Scout camp in Massachusetts. The camp had a natural amphitheatre near the lake used for scouting ceremonies. Wooden benches were set on the hillside, at the base of which was a flat, semicircular space in which stood two "totems" that had plaques nailed to them representing merit badges. In other words, there was already a permanent ritual space available, which simply needed to be recoded for SCA use. This recoding was accomplished by hanging the royal banners from the totems, covering up the medallions.

The ceremony began when an ambassador for the crown prince and princess came into court and announced that their highnesses had arrived "for the annual negotiation of the *danegeld*." A horn was then blown, which was answered by a second, then a third, and finally by a fourth, blown by the prince, who was stationed a few hundred yards away up a dirt road. The coronation procession then marched into the amphitheatre. The procession was lead by eleven spearmen, followed by a choir singing an original song written in praise of Thorvald and Svava. Next walked the prince followed by three knights and a master of arms carrying the princess on a shield. Bringing up the rear were various retainers. Everyone in the procession was garbed as a Viking.

As they reached the thrones the princess was set down; then the spearmen formed a semicircle around the king and queen and pointed their spears at them threateningly. Next the prince said that instead of collecting the *danegeld* they intended to make the kingdom a *Danelaw*. In keeping with the image she projected as a warrior princess/queen, Snook wrote an active role for herself in the ceremony, and she had some of the most martial lines:

Svava - We have already acquired the word bond of our Northern Yarls, Earls and Hearsers. Our long ships are on your shore and we have detained one of your mighty southern households by marrying them off. We offer you this peaceful return to your ancestral lands to rule in our name, enforce our law and collect our taxes.

Thorson - Accept it not and your fields will be salted, your artisans maimed, and your musicians muted. In spring all you will have to look forward too is our banners cresting your hills and our longships on your shores.[46]

The king took the crown off and asked, "Do you intend to kneel and receive this or will you take it from me?" Butler said he would kneel "to the kingdom." He then knelt, swore fealty, and was crowned. Next he crowned Snook, who remained standing. They gave the former king and queen into the keeping of their spearmen for "safe passage." The new king and queen then took fealty from their great officers of state and the landed barons.

After this they sat in state in the royal pavilion and watched the day's fighting, which was an ongoing melee in which each fighter, when he had been killed, had simply to exit the field and then reenter as if resurrected. Members of the populace lined up to give them gifts and tributes and to swear fealty. The king and queen then changed clothes and formed up with their retainers to process back into the amphitheatre for their first court. Before this procession the woman who had acted as their ambassador, acting this time as a chorus, recited a long Viking-style poem extolling their virtues. As she finished, the royalty processed back into the amphitheatre. They wore royal mantles and the king held a live red-tail hawk on his wrist.

During this court the queen named her guard and then she and the king handed out some awards. The now former king and queen were made count and countess, and the ex-queen was made a Lady of the Rose. They finished court by creating a new member of the Order of the Pelican. Once this was over it was time for the feast, which was held in the Boy Scout dining hall, and included toasts, songs, more Viking poetry, and a lot of food, with the royalty sitting at the high table wearing their crowns. Naturally, all performances were directed to them.

Not just the coronation ceremony but the whole day, from outgoing royalty's last court through the feast, was a choreographed piece of theatre that revolved around Butler and Snook. Like Ferdinando and Christine in 1589, they moved through a carefully controlled and coded space, taking possession of their territories and acting out symbolically their ascension before a group of spectators who, because of their presence, were also participants, actors in the theatre of the mock king's rule. This event, employing imagery from Viking sagas, medieval spectacle, Victorian romance, and Hollywood costume dramas, created a piece of theatre in which the desires of the SCA community were acted out with Butler and Snook serving as surrogates for that desire and as objects of affection. As figureheads, the king and queen represent a perfection of the so-called "dream." Those watching the coronation ceremony are by their presence taking part in it and validating the reign.

As Erisman points out, the awards ceremonies fulfill a desire for community by acknowledging and rewarding the contributions of various members, thereby accepting them into the group.[47] But the ceremonies also allow members to focus their escapist desires onto a single act, an act of submission to an absolute authority who, ideally, can be trusted to act with the interests of the kingdom and populace at heart. This act of submission, an important part of the myth of kingship, is crucial to the SCA. If the SCA represents a rejection of modern institutions, then one of those institutions being spurned is democracy. There is no voting for the office of king. There is no campaigning. There is no need to make promises. The king proves his worth by besting his opponents on the field of combat and that is all. It is a fairly pure form of "might makes right." This is also an impulse found, as to be expected, in Tolkien. In *The Hobbit*, the men of Lake Town throw out their mayor, a duplicitous politician, and install Bard, a hero who had just defeated a dragon, as their king. They will have no more elected politicians because they believe a hero—a king—can better protect them.

Although some in the SCA find this objectionable, nonetheless it is an interesting variant on the king game. It is a great relief to have somebody else worry about your problems, and the SCA has resurrected the medieval idea of the king as surrogate as part of their game. When the king has the right to make all the decisions no one else is really responsible for them, but at the same time everybody has to live with whatever the king decides. The SCA, founded in the midst of the Free Speech Movement and the Vietnam war, represented a desire among its members for a system of government they could trust to be just and fair, but also one that was more transparent and less complicated than contemporary American democracy. A mock king, who is the physical embodiment of all his people, a benevolent father figure acting only in his children's best interest, fits that bill.

Theatrics in the SCA

Performance in the spectacle sense—court ceremony, procession, combat, etc.—is integral to how the mock kings of the SCA perform their roles, just as it was integral to the performance of kingship in the Middle Ages. It is somewhat surprising, then, that the theatricals of the Renaissance and medieval courts— plays, masques, dance and music—are nowhere near as important in the SCA as they were historically. As Stephen Orgel writes in *The Illusion of Power,* "Dramas at court were not entertainments in the simple and dismissive sense we usually apply to the term. They were expressions of the age's most profound assumptions about the monarchy."[48] Orgel argues that theatre was a tool of policy, in which a play had, in a sense, two audiences: the king watching the play and the court watching the king watch the play. Dance and music were also an important part of court life, not only for entertainment but also as activities through which to present allegories of royal power. Theatricality permeated court life in the Middle Ages and Renaissance. Only on occasion does SCA royalty approach the full potential of the performative nature of their court by centering their court activities on truly theatrical spectacle, in the way that Farrell did. Rarely is this theatricality taken beyond the coronation itself into the types of court theatrics that would have been found in the late medieval and early modern periods, where theatrical display, dancing, music, and spectacle were tools in the monarch's performance of power.

Many people in the SCA don't recognize that dressing up in medieval clothes and going to SCA events is performative because it seems so normal to them. Most of them have trouble even admitting that it is theatrical, since theatrics involve artifice. However, there are times when their medieval selves stage performances within their SCA performances, which represent a type of double coding that often is much closer to the "real" Middle Ages than anything else the SCA does. Up until now, with the exceptions of Farrell's coronation plays, this book has discussed those types of performance that do not fall into the realm of what is normally called theatre—interpersonal performance, ritual, combat, ceremony—though all of these are part of the *theatrum mundi* of the SCA. However, the SCA is also an excellent laboratory for experimentation in medieval and Renaissance drama. Storytelling, singing, instrumental musical performance, and dance are common. On a larger scale, masques, plays, and even processional theatre are all part of the SCA fabric.

It is worth noting the importance of procession in the SCA because it was such an important form of theatrical expression in the Middle Ages. As Kathleen Ashley observes in *Moving Subjects: Processional Performance in the Middle Ages and Renaissance,* "Procession was, very simply, the privileged mode of public expression in the late Middle Ages and Renaissance."[49] She goes on to note that procession was also an important part of the king game. "Typically, one of four mock leaders—a Robin Hood, a summer king and/or queen, a morris captain or a haggler—would usurp authority from the local priest for a day[.]"[50] The SCA does a fairly good job at recreating this type of medieval performance. As discussed above, crown tourney includes a procession of fighters, and Pennsic has several processions and parades including opening ceremonies, the Fool's Parade, and the Japanese fertility ritual. In addition to these, grand marches and coronation processions make procession the most common performance type in the SCA, much as it was in the Middle Ages.

Pennsic in 2004 also saw numerous bardic circles. Every night in the barn people danced court and country dances to live music played on medieval-style instruments. Wolgemut, a professional medieval-style bagpipe and crumhorn band from Germany, made their annual appearance (though Homeland Security for some reason held their instruments up for several days). No fewer than three commedia troupes performed. The performing arts have their own track of classes called Coxcomb Academy at Pennsic. According to the Pennsic website, their classes represent "a comprehensive one week course in performing. . . . This core program is for ANY performing discipline, whether you are an actor, singer, storyteller, dancer, juggler, or goldfish eater."[51] Classes include techniques such as juggling, prestidigitation and improvisation, as well as classes in medieval and Renaissance performance genres such as mumming, jigges, masque, and commedia, and they have their own stage set up in a small amphitheatre. A second stage, on which every conceivable type of performance took place, was set up in a performing arts pavilion near merchants' row.

Some knights in the SCA have a real problem dancing. As mentioned earlier, although knights in the Middle Ages were expected to know how to dance, and although the SCA's policies state that all peers should be able to dance, few knights dance more than once in their SCA careers—once being enough to show they have done it so when their name comes up for knighthood someone can say "Yeah, I've seen him dance," (play chess, recite a poem, etc.). One king of the East, who had a fourteenth-century persona and who was an avid dancer, issued an edict that required all of his knights to dance in his presence during his reign. At his coronation a ball was held in which several of his knights danced, often for the first time since their knightings. One duke made a joke of it during a partner's dance by cutting out the queen and dancing with the king himself, like a transvestite knight using camp to reinscribe his masculinity while performing what he considered to be a feminine act.

In one of the most interesting royal performances a king and queen, who had Viking and Renaissance personae respectively, decided to employ masque as an integral part of their court. The centerpiece of their reign became a masquerade they staged at their crown tournament, in which everyone was supposed to come as a deity from Roman mythology. People donned their most elaborate garb and carnival masques, and a game was made of trying to guess which god each person was supposed to be. It was one of the few times that an SCA court has approached the type of theatricality and spectacle that would have been employed in the Middle Ages or Renaissance.

Bardic Activities

As the feast, with its opportunities for dance, musical performance, and masquing, is the predominant evening activity at events east of the Mississippi, west of the Mississippi, where they camp more often, campfire singing is the norm. In the early days of the SCA the crown would host an official kingdom "bardic circle." There is a loose structure to this: going around the circle in order, everyone present has to contribute a story, poem, or song. There is often a "regular play list" that includes medieval-style folk songs (such as "Scarborough Fair"), traditional ballads, IRA songs, and lots of drinking songs. Songs by such bands as Fairport Convention, Steeleye Span, and Jethro Tull are also common. The SCA is happy to employ Victorian or even contemporary music if it expresses the ideals or romantic imagery the SCA seeks. Even some Top 40 songs, such as David Bowie's "Heroes," are occasionally sung at bardic circles, to the chagrin of serious reenactors.

SCA members also filk. Filk (both a noun and a verb) is a performance genre developed at science fiction conventions that was quickly transferred to the SCA. The apocryphal explanation for the word says that it is a combination of the words "folk" and "filch," indicating that a filk song is a song that has been appropriated for popular use. However, Kathleen Sloan, a well-known filk singer from science fiction fandom, insists it was simply a typo for the word folk.[52] Another filk singer, Karen Anderson, defines it as "a humorous parody of a folk song,"[53] but notes that the phrase has been expanded to include all folk-style songs written about science fiction or fantasy topics (including SCA topics).

Most songs written on SCA topics, especially from the early days of the SCA, are filk songs set to contemporary tunes. SCA filk singers appropriate popular tunes and change the words to tell stories of SCA adventures. Typical is a song by Hollander to the tune of Simon and Garfunkel's "Greenback Dollar" called "The Mercenary Song":

The first time I ever hired out for pay
My luck it wasn't too good
For Creachin hired me to fight against Ostgardr
I watched the slaughter from the wood, my lord
I watched the slaughter from the wood
Oh I don't give a damn about a chain or a white belt,
Money's the stuff for me
For a willing wench and a keg of beer
Are things you cannot get for free, my lord,
Are things you cannot get for free.[54]

Filk is disparaged by the reenactor wing of the SCA, most of whom prefer to hear only medieval songs or works in a period style, but it is an important element in SCA culture. By co-opting tunes from popular culture SCA members not only appropriate consumable culture for a subversive use, they build community by putting SCA history and ideals into cultural forms that contemporary SCA members can relate to and tunes that they can all sing along with. Like the tropes taken from movies and literature, filk songs are able to reach members on an emotional level that medieval-style tunes cannot attain. Performing poetry or music in a medieval style is too academic for most SCA members, and therefore it is alienating. The audience is forced to think about the musical form and recognize it as a museum piece. People who compose works in a medieval style are highly regarded for their skills, but the songs they write are never as popular as filk songs. Not everybody understands how a fourteenth-century canso should be structured, but everybody knows the tune to "Born in the USA."

Storytelling is the other activity to be found at bardic circles. If the SCA is a group where people can write their own myths with themselves as the heroes, then obviously their stories need to be told. The adventures of SCA life, especially SCA fighting, are the basis of what in the SCA are referred to as "No shit" stories, so called because the stereotype form of the story starts out "No shit, there I was . . . " The story usually goes on to tell how the person telling it was in a battle, surrounded by enemy, and somehow extricated himself. It is, quite simply, a heroic tale told by the hero himself. As Erisman points out, "'No shit, there I was . . . ' stories are so common in the SCA that they are even found at official public performances such as bardic circles where, like filk songs, they bring the modern world of the SCA into a hybrid conjunction with the romantic medieval world the group creates."[55] The "No shit, there I was" story not only has a medieval precedent but, as Andrew Taylor points out, it had a serious function in medieval society. Writing of the stories told to Froissart by the squire Bascot de Mauléon in the *Chronicles*, Taylor writes:

> Chivalric conversation was institutionally sanctioned because it enforced chivalric ideology. Through their discussions, young men learned genealogical history, heraldry and court ceremonial; they learned the complexities of feudal obligation; they learned appropriate model speeches; and they learned crucial chivalric values. These values, of which courage and loyalty were perhaps the most important in war, had to be so deeply ingrained that a knight would ignore common sense and natural instinct and persistently risk his neck instead of simply running away. So, from an early age, the future knight was raised on tales of military glory and taught a certain stance toward violence and toward fear: the one thing chivalric literature virtually never mentions directly.[56]

This is, in many ways, the purpose of chivalric conversation in the SCA. It teaches SCA fighters how they are expected by their society to behave, with loyalty and courage in battle, even if the battle is all for show. Often this type of performance leads into a debate about the nature of chivalry in the Middle Ages and the SCA. Most SCA members are extremely well read. As noted earlier, 52.4% of the respondents in Lenehan's study had college degrees and 40.4% were still studying. Learning about, and debating about, chivalric culture is an important pastime in the SCA, especially among members of the chivalry. At one Estrella War I arranged to camp with Butler (who has a BA in Philosophy),

Hollander (a professional academic), and Scott (well known for his writings on chivalry within the SCA). One night the three of them spent about five hours around a campfire debating whether or not fencing was appropriate for the SCA, whether the SCA's period should be narrowed, what the differences were between twelfth-, fourteenth-, and sixteenth-century feudalism (and why they skipped the odd centuries I have no idea), and how to act as a knight if your persona is a Viking. The common thread throughout this wide ranging discussion was what Taylor would call "Chivalric Discussion" stories and examples used to illustrate how a knight should behave. This type of debate is even more common on SCA internet discussion groups.

Theatrical Performance in the SCA

There are two types of theatrical performance in the SCA. The first is performance of extant medieval and Renaissance scripts. The second is performance of plays written by and for SCA members, usually in a contemporary style. The two types of plays have very different purposes and effects on their audiences.

I have witnessed a performance of the fifteenth-century vernacular comedy *Pierre Pathelin*, and even a pared-down production of the famous morality play *The Castle of Perseverance* at SCA events. *Commedia dell'Arte* is common in the SCA. At Pennsic people will occasionally put on a Shakespeare play. A lot of SCA performance of original source material involves masques, and performance of masques tends to reinscribe the social order, which was, of course, masque's original purpose. Another medieval performance genre that is sometimes performed at SCA events is mumming, a type of resurrection play, in which a hero is slain and then resurrected by a doctor or magician. This type of play, as Chambers notes, was a Christmas play and the form survived into the nineteenth century (in fact it survived into the twentieth).[57]

Although SCA performance of medieval texts often helps to reinscribe the SCA social order, performance of contemporary SCA plays tends to have the opposite effect. Original SCA plays tend to be satires that subvert the SCA paradigm. In one popular series of SCA plays, *Our Kind,* Goldwyn of Britain set out to deflate self-important SCA peers through the use of highly stereotypical characters such as "Lady Cupcake" and "Bruno the Barbarian." In *Our Kind* he created a popular character named Mistress Laurel Seamchecker, a stereotypical know-it-all Laurel, around whom he wrote two more plays. In *Our Kind II: Mistress Laurel Seamchecker Explains It All at You*, Laurel explains the living historian model of the SCA and demonstrates why it is so strongly resisted and so easy to parody:

> And good morning, classless. I am Mistress Laurel Seamchecker, and I'm going to tell you everything you always wanted to know about the Order of the Laurel but didn't have the guts to ask. First and foremost, no member of the Order of the Laurel has ever made a mistake. We only pretend to so the rest of you won't feel bad. While the rest of the Society is intent upon recreating the

Middle Ages, we take that idea one step further: we want to recreate the Society—not as it is, but as it should be. Since our first name is "society," that means you have to learn to get along with other people, even if you can't stand them.[58]

She then goes on to prostrate herself before "Queen Lowbodice."

The most popular, and prolific, SCA playwright was Larry Hyinck/Master Gerhardt von Nordflammen. A punk rocker in mundane life, he portrayed a landsknecht at SCA events and railed against what he saw as SCA hypocrisy in his broadsides, poetry and, most effectively, plays. Although some of his scripts were on medieval subjects, most of his work was about SCA members. In one play, *The Fabulous Furry Fealty Brothers,* Hyinck adapted the 1970s underground comic *The Fabulous Furry Freak Brothers* in order to address a scandal in which three SCA knights had been accused of fighting while high on drugs. The three knights were turned into Duke Phenobaberous, Count Sir Funkline, and Fat Flaky Fealty, while their accusers, all members of the "Old Guard" of the SCA, became "The Society of Blue Noses." People were easily able to recognize themselves in the performance, and all of them were savagely parodied.[59] In *The Queen's Tale*, Hyinck created the story of a young girl at her first SCA event who, prodded by a couple of fools, sleeps with a series of men until, by the end of the event, she becomes Crown Princess.

One of Hyinck's most influential plays arose out of a conflict involving members of the SCA's Board of Directors. In 1982 a member of the SCA Board published a study titled "Trends of Change," in which he proposed that the SCA would someday need to change its structure to a more contemporary model. His main suggestion was that rank, instead of being handed out at the whim of royalty or won in a tournament, would be awarded on the basis of participation and the amount of time someone had been in the SCA. The board rejected the proposal and an ensuing fight led to a lawsuit in which the author of the tract accused the SCA of violating its tax-exempt status by being a social organization and not an educational organization (the lawsuit went nowhere, although the argument is occasionally resurrected). Hyinck responded to "Trends of Change" in his play *A California Vacuum Cleaner Salesman in the BoG Court.* In this play a knight named Leo the Shrieker travels forward in time to a future when the SCA has taken over the world due to a nuclear war. The Board of Directors (now called "The Board of Gods") has instituted all of the suggestions in "Trends of Change." Rank and awards are based on "peerage points," which people earn by length of membership, etc. Fighting is pretty much a side show. A revolt is being staged by the Progressive People's Feudalist United Front, a group from Leo's old barony, who want to revive the "old ways" of honorable combat and feudalism. When Leo realizes that he has a membership card dating from 1982, giving him thousands more peerage points than anyone else, he takes over, fires the board, and decides to set things right just as soon as he can find a king to reign over the area. It turns out the janitor is currently the king. When asked how he got to be king the janitor replies, "80 peerage points and three box tops."[60]

In the introduction to the printed script, Hyinck notes that the whole purpose of the play was to respond to "Trends of Change." He wrote at the time:

> [W]hat the play turned into was an attack on the Hobbyist/Re-creationist wing of the SCA, prompted by me [sic] reading of an interesting little tome called "Trends of Change." I've got to admit, I was pretty worked up about it by some of the ideas contained in this document and even more over some of the psychological "trends" in the SCA I felt it represented. This play, therefore, should be considered in this light. It does not represent a reasoned consideration of the views contained in "Trends of Change," it is not even a satire on those views; satire to my mind is not quite so heavy-handed. Rather, it is a burlesque or a lampoon, akin not so much to slicing at these ideas with a scalpel, as to hacking at them with a meat cleaver. It was meant to chop up the reeking carcass of burgherite combinationalism and toss it into the garbage can where I felt it belonged.[61]

Hyinck was opposing not only the arguments in "Trends of Change" but also other kingdoms whose members, for one reason or another, sought to limit royal authority. Since he came from one of the kingdoms where "The King's Word is Law" was taken as gospel, the fact that in other places peers were (at the time) actively advocating establishing parliaments and even proposing voting for the office of king angered him.

Each of these plays demonstrates how original SCA drama tends to be subversive. The primary purpose of both Goldwyn's and Hyinck's plays was to satirize SCA behavior and expose the "dream" as hypocritical (Hyinck was famous for his disdain of the "dream"). Audience reaction to the plays was mixed: most people enjoyed them immensely, but people who were specifically being parodied were often offended. Just as performance of medieval plays, even satires, reinscribes the SCA paradigm by presenting "period" entertainment for the king or his subjects, original SCA drama tends to be critical of SCA members and undermines their collective fantasy.

Mock Mock Kings

Hyinck saw the SCA, at least partially, as an experiment in feudalism. He argued in several essays that feudalism, based on the mutual exchange of service for protection through the mechanism of fealty, was the best form of government for the SCA (and he said privately that it was the best form of government, period).[62] To this end, while he was opposed to such medieval ideas as parliament, he nonetheless attempted to bring a more medieval idea of fealty to the SCA. The result was something later dubbed "The Westermark Heresy," in which he argued that, instead of peers swearing fealty only to the king as was the SCA custom, they should be allowed to swear fealty to barons if they lived in a barony. As a joke, he resurrected The Progressive People's Feudalist United

Front as a mock revolutionary organization fighting against the tyranny of what he called the "Bilbo Baggins Bullshit Variety" of feudalism.

By challenging the nature of fealty in the SCA, Hyinck had a lasting effect on how SCA members, particularly on the West Coast, viewed their oaths. As Hyinck points out, the SCA oath is actually a combination of homage and fealty together. It is an act of submission, in which the vassal makes himself the servant of the lord and then pledges to be "faithful," but without a corresponding exchange of property common in the Middle Ages. Hyinck insisted (incorrectly) that this was not a true medieval style of fealty, that no vassal would swear an oath in which the limits of fealty were not clearly defined. In fact, according to Marc Bloch, early medieval vassalage was structured in a very similar fashion, with homage and fealty being combined (Bloch notes that while fealty could, occasionally, be sworn without homage, homage, in the feudal period, never existed without fealty).[63]

The type of vassalage that Hyinck was arguing for was the later variety, in which fealty was a carefully defined contract with limitations and duties clearly established for both parties, and which was primarily a business contract in which the vassal exchanged service for a source of income. The lord either agreed to maintain the vassal, providing food, shelter, and means, or else gave the vassal a piece of property from which the vassal could earn an income. It was not always a farm. The vassal could, for instance, be put in charge of a town gate and earn an income from the tolls charged to enter the town or on tariffs on incoming goods. In 1110, for example, Bernard Atton, Viscount of Carcassonne swore fealty and gave homage to Leo, the Abbot of St. Mary of Grasse, in front of witness and on "holy relics." The official version is in the form of a contract transcribed by one John the Monk giving details of the spoken oath. It is several pages long. In it the viscount promises to defend the abbey against any enemies, swear homage to any subsequent abbots, and keep the castles faithfully. The contract goes into great detail as to what each party's rights and obligations are, down to the detail that "when the abbot shall mount his horse I and my heirs, viscounts of Carcassonne, and our successors ought to hold the stirrup for the honor of the dominion of St. Mary of Grasse."[64] The oath goes on to outline such obligations as how much fish, meat, and eggs must be provided to the abbot and his retinue when he visits Carcassonne. Other period oaths go so far as to lay conditions on the vassal's military service noting, for instance, that if one of his lords goes to war with another, what his obligations would be to each.

Hyinck's objection to SCA fealty was twofold: first, that peers were not allowed to swear fealty to the barons, and second, that the fealty oath was too broad. His argument was that, when the king forbade the peers from swearing fealty to the baron, he was denying them a customary right that they had hitherto always been able to exercise. He wrote at the time:

> The whole fiasco emphasizes the fact that, unless a vassals [sic] rights are specified in detail, they essentially <u>have no rights</u> [emphasis in the original] aside from the occasional bone their liege lord deigns to toss them. Its [sic]

time to change this travesty of feudal practice in instituting realistic oaths of fealty reflecting the obligations, rights, privileges and prerogatives of both parties.[65]

Hyinck's argument was very influential.[66] Although they didn't change the words as he had proposed, many peers on the West Coast began to argue that fealty in the SCA should be viewed as a mutual obligation, in which the vassal's obligations to the crown are predicated on the crown's keeping faith with and protecting the vassal. Eventually this interpretation spread to much of the SCA.

Another "heresy," which followed a few years after, expanded on these ideas in a much more subversive way. The shire of Canale played host to a war between the Principality of the Mists and the Principality of Cynagua and, as a joke, the Canale subjects complained that they were being invaded by both armies and declared that they were going to secede and form their own kingdom. In doing so they set up Bray as a mock king in the tradition of the folk heroes discussed by Billington. Soon a group of peers within the West, all of them from the reenactor wing of the SCA, had set up an underground government, a counterculture to the SCA's counterculture. The purpose behind the "Kingdom of Canale" was to present an alternative model for the SCA that had a closer relationship to medieval (particularly fourteenth-century) precedents. The King of Canale handed out peerages and titles that were based on imaginary plots of land and not on a modern award system. His peers carried on intrigues and fought amongst themselves for lands or for succession. Two of them spent months arranging a marriage. Most of this took place away from SCA events, a lot of it online through email discussions, but they did hold an event or two. Several other peers in the kingdom were outraged by this usurpation of royal authority, but it was a serious attempt by reenactors to push the SCA toward a more historical model without eliminating its social aspects, and it represented an infusion of the mock king game of the Middle Ages into the mock king game of the SCA.

Both of these instances of resistance, brought about by a desire to make the SCA more historically accurate in some way, represent an inversion of the original inversion, a carnivalesque usurpation of a carnivalesque activity. By challenging the mock king in the first instance, and by setting up a mock mock king in the second, these two minirevolutions attempted to remake the SCA's king game in ways that better reflected medieval practice.

Performance Reconstruction in the SCA

In 1996 I directed two experiments in performance reconstruction that demonstrate both how the SCA interacts with the medieval king game and how it does not. One of these was a summer game and one a winter game, both revolving around the type of festivals Chambers and Billington discuss. Unlike most SCA performances, which are related to the postmodern SCA game through action and reference, these were intended to be experiments in performance reconstruction, attempts to re-create the performance and social conditions of late-medieval and early-modern performances as nearly as possible. My intent was to work within the SCA fabric and academia, the project of the reenactor wing of the SCA, to find out more about medieval and early modern performance.

The first performance was a reconstruction of Samuel Daniels's *The Vision of the Twelve Goddesses,* the first of the Stuart court masques, which I directed for a Twelfth Night coronation, which was part of my master's thesis project.[67] In this experiment we mounted an elaborate production employing an existing wing and drop set at the Shriners' temple in Oakland, California, where Twelfth Night was being held that year. The main purpose of the production was to see if by having the SCA queen dance the queen's role in the masque we would be able to learn something about the social dynamics that existed in the production of Stuart court drama. It was largely successful, as it raised some interesting questions about the queen's participation. The second project was a production of *Robin Hood and the Friar* for the SCA's thirtieth-anniversary festival. This was not so successful, and ended up revealing much more about the SCA than it did about period performance.

As described by Robert Sarlos, performance reconstruction is an anthropological exercise, a means of learning not only about period production techniques but also about audience responses. The biggest difficulty with reconstructing medieval theatre is how to come to a meeting between the medieval and contemporary minds. Sarlos insisted that an attempt should be made to reconstruct the power relationships that existed between actor and audience. Audiences, according to Sarlos, should be steeped in the period from the moment they arrive at the theatre, moving the performance into the house, the lobby, and even outside. For instance, a production of a Restoration comedy might have orange girls in period costume wandering the house before the performance selling and serving oranges to members of the audience. Sarlos even suggested supplying appropriate costumes to the audience free of charge and went so far as to cast the president of UC Davis and his wife as Charles I and Henrietta Maria, in an attempt to recreate the sociopolitical dynamic surrounding the original production of *The Triumph of Peace.*[68]

These attempts are all doomed to failure because, as Sarlos was forced to recognize, the audience will always be a contemporary audience coded as historical but reading the historical as something out of place, anachronistic, and not truly relevant to modern life. But the SCA, as we have seen, is a society where medieval court relationships are carefully cultivated, and a hierarchical structure exists in which the power dynamic Sarlos sought to recreate at Davis is already in place. The dukes, counts, kings, and knights of the SCA are already there, acting out their relationships in an early-modern court atmosphere. Not only that, but many of them already know how to dance at least one medieval dance.

With the *Twelve Goddesses* many elements came together that allowed us to create a good reconstruction of an early-modern court pageant. The hall had a wing and drop Greek Temple set in the fly loft, just like the one called for in the script. While looking for information on Daniels I stumbled across all the original music for the masque. I had an excellent choreographer, numerous costumers, and a crumhorn band at my disposal. However, the most important element in producing the masque was the participation of the queen. As it was played on the night of her coronation, the masque became a celebration of her new reign just as the original had been a celebration of the ascension of James I. It managed to raise the types of questions Sarlos said a performance reconstruction should seek: was the relationship between the queen and the other masquers as important in the original as it was to us, did the original audience see it as a pagan religious ceremony as some of our audience did, how much was spent on the costumes, etc.?

The Robin Hood play, our summer game, was a completely different issue. Robin Hood games, as mentioned earlier, were not games of the nobility unless in the form of a masque. They were entertainments for the peasants and the merchant classes, and the SCA doesn't provide nearly so good a laboratory for this type of experiment. But it does provide one. Over the last forty years a burgeoning merchant culture has grown up around the SCA. Although part of the educational experience of the SCA has always been to reconstruct the arts and crafts of the Middle Ages, it is a lot easier purchase a suit of armor than to make it yourself, and so the SCA has created a market for medieval-style material culture. Merchants selling everything from food to flea market junk to elaborate costumes, furniture, and pavilions can be found at many SCA events. Since the SCA is supposed to be a single-class feudal society, SCA merchants pose a problem by representing a second (bourgeois) class, one with different values and a different reason for participating in the SCA. Because their presence is entirely mundane, in that they are engaging in actual commerce upon which they must pay taxes, interaction with merchants is always a mundane activity that takes place at SCA events.[69] However, the presence of merchants creates a "market faire" ambiance at large events that is generally welcomed. It was this market faire, and this second class of SCA participants, with which we wanted to interact when we presented *Robin Hood and the Friar*.

Our production could not truly be called a "performance reconstruction" because there is no record of the original production to which we could refer (though recent scholarship, unavailable at the time of our experiment, has shed some light on the original performance conditions). It is better instead to look at it as an attempt to reconstruct a specific *type* of theatre. For several reasons, the Robin Hood game (following Wiles's example I use the term "game" rather than the more theatrical "play" in order to emphasize the recreational aspects of this type of folk drama) is the best choice among the various folk drama motifs of medieval England for a reconstruction project. Much scholarly work has been done in the last twenty-five years that has revealed a great deal regarding the various forms the Robin Hood game took in the fifteenth and sixteenth centuries. Furthermore, although similar motifs such as the Abbot of Misrule, the Mock Mayor, and the May King are mostly unfamiliar to modern, especially American, audiences, Robin Hood is instantly recognizable.

The Robin Hood game is a type of folk drama that was immensely popular in southeastern England and in Scotland in the fifteenth and sixteenth centuries (possibly for much longer). The earliest mention of the game comes from 1427, when a group of players was paid 20 pence to perform Robin Hood in front of the Mayor of Exeter.[70] (Chambers is reluctant to refer to the Robin Hood plays as folk drama because we have some surviving texts,[71] but research by Wiles has shown that these were indeed a people's form of entertainment). The early Robin Hood games for which we have records were likely processions, in which a group of men led by Robin Hood would parade through the town entreating people to join Robin's band of outlaws (though the 1427 game was enacted by "players," so it might have involved some form of mimetic representation). The parades were sponsored by the town or the church, and were often used as fund-raisers for the parish. Money was sometimes gathered through the selling of paper livery badges to all who would become one of Robin's "Merry Men." These parades usually took place at Whitsuntide (the seventh Sunday after Easter) and are roughly parallel to the game of the May King or the Abbot of Misrule. In many places Robin Hood seems to replace the May King, while at other times they appear together or in competition with one another. Often a person—sometimes a man and occasionally a woman—playing Maid Marian would march with Robin as his May Queen.[72]

At times Robin and his men apparently would compete with, or get into fights with, people they met along the way, and these competitions came sometimes to be framed within small dramatic narratives that were performed on the village green. Eventually dancing was added and from then on Marian was played by a man (in 1516 according to Wiles). The final stage occurred when the game was taken over by morris dancers, with Robin Hood, Little John, Friar Tuck, and Maid Marian all taking part.

The Robin Hood of the game is much more anarchistic than the loyal thief who keeps the King's forests safe while he is away. The Robin Hood game was folk drama and was concerned less with an ideal Arcadian paradise, which is the fantasy of a privileged noble class, than with the fantasies of the peasantry, namely a carnivalesque escape from civic authority. Robin Hood here is not a noble in hiding (the courtly tradition) but is a peasant and an outlaw who resists social authority. This has led many medievalists, notably Sponsler, to theorize that the Robin Hood game was a peasant attempt to resist and disrupt the social order.[73] Certainly it was seen as threatening by some of those in power. Richard Morison wrote in 1540:

> the lewdenes and ribawdry that there is opened to the people, disobedience also to your officers, is tought, whilest these good bloodes go about to take from the shiref of Notyngham one that for offendyng the lawes should have suffered execution.[74]

However, as Sponsler later agreed, most of the Robin Hood games were sponsored either by the church or town council, and therefore were official activities.

Though they did occasionally break down into riots, all in all they were a sanctioned bit of mayhem.

One way in which the possible transgressive nature of the Robin Hood game was inverted came with the aristocratic co-opting of the game, a practice that Sponsler calls "the most culturally creative response."[75] As noted earlier, Henry VIII loved the Robin Hood game so much he and his court would often play at it themselves, in one instance having Robin and his men "kidnap" King Henry and feast him at their banquet in the forest.[76] This last tradition became, in hindsight, very important to our production.

The text of *Robin Hood and the Friar*, along with *Robin Hood and the Potter*, was printed in 1562 but is surely somewhat older. Wiles suggests that they may both have been written for a revival of the game that took place under Queen Mary.[77] It appears to be a transitional piece between the Robin Hood processional (wherein Maid Marian would often be played by a woman) and the later Robin Hood morris dance, when a man plays Maid Marian. There are elements of the combat game, the type exemplified by the earliest surviving Robin Hood text, *Robin Hood and the Sheriff*, but *Robin Hood and the Friar* ends in a dance. In *Robin Hood and the Friar* Robin's girl is actually not named. The assumption is usually to identify her as Maid Marian, but she could be the well known "Friar's Dam." However, Wiles points out that some scholars believe that Friar Tuck and Maid Marian were absorbed into the May game from the morris dance.[78]

The action follows the famous ballad of *Robin Hood and the Curtal Friar*, but the play is the first known instance in which the Curtal Friar is identified as Friar Tuck. Friar Tuck in the play is different from the better known version of today. The play ends with Tuck admiring Marian lasciviously, calling her:

> . . . a trul of trust, to serue a frier at his lust
> a prycker a prauncer a terer of shetes
> a wagger of ballockes when other men slepes[79]

This Friar is far more lecherous than the kindly priest known to most modern audiences, and the usually pure, chaste Marian (if this is Marian) is highly sexualized. The portrayal of Tuck is, in many ways, more subversive than that of Robin in the way it criticizes the clergy of the day.

Due to time constraints I decided to mount the play in a week, rehearsing only at the event itself (which lasted ten days). I asked Schmidt, who had portrayed Somnus in *Twelve Goddesses*, to portray Friar Tuck. Schmidt is six feet tall, weighs about 300 pounds, and has thick, unruly blonde hair and beard. He is a martial artist as well as an excellent poet and performer. His size was especially important, since I would be playing Robin Hood, and the actor playing Friar Tuck had to be able to carry me on his back and throw me over his shoulder. Schmidt is also blessed with the singular talent of being able to extemporize rhymed couplets, which turned out to be important since he could never remember his lines.

The rest of the cast we assembled at the event. Since this is a rather rough and tumble show and required rather rough and tumble people, I cast fighters in all the roles, which meant that most of the time my actors would be out on the field fighting melees and that they would often come to rehearsal bruised and battered. Remembering Wiles's descriptions of the fighting that often took place at May festivals, I thought this was appropriate. It also meant, however, that my actors could not be relied upon to show up on time for rehearsal, since if they were having too much fun on the battlefield they would forget that they were supposed to be somewhere else. I had to replace one of Friar Tuck's men at the last minute as a result.

Since we had only one week to rehearse, most of our time was spent working on the fights. It is possible that in the original performance Tuck and Robin fought for real. We, however, decided to choreograph the fight for safety's sake. The difficult thing when using SCA fighters in a choreographed fight is coaching them to forget their training, which teaches them to hit each other very hard, and instead encourage them *not* to hit each other. We blocked the play on the second day but were unable to rehearse with everybody as often as I would have liked.

I had gathered together a collection of ten actors, three musicians, and one morris dancer to form the core of the procession. We started out in one corner of the camp and wound our way up to the market area about a mile away. The musicians played, the dancer danced, and everyone cried out, entreating those we encountered to "join our merry band and become one of Robin Hood's men." Our procession grew steadily until, by the time we got to the market, we had about thirty people trailing behind us. This number swelled even more as we wandered through the merchant area. Those who didn't join us waved heartily and wished us good cheer. Bypassing the stage area we went instead to a nearby lawn (the best equivalent to the village green) and stopped the parade. Instinctively, those who had been following us sat down in the traditional (modern) "I'm going to watch a play now" attitude, forming a semicircle, and the scripted portion of our game was underway. It proceeded smoothly until John threw me over his shoulder and into the "stream." Following Wiles, I was doused with a bucket of water to represent the brook, and this got far the biggest laugh and applause out of the audience (the job of dousing me was performed by a girlfriend of mine, who took a particular, almost maniacal joy in drenching me).

The other big laugh came at the end of the melee. Following the example of other play fragments, I ended the fight with Robin being beaten by the Friar and then suing for peace. As in some of the ballads, the Robin Hood of the game follows the "Robin Hood bested" motif; while able to defeat the Sheriff, he usually loses to people of the merchant and peasant classes. In typical comic fashion, the fight ended with John hitting me in the groin and me delivering my next few lines in falsetto.

Our Marian, played by a man, was of the farcical bearded variety, the false woman of whom Falstaff speaks in *Henry IV 1*, when he says "and for womanhood, Maid Marian may be the deputy's wife of the ward to thee."[80] A large-bellied Irish gentleman in a borrowed dress and a veil to partially hide his full beard came out as Marian and giggled and acted coy as Tuck poked and groped him, thus performing Tuck's lust in what we considered to be an appropriate campy mode. The play ended with a country-dance, in which members of the cast pulled people from the audience to dance with (save Tuck and Marian, who of course danced together).

What we had hoped for was to raise questions about how this play would be performed and received in the Middle Ages. The most interesting reaction came from members of the merchant class, those who often don't involve themselves in the mainstream SCA activities. The play had much more meaning to them than to the "nobility." To the merchants we were a group of traveling players who were much more interesting than the courts and tourneys that were going on out by the list field. They recognized Robin Hood as a champion of the "people" and not the nobility, and they reacted to him accordingly. The procession through the market faire was, in many ways, the most successful part of the performance.

However, as an experiment in recreating the social conditions of a performance of the Robin Hood game it was a complete failure. The reason should have been obvious from the beginning but only occurred to me in hindsight: it was impossible for us to be transgressive because Schmidt and I are, within the context of the SCA, peers. Not only are both of us knights, I am a count and, more importantly in this case, a viscount which, as Fox Davies tells us, has an equivalent English title: sheriff. It is impossible to be transgressive when the sheriff plays Robin Hood. We were not peasants trying to invert and thereby subvert the social order; within the SCA game we were aristocrats playing at being peasants. A telling moment came when, as we progressed through camp, we came upon the camp of the Company of St. George, one of the more serious groups of scholarly reenactors in the SCA (who the day before had put on the *pas d'armes* discussed in Chapter 4). The period and place they reenact is early fifteenth-century England, so the Robin Hood game falls within their time period. Standing around the campfire were three knights, all well known to the actors in our company. As we entreated them to join us they laughed and bantered with us good-naturedly but refused to come along, saying, "No: go on and play your little game and have fun." They reacted to us as comrades, members of their own class, who were out playing a game and slumming. They pretended that they wouldn't join us because it was beneath their dignity, but they appreciated the irony of having peers play Robin Hood. To them we looked ridiculous, but we were in no way transgressive.

What had worked in our favor with *The Twelve Goddesses* worked against us with the Robin Hood game, and what we ended up with turned out to be closer to a masque than to a carnivalesque May game. At best it could be described as a leveling, with Schmidt and I coming down to the level of the merchant class. It is much better to compare what we did to Henry VIII and his Robin Hood games. We were the SCA nobility playing at being pastoral peasants. That is a very different type of game than the one we set out to re-create, but nonetheless a period one. What we had created was yet another aristocratic entertainment, and the reaction to it was one of good-natured ridicule from those of our station. We had clearly reinforced the SCA's social order.

What it showed about the SCA, however, was quite different. In the larger contemporary context, our Robin Hood game resembled the SCA itself. The SCA is not a society of the nobility. It is a society of working- and clerical-class people, some scholars, and many computer technicians. It is a May Game in which people play at being noble, fight with staves, crown a king and queen of Love and Beauty, and live out a romantic pastoral fantasy of days gone by. As I have argued throughout, the SCA can better be compared to Robin Hood and other medieval king games than to a chivalric tournament culture: games in which a ceremonial mock king is chosen from among the players and rallies people to his side for a period of festive misrule. Whereas the *Twelve Goddesses* masque fit rather seamlessly into the SCA framework as an entertainment for a mock royal court, and revealed new possibilities regarding early modern court performance, our performance of *Robin Hood and the Friar* told us more about the SCA than it did the Middle Ages, by presenting another model of performance through which to contextualize the modern SCA game.

The King's Hall

In many ways it is in the banquet hall that the SCA becomes its most medieval. Feasting was, after all, an important social activity in the Middle Ages. Structurally, medieval tournaments were more likely to resemble the East Kingdom model, with a tourney followed by a feast, than the West Kingdom model in which everybody camps out. However, feasting also figured prominently in Tolkien as well. One type of feast that is not common at SCA events is a testimonial. They are reserved for major anniversaries, such as when a territorial baron has served in office for a long period of time (baron is the only office in the SCA that has no term limit, and some landed barons have held office for twenty years).

The man whose knighting was mentioned in the first paragraph of this chapter, Dan Hunter/Duke Radnor of Guildemar, celebrated the twenty-fifth anniversary of his knighting in March 2004. Hunter is considered by many (at least on the West Coast) to be the best SCA fighter ever. He is also extremely well liked and admired, and has a keen sense of theatrics. For the twentieth anniversary of his knighting he had issued a challenge that he would hold a *pas d'armes* and face all comers on the battlefield at Hastings, England, and many people made the trip from the United States to attend. For his twenty-fifth anniversary, his household threw him a party. At March Crown, the event where he'd been knighted, they held a banquet for two hundred invited guests. Each guest was given a gift, a large medallion minted for the occasion. They set up two large adjoined marquis pavilions, for everyone to sit under, and hired professional caterers. On each of the tables was set a large, elaborately blown bottle filled with wine (a group of Vikings sat at the back of the room drinking the bottles from every other table and counting out how many they had consumed to laughs and cheers). One by one people stood up to make testimonial speeches, some humorous and some boring. This banquet referenced not medieval banquets so much as much as the "Long Expected Party" from the first chapter of *The Fellowship of the Ring*. Like that banquet, held to celebrate Bilbo's and Frodo's birthdays, it was to celebrate an important anniversary. Both banquets were held out of doors under tents. People had been looking forward to each of them for months. The participants of Hunter's banquet were even each given a gift (the medallions), just like the guests at Bilbo's party. Everybody recognized this referencing of *The Fellowship of the Ring*: when Hunter got up to make his speech thanking everyone for coming, two people, from opposite sides of the room, simultaneously yelled, "Proud Feet!" (quoting a line in the book).

In *The Medieval Stage*, Chambers suggests that it was in the long winter nights, when the snow drifts were thick, and there was truly nothing to do for months on end, that a certain idea of theatre was developed in Northern Europe, an idea of theatre that was not beholden to Latin precedent. According to Chambers, this tradition began with a great winter feast, made necessary by the scarcity of fodder, for which many animals were slaughtered and eaten. It was not a midwinter feast, like Christmas, but took place when the snows first closed off the pastures in mid-November, and gradually the date shifted to midwinter over time.[81] In the communal hall in which the whole household from lord to servants lived, stories would be told and songs sung and occasionally acted out. Mumming, masque, the boy bishop, the feast of fools, and the lord of misrule, all sorts of kings and mock kings and anti-kings celebrated the inversion of the year through an inversion of social order, leading eventually to elaborate celebrations, mimicking the royal courts, and presided over by magnificent mock kings in the mold of Dudley. In the SCA, just as outdoor activities stemmed from a May-day mock king game, indoor activities began as a feast of misrule, gradually layered with ritual and ceremony, until, like Dudley's revels at the Inns of Court, they took on serious trappings of royal authority. With this ritual and ceremony, kings and queens, artisans and artists, knights and ladies, ostentatious garb, dances and theatrics, the SCA has reconstructed medieval court and domestic performance in the hall of the winter king.

NOTES

[1] Billington, 54.

[2] Stephen de Loraine, quoted in Keyes.

[3] Chambers, 260.

[4] Billington, 30.

[5] Victor Turner, *From Ritual to Performance* (New York: Performing Arts Journal Publications, 1982), 13.

[6] Goffman, *Frame Analysis*, 58.

[7] Catherine Helm-Clark, "There Are No Scrolls," *Tournaments Illuminated* Autumn, no. 140 (2002): 12.

[8] However, the fealty oath is not in the original scroll. It wasn't written down until the creation of a standard ceremony book much later. According to one early member, since

somebody always had a copy of *The Return of the King* handy, that person would open it up to the appropriate page and read, inserting Dorothea's variations where needed. See Stephen de Loraine, quoted in Keyes.

[9] Huizinga, *The Autumn of the Middle Ages*, 91.

[10] J.R.R. Tolkien, *The Lord of the Rings* (New York: Houghton Mifflin, 1994), 739-40.

[11] Keen, 44.

[12] Raymond Lull, *The Book of Knighthood and Chivalry*, trans. William Caxton (Union City, CA: The Chivalry Bookshelf, 2001), 25.

[13] Helm-Clark, 8.

[14] Anonymous, *The Ordene de Chevalerie, in Lull, 107-122.*

[15] Huizinga, *The Autumn of the Middle Ages*, 73.

[16] Helm-Clark, 9.

[17] Keen, 28.

[18] Lull, 15.

[19] Chambers, 263.

[20] Saslow, 149.

[21] Later, the creation of the Order of the Pelican for service split the Laurel, and any Laurels who received their peerage for service to the crown were given the opportunity to switch to the new order. When the king decided to knight someone who was already a member of the Laurel, the orders became distinctly separate, so that the title "Knights of the Laurel" has long since fallen out of use.

[22] There's a joke in the SCA that sums up this argument: "If you hit it with an ax and it breaks it's an art, if not it's a science. For example: take a bottle of beer; hit it with an ax; the bottle breaks, but lap it up and it's still perfectly good beer. Glass blowing is an art; brewing is a science."

[23] Billington, 40.

[24] Ibid.

[25] See Patricia Fortini Brown, "Measured Friendship, Calculated Pomp: The Ceremonial Welcomes of the Venetian Republic," in *"All the World's a Stage. . .": Art and Pageantry in the Renaissance and Baroque*, ed. Barbara Wisch and Susan Scott Munshower (University Park: Pennsylvania State University Press, 1990).

[26] Sir W. Dugdale, *Originales Iuridiciales* (London: 1666). Quoted in Billington, 46.

[27] Billington, 49.

[28] Turner, 21.

[29] Ibid., 55.

[30] The West Kingdom History Project is not clear whether or not the Order of the Rose, for women who had been queen, was formed at the second Twelfth Night. Tradition says that it was, and some people remember it this way, but as Helm-Clark points out, there is no ceremony for the Ladies of the Rose included on the ceremony scroll. However, it has been suggested that the scroll might be incomplete. See Keyes. According to the Kingdom of CAID history wiki, the rose was created at this event by the new queen, Sheryl of Thespis. See Compendium CAIDus, Roses, available from http://wiki.caid-commons.org/index.php/Roses. Accessed 19 September 2009.

[31] Eco, 68.

[32] The SCA actually adopted that title from the original Renaissance Pleasure Faire, where it is used as a form of address for the burghers of the imaginary town of Chipping under Oakwood. See Keyes.

[33] Huizinga, *The Autumn of the Middle Ages*, 70.

[34] Saslow, 13-14.

[35] Ibid., 15.

[36] Duchess Natayla de Foix, forward to *This Sovereign Stage* by Sir Guillaume de la Belgique, *This Sovereign Stage* (San Diego, CA: Shining Armor Enterprises, 2003) 8.

[37] Saslow, 148.

[38] Ibid.

[39] Roy Strong, *The Cult of Elizabeth* (Berkeley: University of California Press, 1977), 114.

[40] Keyes.

[41] Compendium CAIDus, Roses.

[42] Saslow, 151.

[43] Ibid., 140.

[44] Belgique, 9.

[45] Snook, correspondence.

[46] Lisa Snook, script for the coronation of Thorson and Svava, 2004, author's collection.

[47] Erisman, 275.

[48] Orgel, 8.

[49] Kathleen Ashley, "Introduction," in *Moving Subjects: Processional Performance in the Middle Ages and Renaissance*, ed. Kathleen Ashley and Wim Hüsken (Atlanta, GA: Rodopi, 2001), 10.

[50] Ibid.

[51] Society for Creative Anachronism, *Pennsicwar.Org* (Cooper's Lake Campground, 2004, accessed 2 May 2004); available from www.pennsicwar.org.

[52] Roger Nygard, *Trekkies 2*, Roger Nygard dir. (Los Angeles: Paramount Pictures, 2004).

[53] Ibid.

[54] Frederick Hollander, *Mercenary's Song* (Textfiles.com, accessed 14 March 2005); available from http://www.textfiles.com/music/bardic2.txt.

[55] Erisman, 199.

[56] Taylor, 174.

[57] Chambers, I, 393-403.

[58] Goldwyn of Britain, *Our Kind II: Mistress Laurel Seamchecker Explains It All At You* (Golden Stag Players, accessed 30 May 2003); available from www.goldenstag.net/players/scripts_pdf/OurKindII.

[59] Larry Hyinck, "The Fabulous Furry Fealty Brothers," in *The Second Folio of Gerhardt Von Nordflammen* (Vancouver: Copious Free Time Press, 1984).

[60] Larry Hyinck, "A California Vacuum Cleaner Salesman in the BoG Court," in *The Second Folio of Gerhardt Von Nordflammen* (Vancouver: Copious Free Time Press, 1984), 73.

[61] Ibid., 57.

[62] See Larry Hyinck, "In Defense of Feudalism," in *The Second Folio of Gerhardt Von Nordflammen* (Vancouver: Copious Free Time Press, 1984), 214-28.

[63] Marc Bloch, "Feudal Society," in *The Middle Ages*, ed. Brian Tierney (New York: Alfred A. Knopf, 1961).

[64] Bernard Atton, *Medieval Sourcebook: Charter of Homage and Fealty, 1110* (Fordham University Institute of Medieval Studies, 2000, accessed 14 March 2005); available from http://www.fordham.edu/halsall/source/atton1.html.

[65] Hyinck, "In Defense of Feudalism," 223.

[66] Scott, for instance, is a Master of Arms because he feels, like Hyinck, that SCA fealty is not realistically medieval. As what he considers to be a reasonable alternative, Scott advises people who swear fealty to simply say "I promise not to burn your fields or steal your cattle for six months," (six months being the length of most SCA reigns).

[67] See Michael Cramer, "The Twelve Goddesses: A Performance Reconstruction" (Master of Arts in Drama, San Francisco State University, 1996).

[68] Sarlos, 198-229.

[69] For a time there was an experiment in the Kingdom of An Tir in which a monier minted coins, sold them for a dollar a piece, and then redeemed them at the end of each event for the same amount, in hopes of creating a more medieval ambiance for SCA commerce. Of course, he made a profit because not all of the coins would be redeemed. When the SCA refused to officially sanction his activities, fearing legal ramifications, he sued them and the whole thing got ugly, but it proved that commerce at SCA events out of necessity needs to be considered a mundane activity.

[70] Wiles, 43.

[71] Chambers, 178.

[72] Wiles, 23.

[73] See Sponsler, 25-7.

[74] Anonymous, *Robin Hood and the Sheriff of Nottingham* (Western Michigan University, 1997, accessed 2 May 2004); available from http://www.lib.rochester.edu/camelot/teams/sherint.htm.

[75] Sponsler, 46.

[76] Ibid. 47.

[77] Wiles, 39.

[78] Ibid., 21.

[79] Anonymous, "Robin Hood and the Friar," Ibid., 97.

[80] *1 Henry IV*, 3.3.126.

[81] Chambers, 228-232.

6

Conclusion

According to the Society Seneschal (in a public announcement made at Estrella War 2005), there are over 100,000 people participating in SCA activities worldwide. All of these people share a love for the Middle Ages, but it is never the same Middle Ages. For some it is a love of material culture, for some it is history, for some it is romance, and for some it is fantasy. Some just like to fight. Together what they have created is a postmodern mélange of images, a pastiche of ideas about the Middle Ages. Erisman argues that, rather than a desire to experience the historic Middle Ages, it is this hybrid nature of the SCA that makes it attractive to most of the participants. She notes that at SCA events the contemporary, the historical, and the fantastic exist side by side. "This blend of past and present, history and fantasy, gives the SCA its distinctive flavor."[1] It is this hybrid nature, the pastiche of different ideas of the Middle Ages, that more then anything else marks the SCA as structurally postmodern.

What binds the SCA's game together, and also links it to the Middle Ages, is not a study of history but the king game itself. By establishing their own king game, both winter and summer versions, SCA members have re-created an important part of medieval culture. Postmodernism is supposed to break down master narratives but, in one way at least, the SCA is supporting one popular master narrative, that of the romantic Middle Ages promoted by the Victorians. However, SCA members are not trying to replace the dominant paradigm so much as they are creating an alternative, their own taste culture, a game anyone can choose to play or not. This too is an important element of postmodernism. John Seabrook says in *Nobrow* that whereas old bourgeois modernism looked on culture as High Culture/Middle Class Culture/Mass Culture, Nobrow looks at culture as Identity/Subculture/Mainstream Culture.[2] This is the world as SCA members live it. Their identity exists as part of their subculture, around which swirls mainstream culture. Through their re-creation of the king game they have created a community, or better yet a tribe, which gives them romance, companionship, and identity, a literate/filmic/academic/ludic Middle Ages. And at the center of this Middle Ages is a king, part Aragorn, part Charlemagne, part King Arthur from Malory, and part King Arthur from Monty Python, one that never existed but—for four to six months at least—gets to sit at the head table and rule the (known) world.

Turner writes:

> With the renewed emphasis on society as a process punctuated by performances of various kinds, there has developed a view that such genres as ritual, ceremony, carnival, games, spectacle, parade and sports events may constitute, on various levels and in various verbal and non-verbal codes, a set of metalanguages. The group or community does not merely "flow" in unison at these

performances, but, more actively, tries to understand itself in order to change itself.[3]

Every activity mentioned this quote can be found within the SCA and, indeed, it would be hard to find any part of SCA activity that is not encompassed by Turner's quote. If that is so, what is the SCA saying about itself and what is it trying to change? It seems clear that, through a postmodern collection of romantic tropes and idealized behavior, SCA members are trying to change their own personal world and themselves. Lenehan notes in his study that 75.7% of the respondents in Australia and 83.2% in California said that the SCA had changed them in some way.[4]

Participation in the SCA indicates some sort of dissatisfaction with contemporary society and a nostalgic longing for an ideal past. The establishment of an authority figure in the form of a just king, removed from electoral politics, who has proved his worth in some sort of trial—in this case combat—is the product of a desire for a moral compass to guide people through an increasingly complex and unknowable world. This is a dangerous concept, as it encourages people, at least within the framework of the SCA, to give over a large amount of personal responsibility to an unquestioned higher authority. However, with masters of arms and, indeed with much of the politics surrounding the SCA crowns, members do not give over their free will entirely. The rituals of the SCA allow people to build communities, to mark time, and to code as serious the traditions that they have created and the changes the group undergoes. Part of the attraction of the SCA is clearly in putting one's fate in the hands of another, putting oneself in danger in some way. This is true of the tradition of the crown's word being law, but also of the tradition of letting fighters who have been struck determine whether or not a blow was hard enough: both are acts of submission that require a great deal of trust in the character and actions of another person, often a stranger. This is the core of the SCA's idealized view of a world in which courtesy and honor are the paramount virtues. Born out of anxieties about industrialization, modern society, and the Vietnam war, the SCA has become a haven for many of those disaffected with contemporary society and a place for people to negotiate many anxieties that stem from modernism. A yearning for an agrarian feudal society points up anxieties about the pace and scope of our industrial capitalist world. The tournament culture allows the expression of masculine ideals and masculine bonding while at the same time rendering them (mostly) harmless by making them subservient to feminine ideals and desires. At the same time, the carnival nature of SCA events, the inversion of hierarchies, and the breakdown of social rules and constrictions result in temporary release of tension that serves society as a whole by siphoning off that discontent and allowing SCA members to continue to function within the strictures of the contemporary world when they are not at SCA events. Like the king games of the Middle Ages, the SCA serves the needs of the power structures of contemporary society by allowing members to experience a relatively harmless form of misrule and then return to the place assigned to them within the mundane world.

The SCA refers to itself as "The Current Middle Ages," a concept that Eco addressed in "Dreaming the Middle Ages:"

> Our own Middle Ages, it has been said, will be an age of "permanent transition" for which new methods of adjustment will have to be employed. The problem will not so much be that of preserving the past scientifically as of developing hypotheses for the exploitation of disorder, entering the logic of conflictuality. There will be born—it is already coming into existence—a culture of constant readjustment fed on utopia. This is how medieval man invented the university, with the same carefree attitude that the vagabond clerks today assume in destroying it, and perhaps transforming it. The Middle Ages preserved in its way the heritage of the past but not through hibernation, rather through constant retranslation and reuse; it was an immense work of bricolage, balanced among nostalgia, hope and despair.[5]

Clearly, this is how SCA members view their world. Their Current Middle Ages is a cornucopia of tropes and signs drawn from several different Middle Ages, which exists to help them negotiate their existence in the contemporary world. At the same time, however, as Stephen Knight would point out, too much should not be read into all of this. It is important to keep in mind that king games, carnival, fighting, make-believe, romance, mock violence, drinking, and sex are just plain fun.

NOTES

[1] Erisman, 92.
[2] Seabrook, 66.
[3] Turner, 100-101.
[4] Lenehan, 22.
[5] Umberto Eco, "Living in the New Middle Ages," in *Travels in Hyperreality* (New York: Harcourt Brace Jovanovich, 1986), 84.

APPENDIX I

SCA KINGDOMS (as of 2010)

The West Kingdom
Founded May 1, 1966
Northern California, Northern Nevada, Alaska, and the Far East
www.westkingdom.org

The East Kingdom
Founded June, 1968
Delaware, New Jersey, Eastern Pennsylvania, Eastern New York, New England, Quebec, the Maritimes
www.eastkingdom.org

The Midrealm
Founded September 1969
Michigan, Ohio, Indiana, Illinois, Windsor Ontario, and parts of Iowa and Kentucky
www.midrealm.org

Atenveldt
Founded January 1971
Arizona
www.atenveldt.org

Meridies
Founded January, 1978
Alabama, most of Georgia and Tennessee, and parts of Florida and Kentucky
www.meridies.org

CAID
Founded June, 1978
Southern California, Southern Nevada, and Hawaii. Lays claim to the Baja Peninsula.
www.sca-caid.org

Ansteorra
Founded June 1979
Oklahoma and Texas, minus the Western Panhandle
www.ansteorra.org

Atlantia
Founded May, 1981
Maryland, DC, Virginia, North Carolina, South Carolina, and Augusta Georgia
www.atlantia.org

An Tir
Founded January, 1982
Oregon, Washington, the Idaho Panhandle, British Columbia, Alberta, Saskatchewan, the Yukon, and the Northwest Territories
www.antir.sca.org

Calontir
Founded February, 1984
Kansas, Missouri, Iowa, Nebraska, Northern Arkansas
www.calontir.sca.org

Trimaris
Founded September, 1985
Most of Florida, lays claim to most of the Caribbean
www.trimaris.org

The Outlands
Founded June, 1986
New Mexico, most of Colorado, parts of Nebraska; Cheyenne, Wyoming, and the West Texas Panhandle. Lays claim to Mexico.
www.outlands.org

Drachenwald
Founded June, 1993: Europe, Africa, and the Middle East
www.drachenwald.sca.org

Artemisia
Founded July, 1997: Montana, southern Idaho, most of Utah, and western Colorado and Wyoming
www.artemisia.sca.org

Æthelmearc
Founded September, 1997: Western New York, Western Pennsylvania, and West Virginia
www.aethelmearc.org

Ealdormere
Founded October, 1998
Most of Ontario, Canada

www.ealdormere.ca

Lochac
Founded July, 2002: Australia, New Zealand, and parts of Antarctica
www.sca.org.au/lochac

North Shield
Founded October, 2004: North Dakota, South Dakota, Minnesota, Wisconsin, and the Upper Peninsula of Michigan
www.northshield.org

Gleann Abhann
Founded November, 2005: Mississippi, Louisiana, most of Arkansas, and Memphis, Tennessee
www.kingdomofgleannabhann.org/

APPENDIX II

Major SCA Wars

Pennsic War
Last week of July and the first week of August in Western Pennsylvania
www.pennsicwar.org
www.pennsic.net

Estrella War
President's Day weekend in February, near Phoenix, Arizona
www.estrellawar.org

Gulf Wars
Third weekend in March in Mississippi
www.gulfwars.org

Lilies War
Third week in June in Missouri
www.calontir.sca.org/lilieswar

Great Western War
Columbus Day weekend in October in Southern California
www.caid-gww.org/

APPENDIX III

SCA History according to Olsgaard

Note: Henrik Olsgaard/Duke Henrik of Havn, the first crowned king of the SCA, posted this note to the internet discussion group SCA Chivalry on his part in the development of the SCA in the 1960s and '70s. As with all oral histories, it doesn't mesh exactly with the memories of some other people, but it is an authoritative source as Olsgaard was present at many of the events that formed the unique culture of the SCA. This post from the SCA Chivalry user group is reprinted with permission. The links are to photographs on the West Kingdom History site.

In The Beginning . . .

The First actual SCA CROWN Tournament was held on September, 25, 1966 in the West Kingdom. The winner of this Tournament was subsequently actually Crowned KING, and it had no more than one Knight (I don't recall if the only knight, Sir Ardral, was competing that day) present. There were approximately about 10 or so fighters there and most if not all were competing. The final match was between Fulk de Wyvern and myself, Henrik the Dane. (Here we are in an earlier challenge match, that day: http://history.westkingdom.org/Year1/Photos/3THenfulk.htm

I can be seen wearing the first "real" helmet—a 4 plate conical spangenhelm, with a baseball catcher's mask worn on top of it for face protection during combat, and Fulk wears a fencing mask, the standard of the time. I have a mail corselet on, made of 5/8 inch OD, 14 ga. steel wire rings, covering my chest under my tunic, and am wielding a, soon to be banned, morningstar flail—made of a rubber ball covered with rubber "spikes", connected to an oak wood handle by a chain made of leather links. Fulk wields an axe made from a wooden dowel attached to a 3/4 inch thick unpadded plywood blade. This was before the discovery of rattan by Fulk in 1967. He is carrying a steel heater shield, backed with leather.)

At closing Court, after winning the Tournament, I was presented with this scroll proclaiming me King: http://history.westkingdom.org/Year1/Photos/HScroll.htm

Subsequently it was decided to have the first formal Coronation ceremony, to be held at the next scheduled Crown Tournament, on March

25, 1967. On that day I wore my newly completed, knee length mail hauberk, that had started out, the summer before, as the corselet mentioned previously. Just before my formal Coronation, a passing Equestrienne stopped to inquire about our strange appearance and activity. I went over to her and asked if she would let me try out my new armor on her horse. She agreed and here I am riding her horse, fully armed in the first "real" complete sca armor:
http://history.westkingdom.org/Year1/Photos/MC01.htm

Here the horse is carrying me and about 75 to 80 pounds of steel weapons and armor.

Within 15 minutes of this photo being taken, I was dismounted and standing before the Royal Thrones, expecting to be Crowned, when Fulk, who was holding the Crown said "No man who is not a knight, should be King. Kneal!" [sic] and with that he proceded [sic] to dub me Knight with his Spanish made, hand and a half, broadsword. I knealt [sic] as Henrik The Dane and arose as Sir Henrik of Havn, second Knight, to then be Crowned King , with this Crown:
http://history.westkingdom.org/Artifacts/Hats/HCrown.htm

My first Reign ended that day at the proclaiming of the Tournament winner, Richard the Short, as King, at closing Court.

That Reign was actually quite short since, as designated King at the end of the previous Crown Tournament (preceding year, on September 25, 1966), I had not been Crowned and so was without authority in the interim, till Crowned at the Tournament, on March 25.

Afterwards we developed an alternating Tournament schedule, where Crown Tournaments would be followed by Coronation events or Tournaments, so Reigns would last over the length of two Tournament periods, as is standard in our Kingdom today.

Subsequent to the creation of the Society's Order of Chivalry at the second Twelfth Night, in January 1968, by King William the Silent (the third Knight) after his Coronation, Crown Tournaments were held with the Chivalry normally having automatic admittance to Crown lists and other fighters being admitted, usually by invitation only. Over time, local traditions and procedures evolved from those origins, to what they are today.

Please understand that the division between "The Society" and "The West Kingdom" came about rather gradually over a period of several years and so the first reigns of Kings were in "The Society" and as new Kingdoms sprang into being, they developed their own identities and Reigns of Kings and Queens. King William the Silent established the concept of Chivalry in the Society as he Reigned and named members to this body of Chivalry, from among the fighters in the West Kingdom, the only Kingdom in existance, [sic] at the time. Later, Chivalry from The West Kingdom, visited or otherwise interacted with other Kingdoms and created new members there, who created their own successors to this Order.

Sir Henrik of Havn, Second Knight

BIBLIOGRAPHY

The New York Times, 22 December 2002.

Ambrosius, Orlando. *The Courtesy Book*. 3rd ed. Urbana, IL: Folump Enterprises, 1989.

Andrews, Robert. *The Columbia World of Quotations*. Columbia University Press, 1996. Accessed 24 March 2005. Available from http://www.bartleby.com/66/86/35186.html.

Anonymous. *Origins of the Middle Kingdom*. Middle Kingdom, Accessed May 1 2004. Available from www.midrealm.org/midrealm_origins.html.

———. *Robin Hood and the Sheriff of Nottingham*. Western Michigan University, 1997. Accessed May 2 2004. Available from
http://www.lib.rochester.edu/camelot/teams/sherint.htm.

Appiah, Kwame Anthony. "Race. " In *Critical Terms for Literary Study*, ed. Frank and Thomas McLaughlin Lentrichia. Chicago: University of Chicago Press, 1995.

Ashley, Kathleen. "Introduction. " In *Moving Subjects: Processional Performance in the Middle Ages and Renaissance*, ed. Kathleen Ashley and Wim Hüsken. Atlanta, GA: Rodopi, 2001.

Atton, Bernard. *Medieval Sourcebook: Charter of Homage and Fealty, 1110*. Fordham University Institute of Medieval Studies, 2000. Accessed 14 March 2005. Available from
http://www.fordham.edu/hasall/source/atton1.html.

Axton, Richard. *European Drama of the Early Middle Ages*. Pittsburgh: University of Pittsburgh Press, 1975.

Bakhtin, Mikhail. *Problems of Dostoevsky's Poetics*. Translated by C. Emerson, ed. C. Emerson. Manchester, UK: Manchester University Press, 1984.

———. *Rabelais and His World*. Translated by Helene Iswolsky. Bloomington, IN: Indiana University Press, 1984.

Barber, Richard, and Juliet Barker. *Tournaments*. Woodbridge, UK: The Boydell Press, 1989.

Barton, Blanche. *The Church of Satan: A Brief History*. The Church of Satan, 2003. Accessed 27 November 2004. Available from www.churchofsatan. com.

Beck, Tobi. *The Armored Rose*. San Jose: Beckenhall Publishers, 1999.

Belgique, Sir Guillaume de la. *This Sovereign Stage*. San Diego, CA: Shining Armor Enterprises, 2003.

Benamou, Michel. "Presence as Play. " In *Performance and Postmodern Culture*, ed. Michel Benamou and Charles Carmello. Milwaukee: Center for Twentieth Century Studies, 1977.

Billington, Sandra. *Mock Kings in Medieval Society and Renaissance Drama*. Oxford: Clarendon Press, 1991.

184 Bibliography

Bloch, Marc. "Feudal Society." In *The Middle Ages*, ed. Brian Tierney, II, 82-93. New York: Alfred A. Knopf, 1961.

Britain, Goldwyn of. *Our Kind II: Mistress Laurel Seamchecker Explains It All At You.* Golden Stag Players, Accessed 30 May 2003. Available from www.goldenstag.net/players/scripts/ourkindII.pdf.

Brown, Patricia Fortini. "Measured Friendship, Calculated Pomp: The Ceremonial Welcomes of the Venetian Republic." In *"All the World's a Stage . . .": Art and Pageantry in the Renaissance and Baroque*, ed. Barbara Wisch and Susan Scott Munshower, 137-86. University Park: Pennsylvania State University Press, 1990.

Cady, Michael. *Message #426.* SCA-Chivalry, 2000. Accessed April 13 2005. Available from www.groups.yahoo.com/SCA_Chivalry/message/426.

Cady, Michael, and Henrik Olsgaard. *Hastings 2000: Our Experiences at the Battle of Hastings, October 4, 2000.* Stefan's Florilegium, 2002. Accessed February 11 2005. Available from http://www.florilegium.org/files/ CELEBRATIONS/Hastings-2000-art.html.

Calontir, Kingdom of. Accessed 12 May 2004. Available from www.calontir.org.

Cantor, Norman. *Inventing the Middle Ages.* New York: Quill, 1991.

Cardinale, Tina, and Christopher Burns. *In Service to the Dream.* Christopher Burns, director. Los Angeles: Mythos Productions, 2001.

Carlson, Marvin. *Theories of the Theatre.* Ithaca: Cornell University Press, 1984.

———. *Performance.* New York: Routledge, 1996.

———. "The Resistance to Theatricality. " *Substance* 31, no. 98 & 99 combined (2002): 238-250.

Carroll-Clark, Susan. "A Missive from the Editor." *Tournaments Illuminated*, no. 147 (2003).

Chambers, E. K. *The Medieval Stage.* Vol. 1. 2nd ed. Toronto: Dover, 1996.

Cleghorn, Reese. "Of Hounds, Turtles and Old Flags." *American Journalism Review*, no. 19 September 1997.

Clopper, Lawrence. *Drama, Play and Game: English Festive Culture in the Medieval and Early Modern Period.* Chicago: University of Chicago Press, 2001.

Connor, Steven. *Postmodernist Culture: An Introduction to the Theories of the Contemporary.* Cambridge, MA: Basil Blackwell, 1989. Reprint, 1992.

Cox, John. *The Devil and the Sacred in English Drama, 1350-1642.* Cambridge, UK: Cambridge University Press, 2000.

Cramer, Michael. "The Twelve Goddesses: A Performance Reconstruction." Master of Arts in Drama, San Francisco State University, 1996.

Davis, Fred. *Yearning for Yesterday.* New York: The Free Press, 1979.

Dinshaw, Carolyn. *Getting Medieval: Sexualities and Communities, Pre- and Postmodern.* Durham: Duke University Press, 1999.

Dodd, Sandra. "Ethnocentricity." *Thinkwell* 1, no. 1.

Duby, Georges. *William Marshal: the Flower of Chivalry*. Translated by Richard Howard. New York: Pantheon Books, 1985.

Dugdale, Sir W. *Originales Iuridiciales*. London, 1666.

Eco, Umberto. *Travels in Hyperreality*. New York: Harcourt Brace Jovanovich, 1986.

Edwards, Hanna. Interview by author, 6 May 2004, New York, NY.

Erisman, Wendy. "Forward into the Past: The Poetics and Politics of Community in Two Historical Recreation Groups." Ph.D. diss., University of Texas, 1998.

Evreinov, Nikolas. *The Theatre in Life*. Translated by Alexander Nazaroff. New York: Brentanos, 1927.

Eynat-Confino, Irene. "A Stage Upon a Stage: Postmodern Stage Design and Opera." In *Space and the Post Modern Stage*, ed. Eynat-Confino and Eva Sormova. Prague: The Prague Theatre Institute, 2000.

Fisher, William. *The Crusader*. Blogger, 2004. Accessed 24 March 2005. Available from http://christian-patriot.blogspot.com/.

Forgue, Lee. S.C.A. History. Panel discussion at Collegium Occidentalis, Kensington, CA, 19 October 1996.

———. Interview by author, 14 March 2004, Davis, CA.

Forward into the Past: An Introductory Guide to the S.C.A. Kingdom of Ansteorra, Accessed 31 May 2003. Available from www.ansteorra.org/regnum/ hospitaler/articles/fip.htm.

Friedman, David D. *A Miscellany*. 9th Edition. 2000. Accessed 4 May 2003. Available from www.davidfriedman.com/medieval/miscelany_ pdf/miscelany.htm.

Garreau, Joel. *The Nine Nations of North America*. New York: Houghton Mifflin, 1981.

Goffman, Erving. *The Presentation of Self in Everyday Life*. Garden City, NJ: Doubleday Anchor, 1959.

———. *Frame Analysis*. Cambridge: Harvard University Press, 1974.

Grit. "Summer Knights 10/1/2003." *Maxim*, August 2003.

Grossman, Lev. "Feeding on Fantasy." *Time*, 2 December 2002.

Hardison, O. B. *Christian Rite and Christian Drama in the Middle Ages*. Baltimore: Johns Hopkins Press, 1965.

Harman, Willis, and John Hormann. *Creative Work*. Indianapolis, IN: Knowledge Systems, Inc., 1981.

Hassan, Ihab. "Postmodernism: A Practical Bibliography." In *From Modernism to Postmodernism*, ed. Lawrence Cahoone. London: Blackwell, 1997.

Helm-Clark, Catherine. "There Are No Scrolls." *Tournaments Illuminated*. Autumn, no. 140 (2002): 8-15.

Hess, Karl. "Interview with Karl Hess." Interview by Sam Merril. *Playboy*, July, 1976, 55-158.

Heydt, Dorothy. SCA History. Panel discussion at Collegium Occidentalis, Kensington, CA, 19 October 1996.

Hobbes, Thomas. *Leviathan*. Harmondsworth: Penguin Books, 1985.

Hollander, Frederick. *Mercenary's Song*. Textfiles.com, Accessed 14 March 2005. Available from http://www.textfiles.com/music/bardic2.txt.

———. The History and Culture of the SCA. Panel discussion at The Thirty Year Celebration, St. Helena, Washington, 12 June 1996.

———. Interview by author. 15 February 2004, Phoenix AZ.

Horowitz, Tony. *Confederates in the Attic*. New York: Pantheon Books, 1998.

Huizinga, Johan. *Homo Ludens*. Boston: The Beacon Press, 1950.

———. *The Autumn of the Middle Ages*. Translated by Rodney J. and Ulrich Mammitzsch Payton. Chicago: University of Chicago Press, 1996.

Humphrey, Chris. *The Politics of Carnival: Festive Misrule in Medieval England* Manchester Medieval Studies, ed. S. H. Rigby. Manchester, UK: Manchester University Press, 2001.

Hutcheon, Linda. *A Poetics of Postmodernism*. New York: Routledge, 1998.

Hyinck, Larry. *The Second Folio of Gerhardt Von Nordflammen*, 57-76. Vancouver: Copious Free Time Press, 1984.

Isaacson, Rupert. "Knights of Passion." *Geographical*. January 2000.

James, Victoria. *Let's Fight*. The Japan Times Online, 2003. Accessed 27 March 2005. Available from http://www.japantimes.co.jp/cgi-bin/makeprfy. pl5?fl20030504a1.htm.

Jameson, Fredric. "'End of Art' or 'End of History'." In *The Cultural Turn*, ed. Fredric Jameson. New York: Verso, 1998.

———. "Postmodernism and Consumer Society." In *The Cultural Turn*, ed. Fredric Jameson, 1-20. New York: Verso, 1998.

———. "Theories of the Postmodern." In *The Cultural Turn*, ed. Fredric Jameson. New York: Verso, 1998.

Jestovic, Silvija. "Theatricality as Estrangement of Art and Life in the Russian Avant-Garde." *Substance* 31, no. 98-99 (2002): 42-56.

Kaye, Nick. *Postmodernism and Performance*. New York: St. Martin's Press, 1994.

Keen, Maurice. *Chivalry*. New Haven: Yale University Press, 1984.

Keyes, William. *The West Kingdom History Project*. Golden Stag, 2001. Accessed 4 February 2004. Available from http://.history.westkingdom.org.

Kingdom of CAID. *Compendium CAIDus*. Available from http://wiki.caid-commons.org/index.php/Roses. Accessed 16 September, 2009.

Kipling, Rudyard. *A Pict's Song*. 1906. Accessed 26 April 2004. Available from http://whitewolf.newcastle.edu.au/words/authors/K/KiplingRudyard/verse/p 3/pictsong.html.

Kisor, Yvette. Weaving the Web of the Story: Tolkien's Use of Interlace in *the Lord of the Rings*. Seminar at The 39th International Congress on Medieval Studies, 6 May 2004, Kalamazoo, MI.

Kramer-Rolls, Dana. SCA Culture. Seminar at Collegium Occidentalis, Berkeley, CA, 6 March 1993.

Lenehan, Carey. "Postmodern Medievalism: A Sociological Study of the Society for Creative Anachronism." BA Honors Thesis, University of Tasmania, 1994.

Lewis, C.S. *The Silver Chair*. Vol. 6 The Chronicles of Narnia. New York: Harper Collins, 1994.

Liptsitz. George. "Who'll Stop the Rain: Youth Culture, Rock 'n' Roll, and Social Crises," in *The Sixties From Memory to History* ed. David Farber. Chapel Hill: University of North Carolina Press, 1994.

Lull, Raymond. *The Book of Knighthood and Chivalry*. Translated by William Caxton. Union City, CA: The Chivalry Bookshelf, 2001.

Magnat, Virginie. "Theatricality from the Performative Perspective." *Substance* 31, no. 98-99 (2002): 147-163.

McSmith, Shannon. Interview by author, 14 March 2004, Davis, CA.

McWilliams, John C. *The 1960s Cultural Revolution*. Westport, CT: Greenwood Press, 2000.

Meyer, P., ed. *Historie De Guillaume Le Maréchal*. Paris: Société de l'Historie, 1891-1901.

Michasiw, Kim. "Camp, Masculinity, Masquerade." *Differences: A Journal of Feninist Cultural Studies* 6, no. 2/3 combined (1994): 146-173.

Milo, Empress. *An Introduction to the ICS*. Imperial Court Internet Services, Accessed 23 March 2005. Available from www.impcourt.org/icis/about/intro.html.

Mondschein, Ken. *The Society for Creative Anachronism*. Disinformation, 2002. Accessed 8 February 2002. Available from http://www.disinfo.com/site/displayarticle2028.html.

Moore, Thomas. Interview by author, 14 March 2004, Davis, CA.

Morril, E.F. The Art of Being. Seminar at The Pennsic War, Slippery Rock, PA, 10 August 2003.

Muhlberger, Steven. Practical Chivalry, 1350: Geoffroi De Charny's Questions on War. Seminar at The 39th International Congress on Medieval Studies, Kalamazoo, MI, 6 May 2004.

Nugent, Benjamin. *American Nerd: The Story of My People.* New York: Scribner, 2008.

Nygard, Roger. *Trekkies 2*. Directed by Roger Nygard. Los Angeles: Paramount Pictures, 2004.

O'Donnell, Patrick. *The Knights Next Door*. Lincoln, NE: iUniverse, 2004.

Orgel, Stephen. *The Illusion of Power*. Berkeley: University of California Press, 1975.

Overing, Gillian, and Marijane Osborn. *Landscape of Desire: Partial Stories of the Medieval Scandinavian World*. Minneapolis, MN: University of Minnesota Press, 1994.

Paxson, Diana. *The Seed and the Tree*. Accessed 15 December 2003. Available from http://www.currentmiddleages.org/3yc/seed.html.

———. "The Last Tournament." In *The Known World Handbook*, ed. Hillary Powers. Milpitas, CA: Society for Creative Anachronism, 1992.

Postlewait, Thomas, and Tracy C. Davis. "Theatricality: An Introduction." In *Theatricality*, ed. Thomas Postlewait and Tracy C. Cambridge, UK: Cambridge University Press, 2003.

Putter, A.D. "Transvestite Knights in Medieval Life and Literature." In *Becoming Male in the Middle Ages*, ed. Jeffrey Jerome Cohen and Bonnie Wheeler. New York: Garland, 1997.

Rainbird, Miriam. Seminar at The 39th International Congress on Medieval Studies, 6 May, 2004, Kalamazoo, MI.

Reinelt, Janelle. "The Politics of Discourse: Performativity Meets Theatricality." *Substance* 31, no. 98-99 (2002): 201-215.

Robinson, Edwin Arlington. "Miniver Cheevy." 1907.

Rodwell, Andrew. "Anti-Modern Performance in the Society for Creative Anachronism." M. A. Thesis, University of Western Ontario, 1998.

Rose, Greg. *An Explanation of the SCA*. Accessed 1 April 2000. Available from http://www.routiers.org/scaexpl.htm.

Sarlos, Robert K. "Performance Reconstruction." In *Interpreting the Theatrical Past: Essays in the Historiography of Performance*, ed. Thomas Postlewait and Bruce A. McConachie, 198-229. Iowa City: University of Iowa Press, 1989.

Saslow, James. *The Medici Wedding of 1589*. New Haven: Yale University Press, 1996.

SCA. *Pennsicwar.Org*. Cooper's Lake Campground, 2004. Accessed 2 May 2004. Available from www.pennsicwar.org.

Schechner, Richard. *The End of Humanism*. New York: Performing Arts Journal Publications, 1982.

———. *Between Theatre and Anthropology*. Philadelphia: University of Pennsylvania Press, 1985.

Seabrook, John. *Nobrow: The Culture of Marketing the Marketing of Culture*. New York: Vintage Books, 2001.

Shakespeare. *Henry V*.

———. *1 Henry IV*.

Silvestri, Margaret. Interview by author, 14 March 2004, Davis, CA.

Sinou, Andre. Letter to author, 25 April 2005.

Snook, Lisa. Script for the coronation of Thorson and Svava, 2004, author's collection.

———. Letter to author, 6 October 2004.

Society for Creative Anachronism. *The New SCA Fighters Handbook*. Milpitas, CA: The Society for Creative Anachronism, Inc., 1993.

———. *The Society for Creative Anachronism, Inc., Organizational Handbook*. Milpitas, CA: The Society for Creative Anachronism, Inc., 2003.

Sontag, Susan. *Notes on Camp*. Partisan Review, 1964. Accessed 11 February 2005. Available from http://pages.zoom.co.uk/leveridge/sontag.html.

Spinrad, Norman, *Science Fiction in the Real World*. Carbondale, IL: Southern Illinois University Press, 1990.

Sponsler, Claire. *Drama and Resistance: Bodies, Goods and Theatricality in Late Medieval England*. Minneapolis: University of Minnesota Press, 1997.

Sterner, Lewis G. and Marcus Konick, ed. *Tales in Verse*. New York: Globe Book Co., 1963.

Strong, Roy. *The Cult of Elizabeth*. Berkeley: University of California Press, 1977.

———. *Art and Power*. Woodbridge, UK: The Boydell Press, 1984.

Tarentino, Quentin. *Pulp Fiction*. Los Angeles: Miramax Films, 1994.

Taylor, Andrew. "Chivalric Conversation and the Denial of Male Fear." In *Conflicted Identities and Multiple Masculinities: Men in the Medieval West*, ed. Jacqueline Murray. New York: Garland Publishing, 1999.

Thewlis, David. "A Brief Look at the Past." In *The Known World Handbook*, ed. Hillary Powers. Milpitas, CA: The Society for Creative Anachronism, 1992.

Tolkien, John Ronald Reuel. *The Lord of the Rings*. New York: Houghton Mifflin, 1994.

Townsend, David. "Ironic Intertextuality and the Reader's Resistance to Heroic Masculinity in the *Waltharius*." In *Becoming Male in the Middle Ages*, ed. Jeffrey Jerome Cohen and Bonnie Wheeler, 67-86. New York: Garland, 1997.

Trapp, Kenneth R., ed. *The Arts and Crafts Movement in California: Living the Good Life*. New York: Abbeville Press Publishers, 1993.

Tronstad, Ragnhild. "Could the World Become a Stage: Theatricality and Metaphorical Structures." *Substance* 31, no. 98-99 (2002): 216-224.

Turner, Victor. *From Ritual to Theatre*. New York: New York Performing Arts Journal Publications, 1982.

Twycross, Meg, ed. *Festive Drama: Papers from the Sixth Colloquium of the International Society for the Study of Medieval Theatre, Lancaster, 13-19 July 1989*. Cambridge: D.S. Brewer, 1996.

West, Kingdom of. *West Kingdom Coronation Ceremony Scroll—2nd Twelfth Night*. West Kingdom History Project, 1968. Accessed 10 May 2004. Available from http://history.westkingdom.org/Year2/Photos/TNScroll11.htm.

West Kingdom College of Heralds. *West Kingdom Ceremony Book*. Berkeley: Free Trumpet Press, 1991.

Wiles, David. *The Early Plays of Robin Hood*. Cambridge: D.S. Brewer, 1981.

Wilson, Richard Guy. "Devine Excelence: The Arts and Crafts Life in California." In *The Arts and Crafts Movement in California: Living the Good Life*, ed. Kenneth R. Trapp. New York: Abeville Press Publishers, 1993.

INDEX

ABOUT THE AUTHOR

Michael Cramer is an actor, director, filmmaker and scholar who has been involved in historical reenactment and re-creation for thirty years. He has published articles and reviews in *Theatre Journal, The Year's Work in Medievalism,* and *Sixteen Century Journal,* among others. He is also the author of *A Confederacy of Whores: Media and Politics in George W. Bush's America,* (Vox Pop, 2006). He lives in Brooklyn and teaches communications at the City University of New York.